MUSICAL JOURNEYS

HOMI DASTOOR

JAMSHYD AND PHEROZA
GODREJ

THE WZO TRUST FUNDS
THE WZO TRUST FOR WOMEN & CHILDREN
THE WORLD ZOROASTRIAN ORGANISATION TRUST

THE YUSUF AND FARIDA
HAMIED FOUNDATION

First published in 2014 by

49/50 Books
33 Peacock Palace
69 B. Desai Road
Mumbai 400 026
India

ISBN 978-81-921367-2-1

Editor & Publisher **Meher Marfatia**
Text Editor **Sherna Gandhy**
Consultant Editor **Farrokh Vajifdar**

Design **Carma Ideas**
Creative Consultant **Sooni Taraporevala**
Processed and printed by **JAK Printers**

MUSICAL JOURNEYS

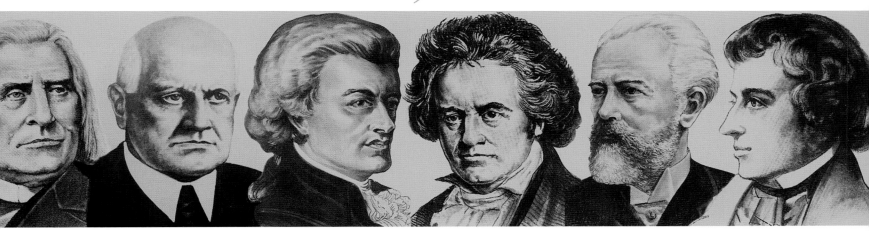

A PERSONAL INTRODUCTION TO WESTERN CLASSICAL COMPOSERS

HOMI DASTOOR

Contents

Foreword

" I salute **Homi Dastoor** wholeheartedly for introducing not only young people but the general public at large to this most painstakingly detailed **introduction to Europe's great composers**. Not only does he describe their musical lineage, but very carefully maps out the logical evolution of music in Europe from the **1600s to the mid-20th century**. Not only does each composer have important points of his life's history carefully explained, but there is also a list of his most important works and explanations of **a few choice masterpieces**.

Anyone who wants an introduction to **the world of Western Classical music** will surely benefit enormously and, I am sure, go thereafter to concerts with **enhanced listening pleasure**. **"**

Publisher's **Note**

Being both the publisher of Homi Dastoor's book as well as his daughter puts me in the position of knowing the man and the music lover. Seeing him author a work like this at the age of 90, mostly from handwritten notes copied from books he couldn't afford to buy as a collegian in the early 1940s, I feel proud. Along comes a rush of memories of growing up with a man whose ruling passion in life – Western Classical music – became a family bond.

Music was everywhere in our home. It boomed grandly from a Grundig player in the hall (which he still has). The volume at which he chose to listen ensured those strains filled each room. Whatever corner of the house we were in, there they were. From Bach to Brahms, Sibelius to Stravinsky, Mozart to Mendelssohn... their prodigious notes second breath to us. And this was literally right from the cradle. Believe it or not, with my pram parked beneath stacks of LPs, I was rocked to sleep with the melodies. Dad recommended this loud bedtime routine widely to friends, describing how the "Merry Widow" Waltz unfailingly saw his baby daughter's eyes scrunch shut within one minute of its opening bars.

Barely a day passed without my brother Phiroze and I being treated to the sounds of this music. The composers who created it became members of our extended family. Dad had clear favourites, Beethoven and Jascha Heifetz. So unabashed a worshipper is he of these virtuosos that he fervently wished his children shared their birthdays with his heroes. Phiroze came in close, born only a day after wizard-of-the-violin Heifetz. I was doomed to more distance, rushing out to greet the world two whole weeks before Beethoven's birthday.

But their birth dates – February 2 and December 16 – came to be indelibly etched in our minds. How could they not, when we actually celebrated them with gusto? It wasn't tribute enough to have the maestros' photographs and marble busts nestle benignly beside the Dastoor ancestral portraits. To mark the great musicians' birthdays, we also happily tucked into festive breakfasts of *sev* and *ravo*, sweet dishes traditionally enjoyed by our Parsi community on auspicious occasions – birthdays, anniversaries and New Year! Guess who ticked these red-letter days on the calendar before they dawned. Hugs and hats off to my wonderful mother who gamely encouraged what was enjoyed by us all.

Long years of a professional life spent at Bombay House (he is possibly the oldest Tata Group veteran still gracing the city) kept him busy with responsibilities. On retiring, he learnt to play the violin, at the age of 75, from 25-year-old Kenneth D'Souza of the Bombay Philharmonic Orchestra. Never too late, he said, smiling as he touched bow to strings.

Never too late, it seems, to author a book either. Solitarily, slowly, writing manuscripts in longhand with neither a computer nor anyone to dictate text to. He researched late into the evening with tired eyes but a lively mind. Even putting pen to paper through a period of relentless pain over a whole year spent trying to beat back an illness.

Why this book then? To spark the same interest in anyone who wants to understand Western Classical music but knows not where to begin. To prove – as our nonagenarian author declares in his "Introduction" here – that there is no mystique to Classical music, it just asks for your time to appreciate it. To be rewarded by the exhilarating and edifying pleasure this ageless music affords for an entire lifetime.

I've been blessed. Mine was the privilege of witnessing at first hand such an enduring passion. I hope it will now inspire you at the turn of these pages.

Meher Marfatia

—30—

the stormy grandeur with which they are all developed. It is supremely lyrical music from beginning to end.
The romantic dialogue of the Second Movement was once compared by Franz Liszt to Orpheus taming the wild beasts. Beethoven's?

Lines from the author's handwritten Beethoven manuscript

Mehli Mehta
Guru to generations of music lovers

" There is really no mystique about Classical music. All that it asks of you is but one thing. Your time. "

INTRODUCTION

Right from my childhood years I have been listening to popular Western music, ranging from Hollywood musicals to the music of the Big Bands of the 1920s, 1930s, 1940s; to the rhythmic foot-tapping Latin American music from Xavier Cugat and Kinsmen, and, of course, to the charming waltzes of Johann Strauss.

And then it happened.

An event that made a momentous, sweeping change and directed my music listening to Western Classical music.

The year was 1942. I was 18 and in the second year of college. I read in *The Times of India* advance intimation of a soon-to-be-shown Hollywood film titled *They Shall Have Music,* featuring Jascha Heifetz, the greatest violinist in the world.

Intrigued, I went to see the film – which I saw subsequently five more times – and was overwhelmed, completely bowled over. The violin performances were so superb, so outstanding, that for several days thereafter the music I had heard kept ringing in my head.

For the next 18 months I went completely crazy. I hungered to know all about Western Classical music. There was no one to guide me. But there was no stopping me either. I first went to the American Library in Bombay (now Mumbai) and read everything I could find on Heifetz. That led me to also read about other top violinists: Kreisler, Elman, Menuhin and Szigeti.

Common sense, however, told me that the best thing to do was obviously to find out who were the great composers. A visit to the J.N. Petit Institute Library on Dadabhai Naoroji Road at Fort fulfilled that need, for there I came across books in a series titled, if I recall rightly, *Lives of the Great Composers.* In making copious notes from those books I was at the library for over three months.

I then went back to the American Library to find some book that would tell me what the music of the great Masters said. After two days of searching, I came across a book that told me exactly what I wanted to know. It was truly a serendipitous find. That book at the American Library – to my great embarrassment I cannot now recall its name – was so heavily loaded with just what I wanted to know, that I realised if I was to make any headway in making notes from it, I would have to visit the library every day for some months. The only way I could do that was by attending college for just the first period when the attendance roll call was taken.

I did just that. Every morning I would leave college after the first period and walk down Hornby Road (renamed Dadabhai Naoroji Road after Independence), with my foolscap-size notebooks tucked under my arm, to the library. Of course, the college sometimes did take surprise attendance roll call in the afternoon. The next day my name would appear on the office notice board, fining me one rupee – which did make a dent in my personal monthly allowance of Rs 25.

It took me nearly six months to take down notes from that book because I had to first read the accounts of most of the compositions mentioned in it before deciding to commit to my notebook those that interested me.

In retrospect the year 1943 – the second year of my bewitchment with Classical music – was particularly rewarding. I eagerly extended my knowledge by reading anything and everything connected with it. However, I regret to admit that in my enthusiasm in this matter, I did not note down those very sources of information from which I was then benefitting.

By this time I felt I knew fairly well many matters concerning Western Classical music, and started attending recitals and concerts held in the city. The revered name of Mehli Mehta was foremost on the lips of music lovers of those days. It was unquestionably the pioneering efforts of Mehli Mehta that kept alive Western Classical music in the country. He was everywhere. The Bombay Symphony Orchestra and the Bombay Chamber Music Orchestra owed their existence to him. Their programmes were carefully selected by him to both woo newcomers to the concerts as well as to demonstrate to those who were already lovers of music that the BSO and the BCO were capable of meeting the challenges of even the works of the Masters.

Mehli Mehta stressed the fact that Classical music must be respected and therefore the audience must come for the concerts in good time. Instructions were issued to close the doors of the concert hall once the performance started. Latecomers were admitted only when the first composition on the programme had been played to its end. Mr Mehta further educated newcomers to the concerts by having two large boards placed at both ends of the stage stating: "Please do not clap between movements."

I then also started reading the *Gramophone* magazine, which fully lives up to its boast of being the best magazine in the world for reviews of recordings and comments on Classical music. Its list of reviewers has always been impressive and their assessments of recordings very reassuring.

Simultaneously, I ventured cautiously into buying records. My parents believed that young people would only learn the value of money if the personal allowance

They Shall Have Music
The film with which it all began

given to them was reasonably restrictive. Those were the days of vinyl discs, so if one desired to buy recordings of a concerto or a symphony, one had to save money over two or three months to be able to do so. But the thrill that came of setting out on that one morning, with enough money to buy a record of a concerto or a symphony, was something I remember to this day.

My first buy was Mozart's Violin Concerto in A Major, K 219 played, of course, by Heifetz, who has since become an icon in my life.

Sometimes, while waiting for some months to collect enough money to buy a large work, my patience would give way and I would phone my friend Sohrab Khambatta to accompany me to James & Co, our favourite music shop, to buy a single disc. At the shop we would listen to eight or nine recordings, mostly of overtures.

When we were sated with all that listening, I would ask my friend his opinion on which record we should finally buy. On one such occasion, he immediately pointed to one disc in a very authoritative manner. I asked why he was so sure of his choice and he said, "Can't you see that the music on this disc goes right up to the end and touches its label?" (Ah, the simple wisdom of those days.)

In April 1946, I joined the Tata group and the starting salary for graduates was Rs 90 per month, with the friendly help of an additional Rs 30 as dearness allowance. This bit of information may make some of you reading these lines smile, but the rupee then was strong and had a long reach (so much so that in the early 1930s a hotel on Marine Drive was charging its clients Rs 16 every day for room, breakfast, lunch and dinner)!

On the salary I now earned, I found I was in a position to consider starting my own collection of recorded music. I also bought my first book on music. *The Victor Book of the Symphony.*

It has been over 66 years since then and my appreciation of Classical music has grown in depth and understanding. One day I decided to review all the knowledge of Classical music that I had so far acquired. In doing this exercise I found that I was comfortable in my knowledge of violin music, but less so of piano and orchestral music. Of operatic music I knew very little, mainly prominent arias from various operas of the kind that The Three Tenors had made popular all over the world. Of chamber music I knew next

> " *For nearly seven decades now I have been listening, engrossed, to this music, and it has truly enriched my life like no other leisure interests could have ever done. I have a missionary-like zeal to ignite such interest in you.* "

to nothing, a fact that I much regretted, knowing how some of the most profound and intimate thoughts of the Old Masters had been gifted to the world in music composed for string orchestras in various combinations.

Soon after I made that survey of the knowledge I had acquired of Classical music by listening to it for well over six decades, I happened to speak about it to my children Phiroze and Meher. They both strongly felt that it would be a shame if all the knowledge I have acquired was to be forgotten. They urged me to seriously consider putting it all in a book. I pondered this for some time and felt there was much sense in what they said. I finally decided to write a book on my lone but happy journey through the realm of Classical music.

So this book that I have written, at the age of 90, and which is now in your hands, is targeted to interest the newcomer in the world of Classical music, just as I had done myself way back in 1942. For nearly seven decades now I have been listening, engrossed, to this music, and it has truly enriched my life like no other leisure interests could have ever done. I have a missionary-like zeal to ignite such interest in you.

All people need to have a cultural dimension to their lives and an interest in Classical music is, indeed, one of the very best ways of achieving this.

There is really no mystique about Classical music. All that it asks of you is but one thing. Your time.

In this connection I confidently submit that if you were to play a CD of popular music and another CD of, say, the Overture to "The Barber of Seville", after listening to each CD six times or so, you will feel somewhat stale listening to the first CD whereas you will feel progressively interested in the Overture because of the build-ups with Rossini's renowned crescendos. Later, as you listen to more Classical music, you will take delight – as in Beethoven's "Appassionata Sonata" – to first hear tantalising hints of a theme still-to-surface, and then revel in it when it is fully presented. Such discoveries in music are endless.

Western Classical music is international music. It is no longer confined to European countries. In recent times we have seen, with great disbelief at first, the vast emerging interest in it in the nations of the Far East. A bonus of cultivating an interest in Classical music is the bond one could well experience some day in meeting strangers having similar interests, in the most unlikely and unexpected situations in life, and end up happily exchanging notes with them.

Books on Classical music have an alphabetical index by which the readers can reach the pages devoted to the composers of their choice. In such cases what happens is that the readers generally track down the pages devoted only to the Old Masters – whose names they already know or have often heard of – such as Bach, Mozart, Beethoven, Schubert, Chopin, Tchaikovsky, to name but a few. Such references, however, do not touch the other major composers who were the contemporaries of the Old Masters, and with whom they interacted in many ways, not just by learning from them, but also by showing their respect and adulation, causing the Old Masters to continue to excel themselves.

Let me offer three examples of the ways in which great composers and their distinguished contemporaries have interacted with and helped each other. The first example is that of Hector Berlioz and Niccolò Paganini. At one stage in his life Berlioz's finances were so distressing that it was his friend Paganini who spontaneously stepped in and saved the alarming situation by giving Berlioz 20,000 francs. With this handsome amount Berlioz, no longer beset by money problems, resumed composing music with a cool mind. It had so happened that earlier Paganini had spoken to Berlioz about a magnificent Guarneri viola that had been gifted to him by one of his admirers and wondered whether Berlioz could compose music for his viola. Berlioz remembered that conversation and did just that by composing "Harold in Italy" for orchestra and viola, and dedicated it to Paganini as his thanks for the help Paganini had given him.

The second example is that of Liszt, already acknowledged as the best pianist of his time, when he first attended a recital by Paganini. At the end of the recital Liszt was so fascinated and overwhelmed by Paganini's innovative fingering and amazing stretches on the strings that he went into a self-imposed sabbatical to further polish his technique the Paganini way. He then declared that he would henceforth be happy to be known as "the Paganini of the Piano".

The third example is that of Schumann who, apart from being a very great composer, was also the founder and editor of *The New Music Journal*. The *Journal* was avidly read throughout Europe and abroad. Schumann had a natural gift of assessing the latent worth of many upcoming composers who approached him with copies of their compositions and asked for advice and guidance. Schumann's write-ups and opinions on all music matters were greatly respected. It was he who divined the raw talent of young Chopin by only listening to a minor composition of his and made the famous announcement in his *Journal*, "Hats Off, Gentlemen – A Genius!" Schumann also intuitively sensed the future greatness of Brahms by referring to him as "the young eagle".

In this book, therefore, you will read the accounts of the Old Masters along with those of their distinguished contemporaries. Read it then as you would any other story. In the chapter titled "A Survey of Western Classical Music from 1600 to our Times" you will find a chart that briefly outlines the course of this music from the 16th century and shows the names of the Old Masters along with those of their major contemporaries.

It is heartening to see several serious efforts in Mumbai to initiate newcomers to Western Classical music. (Noteworthy elsewhere in the country are the Delhi School of Music and the Calcutta School of Music which celebrated its centenary this year.) In the forefront of laudable endeavours in Mumbai are the Mehli Mehta Music Foundation (MMMF), the National Centre for the Performing Arts (NCPA), Furtados School of Music with branches across India and the True School of Music.

Admirably pursuing its aim of providing music education for children and presenting quality concerts, the MMMF is renowned for organising Sangat, its annual Chamber Music festival. The NCPA, in the forefront of promoting Classical Music in Mumbai, not only created the first professional Symphony Orchestra in India with regular concerts every year, but also hosts the London Symphony Orchestra, the BBC Scottish Symphony Orchestra and other distinguished groups.

Hopefully, this book may also make its own small contribution by its declared aim to target the novice interested in getting to know the world of Western Classical music and get hooked on it.

Classics are forever!

Scene outside Mehli Mehta's farewell concert at the Sir C. J. Hall, Bombay

Miniature from the Pontifical of Bishop Erasmus Ciolek, Krakow, 1510
Among the congregation is the Bishop at the centre, with nobles to his left and right and people from the lower classes in the foreground.
Pipers are seen in the high gallery to the left

A Survey of **Western Classical** Music from **1600 to our Times**

*I*taly was the cradle of Western Classical music which arguably owes its very birth and life to the strong and sustained patronage of the Roman Catholic Church.

Since music evoked feelings of grandeur and nobility, giving the human spirit a unique uplift, composers were encouraged by the Church to compose music for the human voice and for the organ. The compositions were mostly Passions, Masses, Oratorios and many smaller works like Cantatas and Motets.

The first outstanding composer was Giovanni Palestrina (1525-94). His claim to immortality lay in his famous Mass (a musical setting of the Roman Catholic Church service), which the Pope declared to be so outstanding that he ordered it to be taken as the pattern for all future music of the Church. Prominent among Palestrina's contemporaries were gifted composers such as Tallis, Byrd, Monteverdi and Allegri. They were followed later by Purcell, Corelli, Couperin and Albinoni.

It needs to be mentioned here that long before the Church emerged as the sole powerful patron of Classical music, human voices raised in song were among the earliest forms of musical expression in the cultures of all the nations of the world, for prayers, rituals and entertainment.

Until the Middle Ages, music had been passed down orally from generation to generation. It was much later in history that music came to be written down. The first musical notations were very likely from the plainchant of medieval monks, who were also among the very early composers with their simple vocal lines celebrating the glory of God.

In the 12th and 13th centuries, outside the influence of the Church were the troubadours, roving companies of singers and poets, ranging from serfs and tradesmen to royalty, who sang of courtly love, of chivalry and adventure.

In contrast there was the *Carmina Burana*, a 13th-century collection of quite lascivious songs about womanising, gambling and drinking, which extolled the baser pursuits of those times.

The French troubadours and their successors progressively opened up a demand for secular music that rivalled the sacred. They developed their music in innovative ways that did not depend upon religious texts. Many, returning from the Crusades, had brought back the Byzantine, Persian and Arabic modes of expression: their music combined the function of churchman and musician, and they thenceforth composed both sacred and secular music. The ethereal with its prescribed modes and the earthly with its folkloristic base became united in music's Classical development.

With the Renaissance came a shift in music's centre of gravity in Europe. The royal and princely houses in Italy, Austria and Germany, became the great new bastions of culture and art, extending their patronage to painters, poets and musicians. Many of these princely houses even had small orchestras of their own which encouraged composers, some of them attached to the court, to experiment with different forms of music (which later led to the development of string quartets and symphonies). Annual competitions were held among the orchestras of these houses, which were keenly contested and did their patrons proud.

The patronage of the royal and princely houses also encouraged new and secular forms of music, among them the Opera, which in time became popular with the general public. This further diminished the role of the Church.

As the control and patronage of the Church thus steadily declined, Western Classical music was liberated and astir with progressive discoveries of new and varied forms of music like string quartets, sonatas and symphonies that captured the genius of the great composers, starting with Johann Sebastian Bach.

In this book you will find biographical sketches on and major compositions of all the master composers and their distinguished contemporaries. These are divided into four sections – (i) their life sketch, (ii) their place in the history of music (either because of their genius or because of their influence), (iii) a listing of some of their major compositions, giving the reader not only an idea of their total wide output but also their versatility and mastery in composing music in various forms whether compositions for unaccompanied voices, chamber ensembles for strings or woodwind, solo

Palestrina presents his Masses to the Pope
They are regarded as the finest music of the Roman Catholic Church

Illustration from French Bible, circa1250
**Medieval musicians at a feast playing a fiddle,
a hurdy-gurdy, a harp and a psaltery**

The Adoration of the Lamb
**A 15th-century panel depicting a choir of angels
in the cathedral at Ghent**

and accompanied sonatas, symphonies, symphonic poems and operas. Such a list may also interest a reader already familiar with some compositions by a particular composer, to pick out items from the list which he feels he would like to hear and may be included in his collection of recorded music, (iv) notes on the composers' select well-known works, this last section being a special feature of this book.

In this connection I wish to state here that I have not hesitated to take down in full (within quote marks) passages, particularly from *The Victor Book of the Symphony,* in respect of many orchestral works because of their superb, lucid analysis of the music which I strongly felt I must share with my readers.

In the "Introduction", I have urged readers to go through the text as if it is the stuff of a profound storybook – the write-ups on all the Old Masters along with those on their distinguished contemporaries – and they will thus learn from them in detail the main features of the Contrapuntal School (1650-1750), the Classical School (1730-1800), and from there the dazzling dawn of the Romantic School (1790-1840) when music powered by Beethoven reached heights never dreamt of before and led to the 19th-century Classicism/late Romanticism and Expressionism (1800-1900).

The period 1900-2000 saw the advent of a unique feature in music, Impressionism, led by Debussy. Many composers of this period also showed great interest in writing programme music.

A significant development of this period was nationalism in music, which saw many great composers also writing music that incorporated the folk melodies and songs of their country or hinted at the spirit of that heritage. Prominent among such composers were Sibelius (Finland), Grieg (Norway), Mussorgsky (Russia), Dvořák (Bohemia), Elgar (England), Brahms (Germany), Liszt (Hungary), Falla (Spain) and Bartók (Hungary).

During this period (1900-2000), literally hundreds of young composers, of varying talents, have approached the public for a verdict on their works. But it takes really a span of 70 to 100 years, for the public, the critics and the music world generally, to finally approve such works as acceptable for the concert halls of the world. And here it is noted that musical moods and tastes change over time, so that what is cautiously accepted as avant-garde today becomes the new norm for tomorrow.

However, given here are names of 18 composers who have already made an impression as I could gather from the *Gramophone* magazine: Samuel Barber, Béla Bartók, Alban Berg, Benjamin Britten, Aaron Copland, Peter Maxwell Davies, Philip Glass, George Gershwin, Frederick Delius, Paul Hindemith, Olivier Messiaen, Witold Lutoslawski, John Cage, Robert Simpson, Michael Tippett, Ottorino Respighi, Dmitri Shostakovich and William Walton.

MASTER COMPOSERS AND THEIR REPRESENTATIVE COMPOSERS

1650-1750 The Contrapuntal/Baroque School
BACH   HANDEL
Scarlatti, Vivaldi, Telemann, Rameau and others

1730-1800 The Classical School
HAYDN MOZART BEETHOVEN SCHUBERT
Auber, Boccherini, Clementi, Cherubini, Field, Gluck, Meyerbeer and others

1790-1840 The Romantic School
BEETHOVEN SCHUMANN CHOPIN MENDELSSOHN
Glinka, Paganini and others

1800-1900 19th-century Classicism/Romanticism
SIBELIUS BRAHMS TCHAIKOVSKY WAGNER
Berlioz, Liszt, Rimsky-Korsakov, Rachmaninov, Grieg, Dvořák, Ravel, Saint-Saëns, Mussorgsky, Borodin, Elgar, Falla, Stravinsky, R. Strauss, Prokofiev, Vaughan Williams, J. Strauss

1900-2000 Impressionism
DEBUSSY
Programme Music
National Music

" The pinnacle of Palestrina's achievement was the Mass, of which he wrote more than one hundred."

GIOVANNI PALESTRINA

Born: Palestrina, Italy, circa 1525
Died: Rome, Italy, February 2, 1594

When Giovanni Pierluigi da Palestrina was 14 years old, a family council was held to determine how and by whom he should be educated. A musical career was chosen. His father owned a house and a vineyard but was not wealthy. His mother volunteered to sell a plot of land she owned to pay for Palestrina's education. She did well, for her son became the greatest composer of church music of his era.

Palestrina had a sweet voice and was organist and choirmaster in Palestrina, a small town near Rome, until Pope Julius III called him to Rome to sing in the choir of the Sistine Chapel.

Accordingly, Palestrina moved his family – he had married the girl of his heart and at 24 was the father of three children – to Rome and was prepared to bask in the Pope's patronage for the rest of his life. But he had been there for only a short time when Pope Julius died. His successor, Pope Paul IV, was told by Palestrina's jealous colleagues that he did not have a good voice, and above all, being a married man he had no right to sing in the choir. Pope Paul thereupon dismissed Palestrina and to salve his conscience allowed him a pension of six scudi as a monthly pension. Palestrina was so upset at this change in his life that he took to his bed with the 16th-century equivalent of a nervous breakdown.

After a slow recovery, he was appointed to St. John Lateran Church as choirmaster. Palestrina and his growing family spent five tranquil years in a little house on the Caelian Hill, happy years untouched by the jealousies and intrigues of Rome.

From this peaceful retreat he was summoned by the accession of yet another Pope, Pius IV, who recalled him to Rome and to the Sistine Chapel. Fortune smiled once more on Palestrina who served 11 Popes altogether. His fortunes rose and fell with theirs.

Major compositions

Palestrina was a prolific composer, writing mainly sacred music such as masses, motets and Magnificats in the *a cappella* style (no instrumental accompaniment) as well as both secular (set to "profane" texts) and sacred madrigals. The pinnacle of his achievement was the Mass, of which he wrote more than one hundred.

Masses
Missa Papae Marcelli
Missa Aeterna Christi Munera
Missa Assumpta est Maria

Motets
Hodie Christus natus est
Tu es Petrus
Adoramus Te, Christe
O bone Jesu

Madrigals
Tota pulchra es ("Song of Solomon")
Veni dilecte mi ("Song of Solomon")
Vox dilecti mei ("Song of Solomon")
Vulnerasti cor meum ("Song of Solomon")

As a great religious composer, Palestrina in his devotional works achieved a serene and ethereal beauty of pure sound

In the dedication of his *First Book of Motets,* in 1563, Palestrina wrote: "The function of music in the Church is the seasoning of devotion by the added delight of sweetness of song and variety of harmony." So well did his music embody this pious belief that a Commissioner appointed by the Council of Trent in 1564 to purify the music of the Church, left Palestrina's compositions unchanged, as being beyond reproach. The purity of Palestrina's "Mass of Marcellus", which he had composed some time before the Council of Trent, moved the then reigning Pope to tears when he heard it after a committee of eight Cardinals had pronounced it fit for papal ears.

Fate struck a massive blow when Palestrina lost, within four years, his beloved wife, two sons and two grandchildren in the plagues then raging throughout Rome. In his grief, Palestrina considered becoming a monk. But he reconsidered and instead took a second wife. In directing her thriving fur business Palestrina profited greatly and used the profits to have copies made of his collected compositions.

Never was money more wisely spent than on the 16 large volumes of Palestrina's works, a treasury of religious music. In the long list of his compositions there was not one that was unworthy. The sacred words could be clearly heard throughout. The polyphonic music with which they were joined could be understood by all. The music won for Palestrina the title "Prince of Music" which is engraved on the simple leaden plate that marked his tomb when he passed on in 1594.

Palestrina's place in music history

Palestrina had a vast influence on the development of Roman Catholic Church music, and his work can be seen as a model and summation of Renaissance polyphony.

The chief characteristic of what has been referred to as the Palestrina style, is that the importance of the words is not entirely overshadowed by the music.

The "Marcellus Mass" is a perfect example of his style. "There is a sensible balance between the 'horizontal' lines of the melody and the 'vertical' lines of the harmony. The contrapuntal voices are not accentuated at the cost of euphony, nor does the harmony hinder a rendering which is full of life. Palestrina's harmonic style is characterised by the frequent use of thirds, and an interchange of the tonic and dominant which makes the tone extraordinarily clean. This is accentuated by an original handling of dissonances, which are used mostly in the descending sequences, and then only for the voices which have unaccentuated syllables. There is no dissonance whatever in the ascending sequence.

"The rhythm of the Palestrina style arises from the composer's desire to build a synthesis of the vertical and horizontal elements. This is not the least of the reasons why Palestrina's compositions are so difficult to sing. But if correctly performed they give an impression of something ethereal and supernatural.

"In Palestrina's church music he discards chromatic progressions which his predecessors and contemporaries used freely; he did this from a devout desire to keep the church modes intact, and his works on the whole gain much in purity and dignity in consequence."

> *To Monteverdi the musical effect was everything.*
> *His guide was truth and truth alone,*
> *and no academic rules were allowed to smother it.*
> *He tied the melody so closely to the words that*
> *it would be 'like a soulless body' if the words*
> *were taken away.*

CLAUDIO MONTEVERDI

Born: Cremona, Italy, baptised May 1, 1567
Died: Venice, Italy, November 19, 1643

Even as a young lad in his teens, Claudio Monteverdi chafed at the restrictions imposed on music by tradition. When he was a student of Marc'Antonio Ingegneri, in Cremona, from whom he received a thorough training, he questioned while dutifully memorising the rigid rules of counterpoint.

Monteverdi employed a fairly complete orchestra and gave its separate groups each a part to play. He brought about many changes in the orchestra. He insisted the violas play with bows instead of plucking the strings and this brought new beauty to the string section. He introduced tremolo and pizzicato techniques to the strings.

As court musician in the service of Vincenzo, Duke of Gonzaga, Monteverdi had many opportunities to broaden his mental horizon. To the Duke's court in Mantua came Galileo, Tasso and other great thinkers.

The music of Monteverdi spans the Renaissance and the Baroque. The corpus extends from madrigals to operas and sacred music.

Monteverdi soon became a great favourite of the Duke and at the age of 40 was commissioned by the Duke to write an opera. The result was "La Favola d'Orfeo" (The Legend of Orpheus) which premiered at Mantua in 1607 and was a great success. Monteverdi gave his singers lovely melodies and interpolated song-like passages into the accompaniment.

Later the same year, tragedy clouded Monteverdi's life. His wife Claudia Cattaneo, the court singer, accomplished harpist and a most genial companion, fell ill and died. Monteverdi was then in the midst of his second opera, "Arianna". Although in sorrow, he drove himself to complete it. The famous Lament in "Arianna", *Lasciatemi morire*, is a cry of grief so profound that it moves listeners to tears. The opera was presented with great success before a huge audience in the Duke's castle in Mantua,

14th-century instruments
**A fiddler and psaltery player
are shown in this fresco**

but it is sad that out of the score only the Lament has been preserved. When his patron Duke Vincenzo died, Monteverdi secured a respected position as the choirmaster to the magnificent cathedral of St. Marks in Venice.

In Venice the arts were flourishing and Monteverdi benefited greatly from them. His masses, motets and other religious writings were heard to good advantage in the vast cathedral. He composed several volumes of madrigals in Venice and operas known now only because he mentioned their titles in his letters. Thus a great deal of Monteverdi's music has been lost to the world.

In 1630 the plague ravaged Europe. Monteverdi vowed that he would make a pilgrimage to the Madonna of Loreto if his life was spared. He escaped the plague and duly made the pilgrimage; thereafter he took holy orders. His assuming the priesthood did not prevent him from continuing to compose operas until his death at the age of 76.

Monteverdi's place in music history

Although nearly 400 years have passed since Monteverdi's death, he is one of the most revolutionary personalities in the history of music. When he was young, contrapuntal vocal music was still at its height. The problems of blending many voices, melodic form and musical structure had mostly been solved, but the music mainly lacked expression and 'life'. Individual emotions could never be properly expressed by polyphonic choir.

"At about this time, composers in Florence were groping their way towards an entirely new musical style. Their aim was to re-create the old Greek drama by giving expression to individual emotions through a single voice singing a melody accompanied by instruments. This development created opera. But the recitative, the 'spoken song' as first attempted in Florence was dry and stiff and lacked 'living' expression.

"It was Monteverdi who gave life to the new form by recklessly breaking all the old rules of composition, if it was necessary to do so in order to make music realistic. To him the musical effect was everything. His guide was truth and truth alone, and no academic rules were allowed to smother it. Monteverdi tried to tie the melody so closely to the words that it would be 'like a soulless body' if the words were taken away. Both melody and harmony are born from the words and to give life to a dramatic situation Monteverdi used harmonies of unprecedented boldness. In everything Monteverdi sought truth and expression. For the first time in history he used the orchestra to create contrasts in colour.

He wrote for specific instruments and gave each of them their own separate task and characteristic voice. In order to increase the expressiveness of string instruments he invented tremolo and pizzicato; and he created new rapid and exciting rhythms for all the instruments."

Major compositions

Sacred Works
Vespro della Beata Vergine (Vespers)
Mass of Thanksgiving

Madrigals
Hor ch'el ciel e la terra
Non havea febo ancora
Lamentos della Ninfa
Zefiro torna
Lettera amorosa
Lament of Arianna
Beatus Vir
Saseta Maria
O chiome d'or

Operas
La Favola d'Orfeo, 5 Acts (1607)
L'incoronazione di Poppea (1642)

> " *It is a fact of music history that several compositions of Vivaldi so influenced Bach, that the latter arranged them for organ and other instruments.* "

ANTONIO **VIVALDI**

Born : Venice, Italy, March 4, 1678
Died : Vienna, Austria, July 28, 1741

A contemporary of Bach, Antonio Vivaldi not only influenced Bach, but himself composed notable concertos for stringed instruments.

His father Giovanni was a violinist in the Cathedral of St. Marks in Venice and took his son there when the child could barely toddle. The boy fell in love with the music and with the Church. He began studying for the priesthood at the age of 15, becoming fully ordained at 25 in 1703.

Young Vivaldi studied the violin with his father and in later years became an outstanding virtuoso of that instrument. At the age of 32 he entered the service of Landgraf Philipp van Hessen-Darmstadt, a German prince then living in Italy. He remained in the Prince's service from 1707 to 1713 and then returned to Venice where he became first violinist at St. Mark's Cathedral.

Vivaldi was director at the same time of a foundling home, the Pio Ospedale della Pietà, where he organised and conducted an all-girls choir and orchestra, a pioneering effort that bore excellent results. The ladies – performing behind a modest screen – took to playing all types of instruments with great enthusiasm, and their performances won many awards in competition with orchestras from other churches.

In addition to his priestly and directorial obligations, Vivaldi – known as "il Prete Rosso" (the Red Monk) because of the colour of his hair – composed voluminously and, in fact, became better known than Bach in his own day. He composed 40 operas and hundreds of religious works. His best-known works, numbering over 400, were concertos and sonatas for stringed instruments which received fine performances and appreciative audiences.

Vivaldi fell out of favour with the Church in characteristic fashion. While officiating at Mass one day, he was seized with an irresistible desire to write down some music that occurred to him. So unbearably did his fingers itch to exchange the rosary for the pen, that just for a moment, he succumbed to the temptation. In the middle of the service, he slipped into the sacristy, wrote as fast and as much as he could, and returned to his duties, hoping that his absence had gone unnoticed. But it had been noticed and he was dismissed from the Church, went into retirement, and died a few years later in poverty.

Vivaldi's place in music history

Of Vivaldi's compositions for strings and voices, the 20th-century Italian composer Alfredo Casella wrote:
"The prodigious wealth of musical invention; the dramatic force which recalls so imperatively the brilliance and fire of the great Venetian painters; the mastery of chord polyphony; the marvellous dynamism of the instrumental part, the incessant movement of which, independent of the voices and chorus, plainly forecasted the Wagnerian style (of opera) and finally, the high quality of the emotions which animated the works, all these put Vivaldi in a wholly new light."

It is a historical fact that several compositions of Vivaldi so influenced Bach, that the latter arranged them for organ and other instruments. The compositions themselves were catalogued in the 20th century under RV numbers, RV being abbreviated from Ryom-Verzeichnis (after the musicologist Peter Ryom).

Notes on select works

Vivaldi's compositional output was so vast that, apart from the very few mentioned below, the rest may be summarised in separate lists.

The Four Seasons

Vivaldi's best-known work, this constitutes a landmark in the history of programme music. They are the first four of 12 concertos that make up his Op. 8. They are scored for solo violin, strings and continuo, and each of the four is prefaced by a brief poem, probably written by Vivaldi himself, in which various episodes are related to the music by key letters at the side which are repeated at the appropriate places in the score.

Here are the four poems as translated by Christopher Hatch in the English edition of Marc Pincherle's monograph on Vivaldi.

Music embellished by art
**In earlier centuries a musical score was also a work of art.
This exquisite example of the illuminator's decorative skill is taken from a
Gregorian choir book of the 15th century**

Spring (No. 1 in E)

"Spring has come and the birds greet it with happy songs, and at the same time the streams run softly murmuring to the breathing of the gentle breezes. Then, the sky being cloaked in black, thunder and lightning come and have their say; after the storm has passed the little birds turn again to their harmonies... Here is a pleasant flowery meadow, the leaves sweetly rustling, the goatherd sleeps, his faithful dog at this side. Nymphs and shepherds dance to the festive sound of pastoral musette under the bright sky that they love.

Apollo and the Muses
In ancient mythology the Sun God, Apollo, was also the God of Music and Poetry

Among the happiest touches of realism are the barking of the goatherd's dog (repeated in harsh notes on the violas) in Spring, and the chattering of teeth at the beginning of Winter, and the later slides, skids and bumps on the ice.

Other Compositions

"La Tempesta di Mare,
  Op. 8 (No. 5 in E-flat)
"La Notte" (G Minor)
  (for flute, bassoon and strings)

Concertos

No. 2, G Minor: "L'Estro Armonico"
  (2 violins, cello and strings)
No. 8, A Minor
No. 9, D Minor
No. 11, D Minor
Op. 7, No. 4, F Minor "L'Inverno"
  (violin and strings)
Op. 10, No. 3, D Major "Il Gardelino"
  (flute and strings)
Mandolin and strings concertos
Oratorio: Juditha Triumphans
Secular Cantatas

Summer (No. 2 in G Minor)

"In the season made harsh by the burning sun the men and herds languish, even the evergreens are hot. The cuckoo unlocks his voice and soon the songs of the turtle dove and the goldfinch are heard. Soft breezes breathe, but unexpectedly the north wind from its quarter seeks out a quarrel, and the shepherd weeps as he is overwhelmed by fear of the gusts and of his fate. Fear of the flashing lightning and the fierce thunder denies his tired body any rest while his furious troop is on the move. How justifiable is his fear? The sky lights up, the awe-inspiring thunder brings down the fruit and the proud grain.

" Vivaldi's best-known works, numbering over 400, were concertos and sonatas for stringed instruments which received fine performances and appreciative audiences. "

Autumn (No. 3 in F)

"With songs and dances the peasants celebrate the happiness of a fine harvest, and after being greatly kindled by bacchic spirits, their rejoicing ends with sleep.

Thus everyone quits both his singing and his dancing. The air is pleasant and moderate, and the season invites everyone to the agreeableness of a sweet sleep. At the break of day the hunter goes to hunt with guns, dogs and horns, he puts the wild beast to fight and tracks him down. Tired and terrified by the loud noise of the guns and dogs, the beast, in danger of being wounded, longs for escape, but is overcome and dies.

Winter (No. 4 in F Minor)

"To tremble frozen in the icy snow, to be buffeted by the wild winds, to stamp one's frozen feet, to have excessive cold set one's teeth to chattering. To pass to a fireside of quiet and contentment, while outside the downpour bathes all. To walk carefully on ice, going slowly for fear of falling. To slip and fall sharply to the ground, and start again on ice, and run until the ice breaks apart. To hear the south wind, the north wind, and all the other winds unloosed in battle; such is winter, these are the joys it brings."

JOHANN SEBASTIAN **BACH**

Born: Eisenach, Germany, March 21, 1685
Died: Leipzig, Germany, July 28, 1750

A man to whom music owed almost as great a debt as religion owed to its founder," Robert Schumann declared of Johann Sebastian Bach. Indeed, all the great composers who followed Bach – including Handel, Haydn, Mozart, Beethoven, Schubert, Schumann, Mendelssohn, Wagner, Sibelius – looked up to Bach and venerated him as their Master.

When Bach was 19, his passion for music was discouraged by an elder brother, Johann Christoph, who tried to keep him away from copying the musical scores the family possessed mainly because copying paper was costly and difficult to obtain. Nevertheless, after the rest of the family had retired to bed for the night, Johann Sebastian would remove the sheets from the cabinet in which they were kept and proceed, by the light of the moon, to copy down laboriously all this music for his own reference and enjoyment. In later years too Bach worked late into the night in rather subdued lighting conditions. Not surprisingly, towards the end of his life he lost his eyesight. Only a few days before his death, however, he miraculously regained it.

At the age of 22, Johann Sebastian married his second cousin Maria Barbara Bach, by whom he had seven children. The family settled in Weimar, under the patronage of Duke Wilhelm Ernst. He lived here for nine years, during which his fame as an organist grew. Bach even attended to the church organ when it needed repair. It was during this Weimar period that he composed and played many of the magnificent series of organ works.

Johann Sebastian Bach was the first musician to use all five fingers in playing; at that time musicians, as a rule, played with only the first three. It is to Bach, therefore, that we owe the modern system of fingering. He played the organ so extraordinarily well that under his hands the instrument almost seemed to speak to the listeners. Bach also played the clavichord and sang in the choir.

His steady development both as musician and composer was owed to successive positions and portfolios he held, first in Köthen and then in Leipzig. In the court of Leopold, Prince of Anhalt-Köthen, Bach found a close-knit orchestra of 18 excellent players awaiting him. Prince Leopold himself played in the orchestra in which Bach directed. The six Brandenburg Concertos, the Suites and many other beautiful works for small orchestras stem from these inspired days. His secular compositions included the "Wedding", "Peasant" and "Coffee" cantatas, much enjoyed for their high contrast to his sacred music, their sheer fun and robust orchestration.

After the death of Prince Leopold, Bach moved to Leipzig and was appointed Cantor of the Thomasschule or St. Thomas School. Despite his onerous official duties there, he somehow found time to compose the magnificent Passions – St. John's, St. Matthew's and St. Mark's; the great Masses; the Christmas, Easter and Ascension Oratorios; and a number of cantatas, chorales, motets and minor religious music. Among the other well-known works he composed were the six Partitas, the "Italian Concerto", the second part of the "Well-Tempered Clavier" and "The Art of Fugue".

He composed other well-known pieces during this period such as the "Goldberg Variations" written in response

> *" Bach was the first musician to use all five fingers in playing; at that time musicians, as a rule, played with only the first three. It is to Bach, therefore, that we owe the modern system of fingering. "*

to a special request from the wealthy Russian ambassador to the Dresden court, Count Kayserling, who suffered from chronic insomnia. The music-loving Count found relief listening to the Variations played to him on particularly bad days by his very own harpsichordist Johann Goldberg. Goldberg, Bach's pupil, was himself an excellent performer, whose brilliantly improvised "Aria" provided the basis of Bach's 30 Variations.

Bach's wife Maria Barbara died suddenly in 1720. In 1721, before leaving for Leipzig, Bach had taken a second wife, the gentle young Anna Magdalena who brought him great happiness. They had 13 children of whom six survived into adulthood.

Towards the final months of his life, Bach visited the Court of King Frederick II of Prussia in Potsdam where his son Carl Philip Emanuel was court musician. There he was invited by the King to try his new Silbermann piano. Bach liked it so much that he improvised on it a six-part fugue on a theme assigned to him by the King. On returning from Leipzig, Bach copied out the fugue and sent it to King Frederick with a letter of thanks. Indeed, this is one of Bach's most remarkable fugues.

Shortly after this visit to Potsdam, Bach was stricken by blindness. Operations only aggravated his condition. He suffered for three years before a paralytic stroke occasioned the final calamity. And with resignation Bach accepted the invitation extended in his beautiful chorale "Come, sweet Death".

Bach's place in music history

Bach is regarded as the greatest representative of the Contrapuntal period in music, so called as the music of this period was especially rich in counterpoint – a word meaning, in its literal sense, "many-voiced" music that contains several strands, each with its own melodic interests, the whole fitting together in effective combination.

It has been said that even if all the music written during the Contrapuntal period were to perish and only the music of Bach remained, we would not lose much. The reason is that the composers of that period generally concerned themselves solely with perfection of form. They wrote fugues, for example, with meticulous craftsmanship, as if ingenuity in their construction and development was all that mattered. Some musicians of

The Bach family crest

that time did contend that Bach's music was unemotional and that he was too much of a cool formalist. It is true that Bach lived in an age which preferred restrained expression but his music is sincere and contains much that is deeply emotional and mystical.

Bach's organ compositions are the most perfect of their kind ever composed, and it is the ambition of every serious student of music to play his 48 Preludes and Fugues. No comment on Bach's compositions can avoid mention of his Passion Music which is so great that societies have been specially formed to sing it. His "Mass in B Minor" is another major work of enthralling music.

Away from Church music, Bach studied the works of his contemporaries. Several of their compositions which held special appeal for him were duly adopted and transcribed as organ works. Those of Vivaldi were favourites with him for extending his repertoire of transcribed pieces for his beloved organ.

Yet, strangely, for almost a century after his death, Bach's music suffered an eclipse, until musicians such as Mendelssohn and Schumann rescued it from obscurity and placed it once again before the public. Bach's music has now come to be regarded in many respects as more modern than that of the so-called "Moderns". Such was the awe-inspiring genius of this Master that though he died in 1750, his music still sounds to our ears as fresh as if it has been composed only yesterday.

Finally, no discussion on Bach's music can be deemed complete without reference to the inspired efforts made by the conductor Leopold Stokowski to bring many of Bach's smaller works to the attention of the public. As a virtuoso of the organ, Stokowski naturally studied intimately the music of Bach for many years. He had perceived the peculiarly adaptable features of much of Bach's music and virtually re-wrote for orchestra

not only several of the mightiest works, such as the "Passacaglia in C Minor", the great "Chaconne", and the "Toccata and Fugue in D Minor", but many obscure and relatively unknown smaller works as well. Stokowski's orchestral transcriptions had been in vogue from the 1930s to the 1950s. Under his spectacular conductorship the Philadelphia Orchestra attained its greatest fame as the foremost virtuoso ensemble. It was further said that each performer in that orchestra was a virtuoso soloist in his own right.

Critics were not unanimous in their enthusiasm for such Bach transcriptions. They resented the heavy opulence of the colours that Stokowski had applied the convolutions of a Bach fugue. The backlash came from several purists who had specialised in Baroque music, returning not only to Bach's original scoring but also carefully researched performances on original instruments of the times.

The music of Bach is an accurate parallel of modern times in as far as any music is a reflection of contemporary life and thought. It represents this in a variety of ways – in the intricacies of the processes, in the complexity and accuracy of its mathematical elements, in its purely scientific and mechanical aspects and in its architecture. Having transcended time, it has pervaded all tastes and climes.

Bach's prolific musical output was systematically catalogued in the second half of the 19th century. In 1950 it was augmented and re-arranged by the Bach-Werke-Verzeichnis (Catalogue of Bach's Works) with BWV numberings. It lists 1126 compositions classified by categories: cantatas, choral works, chorales, organ works, keyboard works, lute music, chamber music, orchestral music, and canons and fugues.

Bach in his family circle. God, music and the family were his entire world, it is said

Notes on select works
Partita No. 2 in D Minor (BWV 1004)
with its appendage – the Chaconne

The most famous of the set of sonatas and partitas is the Partita No. 2 in D Minor (BWV 1004) because of its appendage, the mighty Chaconne, which has been universally accepted as the most difficult piece ever written for unaccompanied violin. It is exhaustingly long at 14 minutes and consists entirely of a single succinct musical progression repeated in dozens of variations to create a dauntingly complex architecture of sound. It is said to be "a celebration of the breadth of human possibility".

After listening to the Chaconne, Johannes Brahms wrote to Clara Schumann: "On one stave, for a small instrument Bach writes a whole world of the deepest thoughts and most powerful feelings. If I imagined that I could have created, even conceived, the piece, I am quite certain that the excess of excitement and earth-shattering experience would have driven me out of my mind."

Indeed, no comment on the Chaconne can surpass the following quotation from Philipp Spitta's biography, *Bach*: "The listener must regard this Chaconne as some phenomenon of the elements, which transports and enraptures him with its indescribable majesty, and at the same time bewilders and confuses him. The overpowering wealth of forms pouring from a few and scarcely noticeable sources, displays not only the most perfect knowledge of the technique of the violin, but also the most absolute mastery over an imagination the like of which no other composer was ever endowed with."

The Partita proper consists of the classic allemande, courante, sarabande and gigue. Its appendix, the great Chaconne, which is as long as the preceding four movements put together, is the longest single movement in the six sonatas and partitas for unaccompanied violin, and is without question the most celebrated piece of unaccompanied string music ever written.

The chaconne was originally a dance, but Bach and his contemporaries were little interested in its dance-like implications. For Bach, the Chaconne was a series of variations on a ground bass, always in 3/4 time with a slow, solemn theme in the manner of a sarabande. The theme and the ground bass occupy the first eight measures. Twenty-nine variations follow, all highly contrasted in character; some are figurative and brilliant, some are densely polyphonic. Bach divides these 29 variations into three grand sections: the first 15 are in D Minor, the next nine are in D Major and the remainder in D Minor once again.

The Chaconne (Bach – Stokowski)

"In its transcribed version, the Chaconne brings into brilliant reality the imaginings of the sensitive person who hears or plays the music on the violin. Who has not thought, perhaps subconsciously, 'There is that passage, it sounds like an organ' – but it does not sound like an organ; only like a violin straining for unattainable sonority. Who has not succumbed to the illusion of a whole band of violin playing because of the deftness of one violinist and the miraculous formulas of Bach's counterpoint? But in the orchestra there is not the illusion, but the glorious and

Bach at the organ
The great composer was also a brilliant organ virtuoso and respected teacher

Major compositions

Choral
St. Matthew Passion
St. John Passion
Mass in B Minor
Christmas Oratorios
Other religious works (cantatas, motets, etc)

Secular Cantatas
Wedding Cantata
Peasant Cantata
Coffee Cantata

Bach – Stokowski arrangements
Prelude in E-flat Minor
Chaconne
Fugue in G Minor ("Little")
Fugue in G Minor ("Great")
Toccata and Fugue in D Minor
Passacaglia in C Minor
Sarabande from English Suite No. 3
Adagio from the Organ Toccata in C Minor
Sarabande from the First Violin Suite

Instrumental
6 Brandenburg Concertos for Orchestra
4 Suites for Orchestra
6 French Suites
6 English Suites
Concerto in Italian Style
Chromatic Fantasy and Fugue
Violin Concertos in E and A Minor
Double Violin Concerto in D Minor
Goldberg Variations
The Art of Fugue
The Well-Tempered Clavier – Books 1 & 2
 (containing preludes and fugues in
 every key)

Chamber Music
6 Sonatas and Partitas for unaccompanied
 violin (1717-22) (BWV 1001-1006)
No. 1, G Minor
No. 2, B Minor (Partita No. 1)
No. 3, A Minor
No. 4, D Minor (Partita No. 2) – Chaconne
No. 5, C Major – Prelude
No. 6, E Major (Partita No. 3)
Cello Suites (6) (BWV 1007-1012)
Sonatas for flute and clavier
Viola da Gamba and clavier
Violin and clavier (Six Sonatas)
Flute, violin and continuo
Prelude and Fugue, E-flat Major
Fantasia, C Minor
Fantasia and Fugue, A Minor
Toccata, D Major

Concertos (in the style of Vivaldi)
Innumerable Fantasias and Fugues
Preludes and Fugues
Toccatas and Fugues
Organ Works

The Bach monument at Eisenach

almost tangible reality; there is a band of strings, of brasses and wind, expanding to full stature the magnificent figures that Bach, perforce, has set down in miniature.

"The basic theme of the work is gravely pronounced by the lower strings at the beginning; and at once the marvellous flow of ideas in seemingly endless abundance rises from the solemn subject. There can be no adequate description of the wonder of this music. In a peculiar fashion it explains itself; it is always clear, articulate, rounded, rich and perfect. There are succeeding waves of power, and waves within waves, that ultimately reach a towering crest of sonority. There are little subsidiary motives; a second thematic idea in flute and other woodwinds, a third in horns and trombones and, towards the end, prodigious outpouring of sound that is never noisy of tone, superlatively full yet

Score of the Chaconne, Partita No. 2 in D Minor (BWV 1004)
This work is universally accepted as the most difficult composition written for unaccompanied violin – 14 minutes in duration, it poses technical challenges for the greatest violinist

not clamorous, in a powerful ejaculation of the basic theme. The end is not yet: there appears once more in the music a divine and somehow tender complacence that recalls again the thought that inspired the vast structure and informed its very measure."

Partita No. 3 in E Major (BWV 1006)
Preludio, Loure, Gavotte en rondeau, Menuet I – Menuet II, Bourrée, Gigue.

Just as it was customary in Bach's time to end a composition in large form with a gay quick movement, so Bach ends the cycle of unaccompanied sonatas and partitas with an entire work that is remarkable for its lightness and high spirits. The Allemande-Courante-Sarabande-Gigue arrangement is dispensed with, except for the Gigue.

The opening movement is not even in one of the dance rhythms. It is marked Preludio. It is one of Bach's most scintillating studies in the concerto style and it can be heard backstage before many a symphony concert, for orchestral violinists love to warm up on it.

The dances are all of the French courtly variety. First is the loure, a dance in moderate tempo and 6/4 time; second is the gavotte en rondeau. The phrase "en rondeau" signifies that the theme of the gavotte recurs several times, with episodes of contrast between its repetitions.

Next is the pair of menuets. The rhythm is always triple and it is often presented, as it is here, as two distinct and separate movements, the first of which is repeated after the second. The partita ends with a bourrée and a gigue. The gavotte en rondeau is so charming that it appeals to every listener and is often played separately.

Prelude in E-flat Minor
"There is a short introduction of low chords, pulsating like the beatings of pain against the heart; and then from the trembling strings arises a song of such sweet and tender melancholy as human ears have rarely heard, and human voices uttered never. The searching poignancy of this melody presses across and through surrounding harmonies of surpassing loveliness; there, almost imperceptibly, two voices join in eloquent dialogue. Now the music is not without gleams of hope, or at least of resignation; it passes momentarily into brighter, major measures, but dies in the shadowy minor from which it came."

Fugue in G Minor: "The Little Fugue". (Bach – Stokowski)
"Two fugues by Bach are among the most popular in the organist's repertoire: 'The little A Minor Fugue', and the 'great' one which is part of the Fantasia and Fugue in G Minor.

"The 'little' Fugue is a wonderful study in colour and climax. It begins with the pronouncement of the theme by the oboe, and ultimately every section in the orchestra has its comment to make on this theme.

"Meanwhile, a series of climaxes succeed one another toward a final thundering forth of the theme. The jaunty subject of the fugue appears in the major on the entrance of the cellos and again when the sonorous basses have it. But the answering voice, though also in the major mode, leads back to more pronouncements of the main theme, again in G Minor.

"From this point onward, there is a swift growth in intensity and power until the full sonority of the orchestra is called forth in the last climax."

Bach playing for Frederick the Great at Potsdam in the spring of 1747
The music-loving king showed great favour to the composer

Orchestra created a sensation repeated even now with each succeeding performance...

"The two sections of the work are intimately connected. The Toccata (from *toccare*, to touch; therefore a work designed to show manual dexterity) is utterly free in style and blazing with brilliance in every measure. Fiercely emphatic phrases, rushing scales, infinitely varied figures contrasting with masses of tone in full orchestra; in swift succession the timbre of each orchestral choir is exploited and we arrive at a massive but swiftly fading climax.

"Then in the 32nd measure the fugue itself begins. Question and answer are entangled in glowing textures of tone, yet always clear. There are recurring surges and recessions of power, yet each minor climax is greater than its predecessor... the strings indulge in a deliriously joyful cadenza that attains the gamut for brilliance and sonority – and all combine to carry the orchestra closer to a final titanic proclamation. Then, as though exhausted, the tempo is slightly relaxed, and a series of gigantic chords, employing the utmost orchestral resources, bring the music to its thrilling close."

Fugue in G Minor: "The Great Fugue" (Bach – Stokowski)

"This is a transcription of the second part of the 'Fantasia and Fugue in A Minor', for organ. Like the 'Little' Fugue it displays a series of climaxes, with various instruments in the orchestral sections sounding their versions of the theme in contrasting or related timbres. Unlike the 'Little' Fugue, however, progress towards the gigantic climax is not a continuous sweep; passages in pianissimo are adroitly built into its structure that the succeeding outpourings of orchestral power may be the more effective by contrast. Sometimes the woodwinds given the theme commune quietly among themselves, sometimes the brass strikes a blazing slash across the fabric of the music. For the finale, the concerted power of the orchestra is gathered up for a mighty declamation. On the final chord, one of Bach's frequent but always surprising modulations to the major accomplishes by means of harmony what the straining orchestra could not add by sonority – a last incredible brilliancy, an effect of reserve powers suddenly unleashed."

Toccata and Fugue in D Minor (Bach – Stokowski)

"It was written for the organ – for displaying on that noble instrument the powers of which Bach alone, in his time, was master. This 'Toccata and Fugue' is among the first of Stokowski's Bach transcriptions. Its first public performance by the Philadelphia

Passacaglia in C Minor (Bach–Stokowski)

"The Passacaglia is perhaps Bach's greatest organ work. Yet one wonders if, really, it is playable upon even that mighty instrument, with a fraction of the nobility, subtlety and delicacy of shading, the exquisitely flexible rhythm, the infinite variety of colour and the inspiring climax given it by the orchestra.

"The solemn theme that opens the work persists in the bass throughout the first section, while above it is reared a complicated structure of variations, all clearly springing from the melodic essence of the foundation theme, yet each more brilliant than its predecessor.

"The second section of the Passacaglia reveals the variations in the lower internal parts, then the theme in the rich nobility of the brass against the penetrating brilliance of the strings above. Now, for the first time, the theme appears in the upper voices, assigned to the woodwinds. Again, it is presented by the violins, with the contrabasses ponderously giving out their particular version.

"Tone colours of which no organ is capable, tones that only a living hand and breath of life can produce, are now invoked by the conductor in this magnificent orchestration. The warm tones of the horns boldly proclaim the theme, with the incisive voices of strings and oboe sharply contrasted. A new figure, involving rhythmic and dynamic as well as melodic and tonal variation, is given to the strings. Syncopation disturbs and modifies the rhythm of the variations and the theme itself, now in the basses, is subjected to a rhythmic mutation that adds to its compelling force.

"The third section of this Passacaglia unfolds new and wonderful treatments, and reveals a sustained, passionate utterance in strings that is overpowering.

"Presently the fugue begins, its first subject (it is a double fugue) comprising the first half of the Passacaglia theme proper and the other subject a new figure in eighth. The complete theme of the Passacaglia does not appear again in the music.

"The fugue is the strictest and the most mathematical of contrapuntal

" Bach's organ compositions are the most perfect of their kind ever composed, and it is the ambition of every serious student of music to play his 48 Preludes and Fugues."

devices, yet there are occasions in music, and countless examples in Bach, where by inspired genius it is made the vehicle for the most intense emotional expression. Never in all his music did Bach employ it more felicitously than here. It begins simply enough, but in its convolutions steadily approaches a climax of soul-shaking power... The trumpets pierce like a single golden ray. The orchestra drives forth a gigantic mass of tone as palpable, almost, as richly graved and many-coloured stone. It reaches a peak of brilliance and sonority beyond which it seems mind cannot go and ear cannot hear – and touches one last soaring pinnacle at the end."

Brandenburg Concerto No. 2 in F Major

The first movement opens with sheer simplicity and clarity, apart from its delightful sprightly rhythm and prolific invention and variety.

"It sparkles, it trips with elastic step infallibly through twining measures and colours rich and bright, like a moving chiaroscuro, sweeping swiftly across the page. The trumpet, undeniable leader of the solo quartet, enters first on a clear and long-drawn note... now the violins in a sprightly figure, the oboe with its somewhat tearful voice in a parallel phrase and finally the flute, spurting jets of bright tone like a silver stream against the massed colour of the string choirs.

"Imitation, thesis and anti-thesis, contrast and parallel... half the melodic

Bach reading proofs of his organ music
The composer worked late into the night in subdued lighting which made him almost blind

It has been said that even if all the music written during the Contrapuntal period were to perish and only the music of Bach remained, we would not lose much.

devices known to the master are resorted to with almost bewildering brilliance. And through it all, a fine elastic rhythm, urging on where a scholar's delight in perfect symmetry might tempt him to linger – a rhythm strongly supporting the delicately balanced structure above it. Yet, at the division of the movement, the loveliest music is still to come.

"Now the quartet appears in both internal and external contrast and at each succeeding shifting of tone colours one wonders which is the loveliest. A modulation to the minor effects no change in the exuberant spirit of the movement;

rather, its sobering tones give stronger contrast to the joyous return to the main theme, in the buoyant F Major, on which the movement closes. A broadening of tone, an extension of the rhythmic stride, a bright major tonic chord and the movement is ended.

"The bold tones of the trumpet in the solo group are less in evidence as the tender sentiments of the second movement supplants the exuberant joyousness of the first. Now a lovely song is woven of strands charmed from violin and oboe, and still again from the flute, while the deeper strings of the orchestra pursue their quiet course through broken chords, ever moving and vital. Again, which voice is loveliest? Again, which confluence of voices shall most deeply enchant our ears? Which of these voices – oboe, flute, violin – shall triumph in the gentle conflict?

"In respect of the third movement, it is difficult to explain the insight of a conductor who guides his musicians through the intricacies of the magnificent fugue involving the solo group throughout the final movement. Four voices, three of them among the weakest in the orchestra, woven in most intricate counterpoint, against massed sonorities of the string choirs – yet each voice is crystal clear, each thread of tone shines independently in its own colour, and still blends with its background. That is Bach.

"The fugue incidentally, is of the type known as a 'free' fugue, in contradistinction to the strictest form of the fugue, which must contain all elements of this contrapuntal device, and then in regular sequence. One would rather think that Bach, facile as he was in the most difficult labyrinths of harmony, was a trifle impatient, out of his own exuberance, with the confines of strictest form. Be that as it may, he

has created in this movement, within restrictions which would be paralysing to a present-day composer, an expression of dashing high spirits."

Brandenburg Concerto No. 5 in D Major

"In this concerto, violin, flute and piano are treated as solo instruments in all three movements, although combined with extraordinary beautiful effort in the second. The thematic material of the first movement is presented at once in the strings and more powerfully in the ensemble. The solo violin and flute have frequent responsive phrases, posed against the concerted voices of the whole orchestra group. There is a long, elaborate and difficult solo for the piano; the original scoring had demanded a virtuoso harpsichordist.

"The second movement, grave and full of emotion, takes the form of a trio for the solo instruments, in which their separate voices are intricately woven in most expressive melody.

"The third and final section is a marked and not unwelcome contrast, and with almost abandoned swift rhythms, bright tunefulness and more sonority than has heretofore appeared in the concerto."

Fugue in C Minor

"It is a far cry from the 'Well-Tempered Clavier' of Bach to the great orchestral instrument of today, with its more than hundred voices, its infinite variety of tone colours, its flexibility and its power. Bach, of all the classic composers, would have revelled in it and exploited its possibilities as no one else could have done. This little fugue, originally a student's exercise, becomes in Stokowski's brilliant transcriptions a glowing and powerful episode. Not forgetting the essential humour and joviality of the fugue, the transcriber seizes upon its intrinsic dramatic possibilities also, and from the statement of the theme by the violin at the outset, he builds to a gigantic climax involving the full powers of the orchestra.

"Here are rhythms within rhythms, strings and woodwind and trumpet in subject and answer, with elements of the original theme constantly reappearing and keeping in motion the complicated tissue woven by Bach and coloured by the orchestrator. Now there is a simple statement of the jolly subject by the unassertive woodwind voice; now low scales are drawn across the page; minor climaxes rise and fall – until finally the long-restrained trombones and tuba assert the main subject in the bass and the whole orchestra joins in gigantic chords, the last of which, suddenly moving from minor to parallel major, ends the fugue in a golden blaze."

Sarabande from the English Suite No. 3

"The sarabande which Stokowski has transcribed for orchestra is extracted from Bach's Third English Suite. The suite, in Bach's time, was a grouping of movements in dance rhythms, rather less formal than overture and sonata. The sarabande was very frequently chosen as one of the movements, primarily because of the intrinsic dignity and grace of its rhythm, and also because it furnished a desirable rhythmic contrast with the more robust measures of the popular dance forms.

"The extended rhythmic impulse of the sarabande, being as it is in slow 3/4 time, does not adapt it to the contrapuntal style, and the movement consequently assumes the character of an eloquent but simple song. In the orchestral transcription the lovely melodic line is maintained in all its purity, yet its curves are accented delicately with colours drawn from a variety of instruments. The rhythmic element is preserved by subtle yet simple means – an occasional rolling arpeggio from the harp that gives a moving impulse and at the same time applies a fugitive brilliance."

Performing the Partitas

Bach's partitas and sonatas for unaccompanied violin are not only punishing tests of the technical prowess of their performers but also demand insightful readings of their compositional elements.

In this connection it is interesting to compare how the two towering violinists of the 20th century – Jascha Heifetz and Yehudi Menuhin – have played and recorded for posterity their separate approaches to the Bach partitas and sonatas.

Heifetz, ever alert to fulfilling the composer's intentions, takes note of the fact that the various movements of the partitas and sonatas carry the label of dances and accordingly stresses their precision of rhythm, while Menuhin prefers an idealistic approach, a profound quasi-spiritual interpretation.

Menuhin was a world-famous child prodigy at the age of 12. Unfortunately, his adulthood was beset with problems. He frankly admitted later to having had to re-learn many technical aspects of violin playing.

Heifetz, on the other hand, had a smooth transition in life and with his prodigious technical superiority, consolidated his reputation as foremost among the greatest violinists of the 20th century. He died in 1987 and to this day there has not possibly emerged any noteworthy challenge to his prime position. In fact, many of his eminent colleagues, led by Itzhak Perlman, have come to regard him as a heaven-blessed artiste. When the music world celebrated Heifetz's birth centenary (1901-2001), the editor of *The Strad* magazine, Eric Wen, writing in the *Gramophone* edition of October 2001 also hailed Heifetz as "the violinist of intuitive perfection".

Yehudi Menuhin and Jascha Heifetz interpreted Bach's partitas differently

George Frideric Handel

GEORG FRIEDRICH
HANDEL

Born: Halle, Germany, February 23, 1685
Died: London, England, April 14, 1759

*A*lthough their son is now counted among the greatest composers of the Baroque age, Georg Friedrich Handel's parents were indifferent to music. Indeed, his father was actually opposed to his becoming a musician and young Handel resigned himself to becoming a lawyer.

At the age of 7, however, Handel taught himself to play the clavichord, practising on a small instrument smuggled into the attic. When his father took him on a trip to visit his acquaintance, Duke Johann Adolf I, his playing so delighted the Duke that Handel's father was persuaded to seek a music teacher for his son. Handel also learnt to play the violin, oboe and organ and studied harmony, counterpoint and composition with Zachow, the best teacher in Halle.

When his father died, Handel was 18. Without hesitation he dropped the detested law and accepted a position as organist in the Dom Church. He served several years' musical apprenticeship in Hamburg, capital of German opera, played the violin in the orchestra and composed his first opera. It was also in Hamburg that he fought his famous duel with a rival harpsichordist. A coat button, which deflected his adversary's sword, saved his life.

As his first opera "Almira" was a success, Handel followed it up with a second opera, "Nero", which also proved to be a success. Jealous rivals, however, made his life in Hamburg difficult and in 1706, at the age of 21, he left Germany and went to Italy.

Once there, he fell in love with Italian opera and felt at home wherever he travelled in that country. He composed an opera, "Rodrigo", Italian in text, musical style and feeling. This brought him to the attention of wealthy Italian sponsors.

In 1710, Handel returned to Germany to become Director of Opera in Hanover where his opera "Rinaldo" was to be performed. His first act

The Little Handel
This famous painting depicts the scene one night when the family, awakened by noises from the lumber room, found young Handel diligently practising on an old harpsichord

there, however, was to request leave of absence to go to London where it would also be performed. "Rinaldo" was a great hit in London. The English were lovers of Italian opera and this German, who wrote like an Italian with a German accent, suited them perfectly. Handel settled in London in 1712 and lived there till his death. He changed his German name to the English equivalent, George Frederick, and became a naturalised British citizen in 1726.

He was very successful in London and composed 15 operas, all of which did well. Then, in 1728, John Gay's "Beggar's Opera", an English ballad opera, took England by storm and Handel's operatic works unfortunately played to empty houses.

At the age of 52, Handel suffered an apoplectic stroke and was ill for some months. When he returned to London after having taken the cure in Aix-la-Chapelle, he was bankrupt but restored in body and in spirit. He decided to regain his lost prestige by way of the oratorio. Each year, from 1738 to 1751, he produced an oratorio, sometimes two, and the English loved them all as they had loved his operas earlier.

For the last seven years of his life, Handel was blind. His oratorio about the blind Samson was prophetic of his own fate. But he continued to play the organ and conducted to the last. Handel was buried in London's Westminster Abbey with all the pomp and ceremony that England bestows upon her favourite sons.

Handel's place in music history

Handel's greatest claim to be remembered for all time is his oratorio "Messiah". The world's most famous oratorio, the "Messiah" is regarded as one of the miracles of human achievement. So powerful are the emotions stirred by its noble music, that (so a version of the story goes) at one of its first performances in England before King George II, the king was so moved by the "Hallelujah Chorus" that he stood up. Seeing their sovereign standing, the audience followed suit. Ever since then it has become the tradition at every performance of the "Messiah" for the

whole audience to stand up at the singing of the "Hallelujah". Handel himself said of the "Hallelujah" – "I did think I did see all Heaven before me, and the great God himself."

The most frequently played of his harpsichord works is the "Chaconne" in G, from the second set of Suites (No. 2), and the air with variations from Suite No. 5 in F, which has become famous under the title "The Harmonious Blacksmith".

Well known too are his "Water Music" and "Fireworks Music". The latter was commissioned by King George II to accompany a spectacular fireworks display to celebrate the Treaty of Aix-la-Chapelle. Even its rehearsal in London's Vauxhall Gardens, caused an impromptu audience of 12,000 to stop traffic for three hours.

Major compositions

40 Operas
(including "Rodrigo" and "Rinaldo")

19 Oratorios (including the "Messiah", "Saul", "Samson", "Solomon" and "Judas Maccabaeus")

12 Organ Concertos

12 "Concerti Grossi" for strings

Sonatas for violin, viola, oboe, etc.

Harpsichord "Chaconne" in G

Viola da gamba Sonata

Oboe Sonatas

Suites for full orchestra, including the "Water Music" and "Royal Fireworks Music"

DOMENICO
SCARLATTI

Born: Naples, Italy, October 26, 1685
Died: Madrid, Spain, July 23, 1757

*D*omenico Scarlatti's father and mentor, Alessandro Scarlatti, conducted the King's Orchestra in Naples and was highly respected. He noticed his son's talent for music and helpfully developed it.

When Scarlatti was 20, his father sent him to Venice to complete his studies. It was not long after that he realised that unlike his father – who had already written over 150 operas – he was drawn strongly to the harpsichord. The younger Scarlatti soon excelled both in playing the harpsichord and also in composing music for it.

At the age of 32 he declared his independence from paternal control and began travelling extensively all over Europe, gambling recklessly. He supported himself by composing, playing and teaching the harpsichord wherever he went. In Rome he was engaged in a harpsichord and organ competition with Handel at the palace of Cardinal Ottoboni. The harpsichord contest was adjudged in Scarlatti's favour and Handel won the organ event. Scarlatti remained unsurpassed as virtuoso on the harpsichord.

Apart from his many concert tours in Europe, Scarlatti was Court "cembalist" (player of any orchestral keyboard instrument) for varying periods at Warsaw, Rome, Lisbon, Naples and, longest, at the Spanish Court in Madrid. Here he was employed as maestro de cámera to the Portuguese princess and later Spanish Queen, Maria Barbara, from 1729 until his death in 1757.

Scarlatti died leaving his wife and children in dire circumstances, having gambled away all he had amassed through the years. They did not even have the satisfaction of knowing that their husband and father would be remembered as the father of modern piano playing.

> *"Scarlatti was the first person to introduce big skips and wide arpeggios in playing the rapid repetition of a single note to simulate one long legato tone, and the crossing of hands on the keyboard. The crossover of hands added greatly to the brilliancy of his performances."*

Scarlatti's place in music history

Scarlatti's importance in the history of piano playing is supreme. His influence is discernible in the techniques of Chopin, Liszt and Mendelssohn. He was the first person to introduce big skips and wide arpeggios in playing the rapid repetition of a single

> " *Scarlatti remained unsurpassed as virtuoso on the harpsichord.* "

note to simulate one long legato tone, and the crossing of hands on the keyboard. The crossover of hands added greatly to the brilliancy of his performances.

His compositions, many of them based on Italian and Spanish folk songs, are as lovely when played on the modern piano as on the 18th-century harpsichord. Many of his smaller pieces have been arranged in suites for concert performances on the piano. His sparkling compositions are the infinite delight of all who play or enjoy listening to keyboard music.

Major compositions

Domenico Scarlatti's works are catalogued as K numbers, after the American harpsichordist Ralph Kirkpatrick. These now supersede the L (Longo) numbering.

70 operas (including "Tetide in Sciro")

Stabat Mater

Salve Regina

The Keyboard Sonatas are his best-loved works.

The most unfortunate part of Scarlatti's life was the scattering of his over 600 compositions. It was not until his sonatas were collected by Alessandro Longo and published by Ricordi, 150 years after his death, that the true extent of his contribution to keyboard music was fully realised.

A 15th-century harpsichord
In this keyboard instrument quills pluck the strings, causing them to vibrate. The intensity of sound is not modified by pressure of the fingers but by making the plectrum touch a varying number of strings with the same pitch. In its heyday (1500-1700) this was used as a continuo instrument in large and small ensembles. It resembled the modern pianoforte in shape

Josephus Haydn

FRANZ JOSEPH
HAYDN

Born : Rohrau, Austria, March 31, 1732
Died : Vienna, Austria, May 31, 1809

One of as many as 12 children, Franz Joseph Haydn learned early on about the struggle for existence within his own family, where there was never enough food to feed all the hungry mouths.

When he was just six years old, a cousin, attracted by Haydn's "weak but pleasant voice", took him to Vienna to study in its famed choir school. He received excellent training in music there until one day, in a restless moment, he cut off the pigtail of the man sitting on the bench in front of him. For this boyish prank he was expelled from the choir school.

By the time he was 17, Haydn's voice had naturally started to change and his capability as a choir boy was coming to an end. An older boy at the choir school, Spangler, befriended him, allowed him to share his attic room and gave him the music sheets Haydn was too poor to buy for himself. He was forever jotting down musical ideas, which consumed reams of paper.

By the time he was in his early twenties, Haydn had found a patron in Count Fürnberg, with whom he played string quartets. Haydn composed his first 18 quartets for the Count.

His next appointment was music director to Count Morzin, where he directed a small orchestra. Haydn composed his Symphony No. 1 for this group, the first of over a hundred symphonies he would compose during his lifetime.

When Count Morzin could no longer afford the luxury of a resident composer, Haydn gratefully accepted the invitation of Prince Paul Anton Esterházy to be his musical director or Kapellmeister. Later, he was transferred to the retinue of Prince Nicholas Esterházy and remained with that aristocratic family for 30 idyllic years.

The Esterházy household spent the spring and summer months in the countryside in Hungary, close to Vienna. In winter, the establishment moved bag and baggage to Vienna. Haydn loved Vienna. He loved the vivacious ladies there (maybe because he was married to a nagging wife), and the bustle and gaiety of the city's streets. He adored Wolfgang and Constanze Mozart and took part in the string quartets at their Sunday morning musicales.

One year, Prince Nicholas took longer than Haydn thought fair to give the signal to depart for the city. To drive home the point that the exodus to the city was overdue, Haydn invited his patron to hear a new symphony he had composed.

The court assembled in the white-and-gold salon and the performance began. When the orchestra came to the last movement, the players stood up one by one, blew out their candles and tiptoed from the stage. After the last musician had departed, the stage was dark and silent. The Prince saw the point, laughed indulgently and gave the long-awaited signal for departure.

During his Esterházy years, Haydn composed five masses, 11 operas, 60 symphonies, 40 string quartets, 125 cello trios, besides occasional works for birthdays, weddings, funerals, etc. When Prince Nicholas, the most generous and genuinely musical of the Esterházys died, Haydn was almost 60.

It was at about this time that Haydn was called upon to compose what came to be called the "Minuet of the Ox". It happened that one day Haydn was seated at his desk in his flat in Vienna when a neighbouring butcher entered, hat in hand, bowed respectfully and stammered out his request: Would the great Herr Haydn write a minuet for the wedding of his daughter? He offered to pay any price for the music. Haydn, ever obliging,

and with a twinkle in his eye, promised the butcher that he would compose a minuet within 24 hours.

Some days later, hearing the sound of music outside, Haydn stepped out onto his balcony. He saw the wedding procession approaching to the music of the minuet he had composed for the occasion. And right at the head of the procession was a milk-white ox, decked with garlands of flowers. "For you," said the happy butcher, halting the ox at Haydn's door.

In 1791-92, Haydn visited the British Isles where he was fêted and entertained by royalty. He went for a second time in 1794-95. The 12 London Symphonies that he composed there are among his finest works. He was idolised in London and received the degree of Doctor of Music from Oxford University. Haydn graciously returned the compliment by specially composing his "Oxford" Symphony.

Haydn also received several other honours. England inspired him to write his oratorios "The Creation" and "The Seasons" for the Handel Festival which he attended. Haydn jocularly declared, "It is England that has made me famous in Germany!"

During the last four years of his life, Haydn returned to the service of the third generation of Esterházys. But times had changed. Napoleon's armies kept harassing and then bombarding Vienna. In 1809, Haydn was on his death-bed. He asked his servants to sing for him the melody of his "Emperor" Quartet, to which he had written a remarkable series of variations. Sung to the words *"Gott erhalte Franz den Kaiser"* (God save Emperor Francis – the Austrian Emperor), it became the Austrian national hymn. On the wings of that song, Haydn's soul took flight.

Haydn on his way to England
It was during his first visit to England that he composed the 12 "London" masterpiece symphonies

Haydn's musical calling card had its own melody

Haydn's place in music history

Haydn has come to be known in the history of music as the father of most of the instrumental forms such as symphonies and string quartets. Not perhaps very revolutionary, but his long periods of residence at the isolated Esterházy estate elicited this response from him: "There was no one near to confuse me, so I was forced to become original!" He nevertheless greatly influenced his contemporaries, and for many years his symphonies and, particularly, his string quartets served as models to those who came after. Both Mozart and Beethoven freely admitted how much they had learned by studying Haydn's symphonies and string quartets.

Haydn's music has a dainty grace and is bright and genial. Constant melody is the most marked characteristic of his music. He sang into his music his bubbling joy of living, his peasant heartiness, his love of nature and of his fellow men and his innate nobility of character. His sense of humour is also reflected in the appropriate inventive names he gave to many of his symphonies.

Major compositions

Cantatas and Oratorios
Several cantatas including:
"Seven Last Words of Our Saviour on the Cross" (First version for string quartet)
"The Creation" (Haydn's devout religious feelings are revealed here. Starting with a slow mysterious depiction of chaos, the work falls into three parts: Creation of the Earth, Creation of Living Creatures, Creation of Adam and Eve)
"The Seasons", a loving portrait of Nature using music to mimic the flight of birds and the motion of the sea
14 Masses
22 Arias
5 Grand Operas
4 Comedies
36 Songs
125 Symphonies, including:
  Op. 33, No. 2 "The Joke"
  Op. 33, No. 3 "The Bird"
  No. 45 "Farewell"
  No. 50 "The Frog"
  No. 65 "The Lark"
  No. 73 "La Chasse"
  No. 74 "The Rider"
  No. 88 "The Hen"
  No. 92 "Oxford"
  No. 94 "Surprise"
  No. 100 "Military"
  No. 101 "Clock"
  No. 103 "Drum Roll"
  No. 104 "London"
77 String Quartets
30 Concertos (for various string instruments with orchestra)
40 Piano Trios
12 Collections of Minuets
Numerous Sonatas for clavichord
66 Compositions for wind and strings
125 Cello Trios

Concertos
Cello Concerto in C
Clavier Concerto in D
Organ Concerto
Trumpet Concerto in E-flat
Violin Concertos in A, C, G
Sinfonia Concertante in B-flat (oboe, bassoon, violin, cello)

A Haydn quartet
This scene shows Haydn, the violinist turning the pages, playing in a string quartet at the home of his friend Marianne von Genziger

WOLFGANG AMADEUS **MOZART**

Born : Salzburg, Austria, January 27, 1756
Died : Vienna, Austria, December 5, 1791

Wolfgang Amadeus Mozart is considered the greatest natural genius of music; indeed of all art, according to many. Science still strives to offer a convincing explanation for the genius of such prodigies as Mozart.

He was only 3 years old when he started showing an interest in his sister Nannerl's music lessons. His ear was so keen that he could not only discriminate between chords and dischords but could even detect slightest variations in the pitch of a violin.

At 4, Mozart started to learn music and at 5 was composing little pieces. When he was 6, Mozart could play, with remarkable virtuosity, the harpsichord, violin and piano, and could also improvise on simple themes given to him.

Mozart's father, Leopold, was his son's tutor. The problem for him was not how to get his son to practise but how to keep him away from the piano, for the small boy played on for hours on end as other children played with their toys.

When he was 7 years old, Mozart, accompanied by his father and sister, embarked on a concert tour of Europe. Wherever they went young Wolfgang created a sensation. Royalty went out of their way to fawn on this wonder-child. Princess Amalia of Prussia, George III and Queen Charlotte of Great Britain, Louis XV of France and many other royals vied with one another to welcome and honour Mozart.

In France he played for Empress Maria Theresa, hauling himself up to the monarch's lap and, without so much as a blush, accepted a right royal kiss. He played with the Princess, Marie Antoinette, and when he fell headlong over the long sword, a part of the court costume he was unaccustomed to, the princess kissed away his tears of pain and chagrin. "When I grow up I will marry you," he promised her.

In Rome, Mozart astonished everyone by a prodigious feat of memory. He wrote, after only a single hearing, the famous "Miserere" by Allegri. This composition had been the exclusive property of the Papal Choir and no one was permitted to copy it, under penalty of excommunication by the Pope. In the case of Mozart, however, the astonished Pope, Clement XIV, took the only possible course of action – he decorated Mozart with a special ecclesiastic title – the Order of the Golden Spur!

At a concert in Naples, the superstitious Neapolitans declared that it was the ring that Mozart wore, imbued with the power of black magic, which made him play as brilliantly as he did. So Mozart had to take off the ring to prove that he could play the piano in the same extraordinary manner without it. Of particular benefit to Mozart was his meeting in London with Johann Sebastian Bach's youngest son, Johann Christian Bach. Through him Mozart became acquainted with the then latest musical developments.

Mozart was in his teens when, with his mother as chaperone, he visited Italy. Mozart lost his heart to Italy, especially Italian opera. He was elected a member of the Philharmonic Society of Bologna, an honour never accorded to one so young. It was in Italy that Mozart changed his middle name from Gottlieb (Theophilus) to Amadeus which meant the same (Beloved of God).

In Mannheim, Mozart encountered the finest orchestra in Europe and composed many works for it. It was in Mannheim that he also made the acquaintance of the latest pianoforte on which he brilliantly played to the amazement of his listeners all around.

Mozart's second visit to France was an unhappy one. The French aristocracy who had applauded him as a young genius was no longer so enthusiastic. He returned to Salzburg and entered the service of the Archbishop of Salzburg. When the Archbishop took his court to Vienna in the spring of 1781, Mozart found himself in the city he loved best of all.

" 'You see, we have no money in the house to buy firewood, so Constanze and I were dancing just to keep warm,' the sadly poor Mozart would say. "

Soon, though, service with the Archbishop became increasingly distasteful. Mozart resented the curbs on his desire to compose the music that was straining within him to find expression. He also thought he was not being treated as well as he should be. When he went to hand over his resignation in person to the Archbishop, there was a bitter exchange of words between the two. Mozart was verbally abused and, in fact, physically ejected from the Archbishop's antechamber. The ugly episode had a happy outcome, though. Mozart was now able to compose the kind of music that appealed to him.

Soon after, Mozart married Constanze Weber. All musical Viennese who mattered attended the home of the Mozarts and participated in the Sunday morning friendly concerts. Haydn, Mozart and two friends played string quartets. Mozart openly declared that he had learned to write string quartets from Haydn. To show his gratitude Mozart composed a set of six quartets and dedicated them to Haydn. Later, on hearing those six, Haydn said to Mozart's father: "I declare to you on my honour that I consider your son to be the greatest composer I have ever heard."

In time, though, these years of triumph and appreciation gave way to years of want and financial constraints, though he continued to compose incessantly. Mozart had no head at all for business. Whenever he was hard up for money he would give a sheaf of his compositions to his publishers and accepted in return whatever amounts they gave him, which was totally unfair when judged against the wonderful music scores he had submitted. Mozart's financial condition kept worsening. There was never enough money to pay for his growing family. Constanze had borne him six children in nine years. Besides, she loved to spend money. One winter morning, a friend visited Mozart and found him and his wife dancing most energetically in their

The darling of the courts
Petted by kings and princesses, as a boy Mozart toured the principal courts of Europe with his father and sister, hailed everywhere as a musical phenomenon

Major compositions

15 Masses, 41 Symphonies
Requiem No. 31, K 297 "Paris"
Cantata No. 35, K 385 "Haffner"
Various arias, songs, canons
Symphony No. 36, K 425 "Linz"
Symphony No. 38, K 504 "Prague"
Symphony No. 40, K 550
Symphony No. 41, K 551 "Jupiter"

Operas
Marriage of Figaro (1786)
Don Giovanni (1787)
Cosi fan tutte (1790)
The Magic Flute (1791)

Violin Concertos
No. 3, G Major, K 216
No. 4, D Major, K 218
No. 5, A Major, K 219
Sinfonia Concertante in E-flat,
  K 364 (violin, viola)
Bassoon Concerto, K 191
Clarinet Concerto, K 622
Flute Concerto, K 314
Horn Concerto, K 447
Serenade in G Major,
  "Eine kleine Nachtmusik", K 525

Piano Concertos (25)
No. 19, K 459
No. 20, K 466
No. 21, K 467 "Elvira Madigan"
No. 22, K 482
No. 23, K 488
No. 24, K 491
No. 25, K 503

String Quartets (25)
6 "Haydn" Quartets
3 "Prussian" Quartets

Piano Sonatas (24)
No. 11, K 331
Fantasia and Sonata in C Minor, K 475

Other works
9 Marches, 25 Dances,
31 Serenades, Fantasies,
Fugues, Rondos, Minuets

Glory days in Vienna
Mozart in the garden of the Emperor's palace at Schonbrunn near Vienna. On the bench lies the score of "The Marriage of Figaro"

parlour. To his surprised friend Mozart offered the following simple explanation. He said, "You see, we have no money in the house to buy firewood, so Constanze and I were dancing just to keep warm."

Mozart's life ended very sadly at the young age of 35. The last composition he wrote was a Requiem Mass commissioned by a mysterious stranger who came to Mozart, heavily cloaked from head to foot in grey. After securing Mozart's acceptance of his commission, the stranger left, without divulging the name of the person on whose behalf he had approached him. To Mozart, already depressed by bad health, this stranger assumed a supernatural aspect. He firmly came to believe that the man had been none other than the messenger of death. Mozart worked on the commissioned Mass in fits and starts, and though he was sick, the vision of the stranger so constantly haunted his fevered mind that he made strenuous efforts to complete it. The end was now very near. The Mass was almost complete. Confined to bed, Mozart invited a few friends to come over to his home and play it for him. He was anxious to hear how it sounded.

On December 4, 1791, Mozart lost consciousness. He died the following day. On the day of his death, a terrible storm raged. As his wife Constanze was too grief-stricken to attend the funeral and as none of his friends were inclined to face the bitter cold outside, only the undertaker and his men were present at Mozart's burial. He died so poor that his body was placed in a pauper's grave. No one cared to note the exact spot where he was buried. And so today the fine marble monument in St. Marx cemetery in Vienna which commemorates the memory of this genius, once fêted and admired by the musical world, stands over an empty grave.

A representation of Mozart's funeral **With no family or friends in attendance, his body ended up in the common burial ground**

Mozart's place in music history

Though Mozart died at the age of 35, he left behind him some 750 compositions. Of these, 626 had been chronologically catalogued as Köchel (K) or Köchel-Verzeichnis (KV) numbers. It has been pointed out that Mozart was an intuitive rather than an intellectual musician. He was the most lavishly endowed of all natural musical talents and composed music effortlessly.

There is the famous legend that Mozart composed the Overture to his opera "Don Giovanni" on the night before its first performance. Actually this is not as astonishing as it sounds for Mozart had the type of mind that could retain any piece of music until it was completed and ready to be finally committed to paper.

In his own time Mozart was regarded chiefly as a composer of operas, and those like his "Don Giovanni", "The Magic Flute" and "The Marriage of Figaro" will continue to be performed as long as people love opera as an art form.

Of all the symphonies that Mozart wrote, the last three are the most frequently performed. All Mozart symphonies are models of form and euphony. It is said that one day a young man asked Mozart for advice on how to compose a symphony. Mozart replied that he believed his questioner to be too young to attempt so serious a composition. The young man protested saying, "But you were much younger than I am when you wrote your first symphony." "True," replied Mozart, smiling, "but then, you see, I did not ask people how to write symphonies. I just went ahead and composed them."

Mozart had the ability to compose an entire symphony or a string quartet, fully scored, in his head. The first drafts of his compositions looked like final copies, divinely dictated. There is none of Beethoven's angry hewing and furious scribbling. His music never lost any of its serenity, sparkle and joyfulness. Dvořák said it all when he declared: "Mozart is sunshine."

No matter what form of music he touched, Mozart's compositions never lost their most distinctive qualities of endless melodic flow and transparency of style. His immortal works have an enduring place in the hearts of all who are attuned to the language of music. He set standards of excellence that have inspired generations of composers who saw him as almost God-like. Tchaikovsky declared, "I love Mozart as the musical Christ." Wagner said, "I believe in God, Mozart and Beethoven." The famed conductor Georg Solti made a very insightful statement: "Mozart makes you believe in God – much more than going to church – because it cannot be by chance that such a phenomenon arrives in this world."

Notes on select works

Eine kleine Nachtmusik (K 525)

This is a serenade for string orchestra. Its four movements are: *allegro, romance, minuet* and *rondo*.

It is Mozart's most well-known work. Even during Mozart's lifetime it was his most popular composition, and it is said that had there been copyright legislation then, Mozart could have well lived an easy and comfortable life to the end on the handsome royalty amounts he would have received.

The first movement is a tiny sonata of crystalline purity of form. Beneath the melodious surface of the following Romance there is murmurous agitation, suggestions of a subdued passion, of a romantic feeling which did not become the fashion until long after Mozart's day. The third movement is a *minuet* and the last a *rondo*. The skipping, sparkling refrain of the *rondo* is the very essence of Mozartian charm, with its echoes of Viennese popular songs.

Sinfonia Concertante in E-flat (K 364)

This is for violin, viola and orchestra. "It is not only one of Mozart's greatest works, it is also the key work that saw the young composer, then 23, attain the level of musical accomplishment that has defined his reputation ever since."

The Sinfonia occupies a pivotal position in the evolution of concerto writing. While it is in the new symphonic style with two solo instruments, it also represents a continuation of the Baroque *concerto grosso* tradition. The soloists play mostly in dialogue, and the work is more a double concerto than an ensemble one. Often the viola takes over phrases heard on the violin, presenting them in a new light, and the soloists join together only at the conclusion of sections.

The opening movement, *allegro maestoso,* is of grand proportions with a double set of themes, the first outlined by the orchestra and the second by the two soloists. When the two solo instruments come to the fore, a more concert-like atmosphere prevails.

The poignancy of the second movement, *andante,* has rarely been surpassed. The opening theme is offered by the orchestra and, in turn, expanded upon by the violin and viola. The dialogues between the two soloists are full of unexpected melodic twists. The final movement, *presto,* is the lightest of the three, bounding along with a carefree verve.

Violin Concertos

Mozart wrote five violin concertos of which the last three (K 216, K 218 and K 219) are best known. They were the first of Mozart's instrumental works to win general recognition throughout Europe. Mozart was a gifted violinist. His father once wrote to him: "You have no idea how well you play the violin. You could be the best violinist in Europe." In a letter to his father after a concert, Mozart wrote: "The audience gaped, all of them, I played as though I was the best violinist in Europe." The violin concertos by the 19-year-old

composer are not conspicuous for any outstanding virtuosity, but for their grace, clarity of form and inventiveness. Bursting with vitality, they express a robust, youthful happiness at being alive.

Concerto No. 3 in G Major (K 216)

Completed in September 1775, it represents the zenith of Mozart's violin concertos. The interplay between the violin and the orchestra is marked by a new and a more intimate relationship. The *adagio,* lovely as a pleasant dream, points to the French style, which again comes to the fore in the *rondo,* where passages in various tempi alternate – a feature common to the final movements of all the last three concertos. Also typical of the finales are the frequent folk song-like passages.

Concerto No. 4 in D Major (K 218) – "Strasbourg"

Completed in October 1775, this concerto is more sensuous than its immediate predecessor. The virtuoso element occurs in the magnificent cadenza which concludes the first movement. It opens with a solemn orchestral introduction; the violin then borrows the first motif and stamps the movement with its plaintive melody. Two dances, a gavotte and a musette, are woven into the *rondo* of the last movement. The musette, a dance of pastoral character in triple time, was a favourite dance in Strasbourg, so Mozart called it the "Strasbourg" Concerto.

Concerto No. 5 in A Major (K 219) – "Turkish"

Completed in December 1775, this is the best known of Mozart's violin concertos: the most nearly perfect as regards grace, spirituality and spaciousness. The first movement is full of surprises – such as the constant changes from cajolery to delightful elegance and hearty good humour. The *andante,* simple to a degree, is the pearl of Mozart's slow movements. The *rondo* is international in character and its main theme, a stately minuet, is interrupted by a fiery Hungarian dance and a piece in mock-Turkish style.

Piano Concertos

Mozart wrote 23 piano concertos. Just as Haydn is called "the father of the symphony", Mozart must rightly be called "the father of the concerto". He gave the concerto definite form. His most significant contribution was the balanced interplay between the solo instrument and the orchestra.

Concerto No. 19 in F Major (K 459)

This concerto has been described thus: "The scoring is light, without trumpets and drums, with the winds having a fair share of interest. If the first movement is more equable and less dramatic than usual the 'slow' movement – actually an *allegretto* – has operatic overtones in its gentle rhythm. All this is brilliantly capped by a finale that alternates the wit of opera buffa – the playful *rondo* theme on piano and wind alone – with mock-serious displays of counterpoint in the orchestral tuttis."

Concerto No. 20 in D Minor (K 466)

"With its turbulence, anger and despair, it is the most romantic of all Mozart's compositions," it has been said. Beethoven played it often and even composed cadenzas for it. The opening *allegro* is the first of Mozart's concerto movements in which the tutti and solo are contrasted in an unabating dualism. After the orchestral exposition the piano enters with a significant new theme, which is never adopted by the orchestra and is developed in opposition to the orchestral material. The writing for the soloist is elaborate, yet it is always motivated by musical rather than purely virtuosic considerations. The Romanze is an exquisite movement conceived along spacious lines. It is in simple *rondo* form with the traditional stormy second episode. The final movement, *rondo allegro assai,* is the least tragic of the three. There is a tranquillity to most of it that is accentuated to the end."

Concerto No. 21 in C Major (K 467)
(The theme from "Elvira Madigan")

"The opening *allegro* is a majestic movement, the orchestra having breadth and grandeur, the solo part dignity and brilliance. The finale, *allegro vivace assai,* sparkles gaily,

and between these two movements is one of the loveliest slow movements in the whole of concerto literature. People reportedly wept at the first performance, and we can imagine them strangely stirred by this elegiac *andante,* a movement said truly to foreshadow Chopin's nocturnes. It is fragments of this *andante* that coloured the 1967 Swedish film *Elvira Madigan,* a chronicle of a hopeless love."

Concerto No. 22 in E-flat Major (K 482)

"This concerto is a reflection of Mozart riding high on a wave of acceptance and appreciation as composer and performer. The concerto combines high good humour in the two outer movements, with moving dignity in the central *andante*. The work is a magnificent showpiece and Mozart made the most of it when he played the solo part at the première in December 1785. 'The *andante* so pleased the audience that it had to be repeated – a rather unusual occurrence,' wrote Mozart's startled but proud father, Leopold."

Concerto No. 23 in A Major (K 488)

Written entirely in the month of March 1786, the concerto begins with the orchestra announcing a large group of lively, graceful themes, which are later taken up and developed along with new material by piano and orchestra together. It is brilliant, happy music

Mozart and Cavalieri
Soprano Caterina Cavalieri was one of the most famed interpreters of Mozart's operas

and shows the sunniest side of Mozart's nature. The slow movement is in a mood of the most touching melancholy. The piano sings beautifully as if all the time Mozart had in mind that most personal of all instruments – the human voice. The exquisite ornamentation of the song never disturbs the simple flow of melody, and the colouring of the orchestra is wonderful and silvery, while the flute and other wind instruments mingle in the most natural way with the tone of the piano. It is one of Mozart's loveliest slow movements. The finale is a *rondo* of endless contrasts in melody.

Concerto No. 24 in C Minor (K 491)

"This concerto is Mozart at his most personal, an uncommonly forceful and tragic work. In the first movement the weight of tragedy falls upon the winds with strings accompanying only. The second movement, *larghetto,* moves in regions of the purest and most moving tranquillity and simplicity of expression and is in *rondo* form. The final movement, *allegretto's* theme with variations, is the only time in the concerto that the piano is heard in a virtuosic role."

Concerto No. 25 in C (K 503)

"Stately and powerful, it is complicated in structure and technically is perhaps Mozart's most difficult piano concerto. Musicologist Alfred Einstein claims that it is not only his greatest piano concerto but also one of his greatest instrumental works. In this concerto victory is attained, symbolised simply and indisputably in the triumphal march theme of the first movement. No other work of Mozart has such dimensions. In no other concerto does the relation between the soloist and the orchestra vary so constantly and so unpredictably.

The death of Mozart
On his death-bed Mozart's thoughts were occupied with the composition of his "Requiem"

"First movement, *allegro maestoso:* The heroic nature of the whole work appears in the first bars. The development is entirely thematic, close-knit and masterly.

"The second movement, *andante,* has the same breadth and spaciousness. The movement is more tender than the first.

"The finale, *allegretto,* has been described as one of Mozart's most serious-minded *rondos.* This movement is passionate rather than heroic."

Fantasia and Sonata, C Minor (K 475)

"Some believe that this sonata, given its fire and passion, surpassed all others previously composed, foreshadowing the monumental Beethoven sonatas that were to come. It is full of apprehensive heartbeats and melodic apparitions of ghostly beauty. The development of the first movement is on a large scale. The big slow movement is essentially a set of variations with richly developed incidents that make it a kind of serious *rondo.* The finale is also a *rondo,* although one that only deepens the tragic tone of the whole work."

Symphonies

In 1788, within the short period of two months, Mozart composed three symphonies: the E-flat Major (K 543), the G Minor (K 550) and the C Major (K 551).

Symphony No. 40, G Minor (K 550)

This symphony is one of Mozart's most tragic works. According to his biographer Hermann Abert: "The symphony gives pregnant expression to the deep fatalistic pessimism which was rooted in Mozart's nature.

"In the first movement, *allegro molto,* the impression of profound suffering is revealed in the first theme and in its final motif the inner tension breaks through with great force. The second theme confirms and strengthens the emotional and sombre mood.

"In the second movement, *andante,* the sense of disquiet broods over everything. Dark ominous-sounding chords increase in intensity to the accompaniment of the hammering rhythms of the main theme.

"The third movement, *minuet,* though dance-like in external form bursts its bounds by its intense emotional content. The sole gleam of light in the whole work is provided by a trio, an idyllic intermezzo.

"The fourth movement, *allegro assai,* has all the elements of the symphony in full revolt. The main motif is in tempestuous mood and the second theme struggles in vain to cast a ray of light. Practically the whole working-out is forte, the mood being further intensified by the main theme's mad chase through different keys."

Symphony No. 41 in C Major (K 551) – "Jupiter"

It is not known how the C Major Symphony came by its title "Jupiter". Mozart's biographer Otto Jahn thinks it has been so called to indicate its majesty and splendour rather than with a view to any deeper symbolism.

"The 'Jupiter' is dignified and solemn as manifested in the brilliant pomp of the first movement. The *andante* reveals the very depths of feeling, with traces in its calm beauty of the passionate agitation and strife from which it proceeds; the impression it leaves is one of moral strength, perfected to a noble gentleness. The *minuet* recalls to mind the cheerful subject of the first movement. There is an elastic spring to its motion, sustained with a delicacy and refinement which transports the hearer into a purer element, where he seems to exist without effort, like the Homeric gods. The *finale* is a masterpiece of Contrapuntal art, which leaves the impression of a magnificent princely pageant."

The Salzburg Festival

Lying in a beautiful mountain district, with many medieval houses and magnificent buildings rich in tradition, the Austrian city of Salzburg early became a centre of vigorous musical activity – particularly in connection with divine service in the city's cathedral. After a period of decay in the first half of the 19th century, the city's venerable traditions were revived in connection with the new Mozarteum.

After the First World War an annual festival was inaugurated in 1920. In 1926, a Festival Hall was built and the Vienna Philharmonic Orchestra began to give concerts here under the foremost conductors of the time. World-famous singers also helped to make the Salzburg Festival a musical occasion of the highest order. Mozart remained the most prominent composer in these programmes, but works of other great composers were also performed.

"The muse forbids the man who is worthy of praise to die."

– Horace

LUDWIG VAN
BEETHOVEN

Born: Bonn, Germany, December 16, 1770
Died: Vienna, Austria, March 26, 1827

The early years of life were hard for Ludwig Van Beethoven. His father, a musician, had heard of the successful concert tour of Europe made by the Mozarts, and with a view to making some money himself by presenting his son to the world as another child prodigy, he started teaching Ludwig, then 4 years old, to play the piano and the violin.

To his disappointment, the boy did not show any extraordinary aptitude for music in spite of several beatings to speed up his learning. It is providential that such cruel treatment from his father did not give young Beethoven a dislike for music, for had that happened, the world would have lost all the tremendous music that he was later to compose and perform. His mother was the only woman Ludwig deeply loved. She died when he was 17.

At 12, Beethoven became court organist, then court pianist and violinist in the orchestra of the Elector of Bonn. The fame of his improvisations on the piano soon spread beyond his home town. Beethoven was fortunate that his general education was supervised by the von Breunings, a cultured Bonn family with extensive social connections. Frau Breuning saw to it that Beethoven attended school regularly and was taught French, Italian and Latin. Beethoven's interest in literature led him to appreciate Shakespeare.

On his first visit to Vienna, Beethoven managed to secure an interview with Mozart who was then at the height of his fame. In the course of this meeting, Mozart requested Beethoven to play the piano for him. Mozart was not much impressed by the 16-year-old youth's playing, wonderful though it was. He probably thought it was insufficiently rehearsed beforehand. Mozart then gave Beethoven a complex theme and asked him to improvise on it. As Beethoven started his impromptu variations, Mozart listened attentively

Therese von Brunswick

" *Shortly after Beethoven's death, a secret drawer was found in his writing table containing three letters written in pencil and addressed to the 'immortal beloved'. Some believe that this refers to Countess Giulietta Guicciardi, while others consider the 'immortal beloved' to have been the beautiful Therese von Brunswick to whom Beethoven is said to have been secretly engaged for two years.* "

and became greatly impressed, especially as Beethoven ended with a perfect fugue. To some of his friends who were present, Mozart declared, "Take note of him. One day he will be famous."

Mozart's prediction more than came true, for in later years Beethoven effortlessly wrote page after page of glorious music the like of which the world had never known before.

When he was 22, Beethoven returned to Vienna with the blessings of his patrons and this time settled there for the rest of his life. Mozart was dead by then and Beethoven opted to study with Haydn. But nothing much came of this proposed arrangement. However, the caring instruction Beethoven received from his teacher Johann Albrechtsberger was invaluable.

In Vienna, Beethoven found noble patrons who were greatly impressed by his improvisations. They took lessons from him and paid well for the special compositions that he wrote for their private orchestras and string quartets.

The Prince and Princess Lichnowsky invited Beethoven to live in their palace and assured him an annual income. They presented him with four fine instruments and even set the fashion of overlooking the many eccentricities of his versatile genius. In a short while Beethoven became the idol of the music-loving people of Vienna. He rapidly built up a formidable reputation as a pianist before gaining recognition as the greatest composer of his time. His fame steadily increased over the years. He had access to the palaces of all the Viennese nobility. He counted princesses and countesses among his pupils. And though he was brusque in his manners and blunt of speech, the Viennese nobility still respected him for they knew that at heart he was a lovable man besides being a very great artist.

Beethoven's affections were usually centred on ladies from the most select Viennese circles, such as the young Countess Giulietta Guicciardi (to whom he dedicated the "Moonlight Sonata"). It is said that their relationship was ended by the girl's family who objected to her marrying a man without rank, fortune or profession. Presumably, similar reasons prevented his marrying Therese Malfatti and Bettina Brentano.

Shortly after Beethoven's death, a secret drawer was found in his writing table containing three letters written in pencil and addressed to the "immortal beloved". Some believe that this refers to Countess Giulietta Guicciardi, while others consider the "immortal beloved" to have been the beautiful Therese von Brunswick to whom Beethoven is said to have been secretly engaged for two years. Beethoven was constantly falling in love, but it was not usually long-lived. And because he had throughout maintained

The house in Bonn where Beethoven was born
His childhood was miserably unhappy here

This regard for democracy is evident in his admiration for Napoleon Bonaparte. Beethoven rejoiced when Napoleon's armies marched from victory to victory. He saw Napoleon as the liberator and champion of the common man, and enthusiastically dedicated his magnificent Third Symphony, "The Eroica", on which he was then engaged, to his hero. Later, when Napoleon seized the throne of France and proclaimed himself Emperor, Beethoven flew into a rage and tore up the title page bearing the dedication of his symphony to Napoleon.

In 1798 came the first sign of that grave tragedy in Beethoven's life – his deafness. For this man, who was the greatest composer and performer of his time, this affliction must have come as something too terrible for words to describe.

At first Beethoven refused to be unduly distracted by the whistling and buzzing sounds that troubled his ears. In any case, he kept his fears to himself for he was afraid that his professional standing would be badly affected if people came to know that he was getting deaf.

Beethoven tried every remedy that was suggested to him by various doctors whom he consulted. But soon things got so much worse that the composer was forced to confess his terrible predicament before the world. After two long years of keeping the dreadful secret to himself, Beethoven finally had to confide in his intimate friends.

His deafness gradually turned Beethoven, a once lovable man, into something of a surly bear. From that time onwards, as Romain Rolland put it, "Beethoven was destined to live on in the immense solitude of his genius and made miserable by contact with a world which he could not understand, even as it could not understand him."

The Maestro at work
With Beethoven composing was not easy. He toiled over every measure sitting for long at his piano

very high ethical standards, there were no sordid scandals that could have brought dishonour or disrepute to his name or those of the ladies he loved. Some measure of the genuine affection in which Beethoven was held by Vienna's nobility can be judged by the fact that the Countess Therese von Brunswick when presenting her portrait to Beethoven inscribed it: "To the rare genius, the great artist, the generous man."

Still, there is no denying that on many occasions, even in his dealings with his patrons, Beethoven was downright rude. On one occasion he was invited to play the piano at a private party held in the palace of one of his patrons. While playing, he was disturbed by the chatter of guests in the front row. He abruptly got up from the piano and stormed out of the room.

On another occasion, he was walking along the street with the great writer Goethe when a royal procession approached. Goethe immediately stepped back and bowed to the Empress and her retinue. Not so Beethoven. Firmly clapping his hat on his head, he walked straight through the royal procession, bowing only slightly to the left and to the right to acknowledge the greetings of some of the princes in the procession. The incident is more an illustration of Beethoven's bad manners than a demonstration of democratic independence. But it does characterise Beethoven's attitude towards the trappings of the wealthy classes: he was undoubtedly a great lover of liberty and felt deeply for the rights of the common man.

Beethoven now commenced to shun the society of his fellow men. He went alone for long walks into the countryside, trying desperately to find in nature some solace for his miseries. He turned inward for an understanding of life's meaning, and found great comfort in the glorious music that was still pent up in his heart and awaiting expression.

Loneliness, it is said, is the invariable lot of great men and constitutes one of the most powerful driving forces that impels an artist to create. In Beethoven's case it was certainly true. Some of his finest compositions were written when his ears had closed to all outward sound and forced him into complete personal solitude.

There are those who believe that it is because, not in spite of, his deafness that Beethoven's genius blazed forth with such intensity and made him the foremost exponent of emotion and expressivity – the massive link between the Classical and Romantic composers.

Beethoven's deafness grew steadily worse over the years. Gradually, he had to give up playing the piano. At one of his last performances before some of his pupils, when Beethoven came to the soft section of a slow movement which he was playing, he touched the keys so lightly that no sound actually came from the piano. He was so deaf by then that he carried on playing unawares, firmly believing that he was treating his pupils to the most sensitively tempered piano playing they had heard.

Though profoundly affected by his inability to hear, Beethoven was not overwhelmed by this great tragedy in his life. He was one of the strong men of the world who fought his fate every inch of the way. When deafness first overtook him, one can but guess at the severe internal conflicts that must have shaken him.

Yet he emerged triumphant from all those sufferings. Fate had halted his career as a pianist, but he could still continue composing. His deafness could not take that away from him.

And compose Beethoven determinedly did – work after work of incomparable beauty such as the "Diabelli Variations", the late string quartets, the "Missa Solemnis" and the magnificent Ninth Symphony. And once again, Beethoven deliberately sought the society of his fellow men, flirted with the young ladies as of old, and talked and joked with everyone as if nothing untoward had happened. True that his laughter was now the laughter of a man unused to happiness; true that his face was now lined with the intense suffering that he had undergone. But Beethoven was determined to show the world that although he had been brought to his knees by a cruel destiny, he was again on his feet with the fighting light in his eyes, flashing defiance unto the stars.

By 1802, Beethoven realised that he had to abandon all hope of improvement in hearing. He was plunged into deep despair, including passing thoughts on suicide that were expressed in a letter which has been called the "Heiligenstadt testament" (after the name of the town in which he was living at that time).

In 1824, at the first performance of his Ninth Symphony, Beethoven was conducting the orchestra. The music had ended but he continued beating time to its closing theme, apparently from memory, until a singer nearby gently took his arm and turned him round to witness the applause with which the people were making the concert hall ring. Tears rolled down Beethoven's cheeks as he bowed to acknowledge the standing ovation. This was to be his last public appearance. Beethoven's life was nearing its end.

When news spread in Vienna that he was dying, friends, acquaintances, and even strangers came streaming to his death-bed. This was not surprising, for Beethoven, way back in 1815, had been given the Freedom of the City of Vienna Award by adoring music-loving citizens, right from the Viennese aristocracy to the common man.

On March 24, 1827, Beethoven received the Blessed Sacrament. When the ceremony was over, he weakly threw out a hand and said: "*Plaudite, amici, comoedia finita est*" (Applaud, my friends, the comedy is over). He lost consciousness two days before he died.

Beethoven died the way he had lived – battling Fate to the very end. On the evening of the day he died, a thunderstorm raged over Vienna. One particularly terrifying peal of thunder awakened even the dying Beethoven who, half raising himself from his bed, shook a clenched fist at the raging heavens and fell back dead.

That clenched fist Beethoven shook with his dying breath at the raging elements was a gesture that symbolised the manner in which he had lived his whole life – as a conqueror, a master of his Fate. As the great Chinese sage Confucius once said: "Our greatest glory is not in never falling, but in rising every time we fall."

Beethoven's life is more than the mere life story of a great composer. It is also the story of the indomitable spirit of man. His funeral was attended by over 20,000 people, among them the cream of Vienna's nobility. So huge was the crowd that troops were called in to maintain order. Great artists of the day vied with each other for the honour of carrying Beethoven's coffin.

The actor Grillparzer delivered the funeral oration: "He was an artist, and

Major compositions

Symphonies
No. 3, E-flat Major, Op. 55 "Eroica" (1804)
No. 5, C Minor, Op. 67 "Fate" (1805)
No. 6, F Major, Op. 68 "Pastoral" (1809)
No. 7, A Major, Op. 92 (1872)
No. 9, D Minor, Op. 125 "Choral" (1817-23)

Overtures
Egmont
Ruins of Athens
Leonora 1, 2, 3

Piano Concertos
No. 3, C Minor Op. 37 (1800)
No. 4, G Major Op. 58 (1805)
No. 5, E-flat Major, Op. 73 "Emperor" (1809)

Violin and Orchestra
Violin Concerto in D Major, Op. 61 (1806)
Romances for Violin and Orchestra
  No. 1, G Major, Op. 40 (1803)
  No. 2, F Major, Op. 50 (1805)

Piano Sonatas
C Minor, Op. 13 "Pathétique" (1799)
C-sharp Minor, Op. 27 "Moonlight" (1802)
C Major, Op. 53 "Waldstein" (1803-04)
F Minor, Op. 57 "Appassionata" (1806)
E-flat Major, Op. 81 "Les Adieux" (1811)
B-flat Major, Op. 106
  "Hammerklavier" (1818-19)
C Minor, Op. 111 (1822)

Violin and Piano Sonatas
F Major, Op. 24 "Spring" (1801)
A Major, Op. 47 "Kreutzer" (1802)

Cello and Piano
Sonata in A Major, Op. 69 (1809)

String Quartets
No. 1, F Major
No. 2, E Minor
No. 3, C Major, Op. 59
  "Rasoumovsky" (1806)
No. 10, E-flat Major, Op. 74 "Harp" (1809)

Bagatelles
A Minor, "Für Elise"
Ecossaises
G Major, Op. 129 "Rondo a capriccio"
  (Rage over a Lost Penny)
Minuet, G Major

Beethoven's main compositions over three periods of his life

The Early Period
(upto 1803)
2 symphonies, 8 violin sonatas, 6 string quartets, 3 piano concertos, 21 piano sonatas (including "Pathétique" and "Moonlight").

The Middle Period
(upto 1817; first signs of deafness appear)
Symphonies 3 to 6, three "Rasoumovsky" quartets, Fourth and Fifth piano concertos, violin concerto, piano sonatas (including "Waldstein" and "Appassionata"), the opera "Fidelio" and the "Kreutzer" violin sonata.

The Last Period
(upto his death in 1827; by 1817 Beethoven was stone deaf)
The Ninth Symphony, "Missa Solemnis", the last piano sonatas (including the famous emotional "Hammerklavier"). The last quartets (12 to 16) are so profound that many consider them to be beyond understanding, including No. 14 in C-sharp Minor which critics regard as the greatest string quartet ever written. The Ninth Symphony's final movement is a triumphant setting of Schiller's *Ode to Joy*. In this symphony Beethoven broke new ground in terms of scale and introduced choral forces into the symphony for the first time.

what he was, he was only through his art… Because he shut himself from the world, men called him hostile, and because he avoided sentimentality, they called him unfeeling. The finest points are the most easily blunted, or bent, or broken. He fled the world because in the wide range of his loving heart he found no weapon with which to resist it. He withdrew from mankind after he had given it everything, and had received nothing in return."

Franz Schubert was one of the coffin bearers at Beethoven's funeral. After the funeral ceremony, he went with a few friends to a tavern for a glass of wine. Raising his wine glass Schubert saluted the memory of Beethoven adding, "And here's also to the one among us, who will next follow the Master." Little did Schubert know that 18 months later he was to be that man.

Beethoven's earthly remains lie today in the Währing cemetery near Vienna. Over his grave is a large white marble stone. On this marble stone is engraved no flowery or lengthy epitaph, but just one self-sufficing, magnificent word: "Beethoven".

Beethoven's place in music history

Beethoven was 22 when he went to Vienna for the second time. During those first years there, a flood of pieces for various instruments and combinations poured from his pen: the "Kreutzer", "Moonlight" and "Pathetique" sonatas, three concertos for piano, the first six string quartets and the first two symphonies. By the time he was 31, publishers were vying for his works in which they recognised a new and authoritative voice. This was music liberated from conventional trammels, free as music had seldom been – original, expressive and powerful.

Unlike Mozart, with Beethoven composing was not easy. He toiled over every measure sitting at his piano. Many a time even in the final draft of a composition he would make last minute amendments. His writing desk was hopelessly untidy, littered with rusty pens and even half-eaten food. In the agony of composing he would rage up and down in his room. Away from his home, Beethoven often sought peace by wandering in the beautiful countryside where he would sit for hours beneath trees with his precious sketch books into which he would scribble any musical ideas that came to him – ideas which he would use, months or even years later, in his compositions.

" Some of Beethoven's finest compositions were written when his ears had closed to all outward sound and forced him into complete personal solitude."

Beethoven's initiative in writing music for instruments beyond their then accepted range (see Box on pg. 61) had several ripple effects. Composers who succeeded him started doing the same, and this soon led musicians to develop greater virtuosity in playing their respective instruments. This, in turn, influenced makers of instruments to better construct and design instruments.

With such music being written for it, the orchestra had to be strengthened by the doubling or trebling of certain instruments, and addition of two or three new instruments. As a result, by the time Beethoven died, the music written for the orchestra was greater in range, richer in texture, warmer in colour and more complex in its harmonies.

In the history of every art there arises at some time a great genius who, in his work, sums up not only all that has gone before him but also anticipates what is yet to come. Beethoven was such a genius in music, for he was not only the greatest representative of the Classical period, but was also the prototype of the Romantics who were to follow – the herald of the age of Schubert, Schumann, Chopin and many others. To quote one admirer: "Through a fortunate accident of time, through a happy orchestration of destiny, Beethoven came into the world at the very crest of music. His work weighted and shaped the summit of the waves towering before they spouted and burst."

Shakespeare and Beethoven are the universal types of geniuses in their respective arts. There is something about them that appeals directly to people, even those untutored in literature or music. The full gamut of human emotions appears to be so completely and effectively covered by both Shakespeare and Beethoven that their works have something to say to every man.

Beethoven wrote music not for an age but for all eternity. He did not pander to the popular taste of his time, since he had too great a respect for his art to do this. Beethoven had an unshakeable confidence in the fact that whatever he wrote would stand the test of time. When someone informed him that the performances of his last quartet had been accorded a cool reception, Beethoven smiled and simply said: "It will please them one day."

Beethoven's compositions are generally divided into three periods. The first period (1792-1803) bears traces of the influence of Haydn and Mozart. The second period (1803-17) reflects his greatest activity. The works are individualistic and bear the impress of his

The Imperial Theatre in a suburb of Beethoven's beloved Vienna

stormy and alternately tender and brusque personality. In his last period (1817-27) – 10 years before his death – Beethoven set norms from which music diverged only with great difficulty.

The very growth of his powers as he moved through life stamps Beethoven as a Master. He gave the world some of its finest utterances in music. His nine symphonies are marvels of that art. His 32 piano sonatas are the finest of their kind in the world and have been described as the New Testament of pianists.

Indeed, Beethoven was so enamoured of the structural outline of the sonata form, that his fondness for it is reflected in many of his compositions other than the piano sonatas. As Beethoven was comfortable as an orchestral composer, the piano sonatas also have a strong orchestral colouring, which makes them quite unique.

In his last quartets Beethoven touched spiritual heights which can scarcely be attained by any other mortal. As the sculptor Jacob Epstein says in his autobiography: "One cannot speak of the last quartets of Beethoven without seeming to gild fine gold. There is nothing else in all the wide realm of art that can quite compare with these works. Here in the last quartets Beethoven seems to have written them for himself alone. They are like the soliloquy of one who having expressed all sorrow, communes with his own soul in a final and withdrawn unique language."

Such was the empirical magic of his touch that Beethoven wrote only one violin concerto which has been long regarded as the greatest ever written. Of the five piano concertos, the fifth, better known as "The Emperor", is easily the most popular piano concerto in the world. Add to all these mighty works, his charming violin and piano sonatas, his powerfully scored opera "Fidelio", his great "Mass in D Minor", and we can only wonder at the vastness of the power within the composer that impelled Beethoven to write so much great music. Truly, had Beethoven written nothing more than these 32 piano sonatas, he would still have been hailed as immortal.

The most significant change noticeable towards the end of the Classical period was in the type of music composed, as distinct from the music composed at its commencement. When Haydn ushered in the Classical era, the music composed was pure and absolute music. But in the closing years of the Classical era, Beethoven was not only the greatest representative of that rich period but was also the prototype for the Romantics who were to follow him.

Beethoven anticipated what Wagner was to declare many years later when he said that it was "in the nature of instrumental music in its highest form to express in sound what is inexpressible in words". And true to the Romantic period, which was later to burn so brightly in the music of composers such as Schubert and Chopin, Beethoven's music depicted a world of inner strivings and aspirations; it became the product of conscious self-expression, one of the main qualities that differentiates the Romantic from the Classical composers. "With Beethoven," Wagner said, "Music commenced to be charged with subjective emotion; with Beethoven music commenced to speak freely of the tempests and the trials and triumphs of the human soul." Beethoven had blazed a new trail in music which, in the Romantic period, was to broaden tremendously and whose direct influence is still being felt well into the 21st century.

What raises Beethoven's genius in music to the level of Shakespeare's in literature is his supreme mastery of musical form. He was able to create vast and complex musical structures stemming from the fundamental building blocks of music itself. For Beethoven, a simple musical figure had manifold implications that could generate an entire symphony. For example, the opening four notes of the Fifth Symphony, the "Fate motif", are especially portentous, since some derivations of them are heard in nearly every bar of the first movement.

Notes on select works

Violin Concerto in D Major, Op. 61

Composed in 1806, this was dedicated to Stephan von Breuning, Beethoven's friend. The concerto was written for violin virtuoso Franz Clement, who gave it its first performance on June 23, 1806.

The concerto was far from complete, and at the inaugural performance, Clement had to play certain sections at sight. The soloist was highly praised but the concerto did not have a good reception. Following the practice of those times, Clement played the first movement, and then one of his own sonatas, which he rendered on one string with the violin held face down! Thereafter, he played the second and third movements.

The concerto was forgotten for almost 40 years, until the 13-year-old Joseph Joachim, later the leading violinist of the day, established its supremacy by an inspired performance in 1844. It was then received with enthusiasm. Joachim played it on several occasions, making the concerto so much his own, that it came to be rightfully regarded as a magisterial composition. The fundamental mood of the concerto is happy. It opens with five soft drum strokes introducing the wonderfully calm first theme. But those five beats startle when they are taken up by the orchestra in its long introduction. The pompous march-like theme, with a kettledrum motif, continues in the cantabile main theme. It all resolves in the most natural way in the world, however, and those five beats haunt the thematic development.

The larghetto, second movement, is like a poetic vocal duet between the orchestra and the soloist. The sublime song of this movement is a theme and variations, with the violin weaving exquisite garlands of melody about the theme in the orchestra. In the violin part here, the emphasis is on lyrical content rather than on virtuosity. The finale which follows without pause is an exuberant *rondo*, simple seeming, but rich in contrasts, and it ends in an irrepressible outburst of high spirits.

The concerto is regarded as the foremost violin concerto and some of the best violinists – Heifetz, Kreisler, Menuhin, Milstein, Oistrakh, Perlman, Stern, Szigeti – have regarded the performance of it in public as the peak achievement of their careers.

In my personal opinion, the concerto's performance by Jascha Heifetz is supreme, embellished by his flawless technique, perfect intonation and superb tone. On the occasion of Heifetz's birth centenary in 2001, Eric Wen, the editor of *The Strad* magazine, wrote a special article on Heifetz in the October issue of *Gramophone*, in which he emphasised that Heifetz was a "violinist of intuitive perfection".

Beethoven also composed two Romances for the violin:

No. 1 in G Major, Op. 40
No. 2 in F Major, Op. 50

Violin Sonatas

No. 1 in D Major, Op. 12, No. 1
No. 2 in A Major, Op. 12, No. 2
No. 3 in E-flat Major, Op. 12, No. 3
No. 4 in A Minor, Op. 23
No. 5 in F Major, Op. 24 "Spring"
No. 6 in A Major, Op. 30, No. 1
No. 7 in C Minor, Op. 30, No. 2
No. 8 in G Major, Op. 30, No. 3
No. 9 in A Major, Op. 47 "Kreutzer"
No. 10 in G Major, Op. 96

The amazing variety to be found among Beethoven's 10 violin sonatas reflects his profound familiarity with an instrument he knew best.

With so much wonderful music that all these sonatas offer, it is admittedly arbitrary to comment here on only two of them: No. 5 in F Major, Op. 24 and No. 9 in A Major, Op. 47.

Beethoven on music

"I am the Bacchus who crushes delicious nectar for mankind. It is I who gives the divine frenzy to men."

"Music is the only spiritual entrance to a higher world of knowledge. So use the lofty significance of thine art that thou shalt follow it from a pure and holy love to ennoble thyself and others, and to kindle in the hearts of all an enthusiasm for what is eternally great and beautiful."

"Music is a more lofty revelation than all wisdom and philosophy."

"Music is the mediator between the spiritual and sensual life."

The F Major, Op. 24, known by its label "Spring", certainly has a vernal touch in the opening theme, spelled out by the violin in the *allegro* first movement. The *adagio* that follows lives up fully to one's expectations of serene beauty. The third brief movement, a *scherzo*, leads to the *rondo* of the fourth movement, which begins charmingly before going on to its energetic moments.

The A Major Sonata, Op. 47, "Kreutzer", is the best known of the 10 sonatas. Its first performance was given by the French violinist Rudolphe Kreutzer, a close friend of Beethoven. (Kreutzer himself was an esteemed composer whose D Minor concerto was then in every violinist's repertoire.)

Romain Rolland in his book, *Beethoven*, wrote: "The Sonata opens with a majestic introduction, ending in a dominant pause." (Tradition has it that Bridgetown, a brilliant English violinist, improvised a cadenza here that Beethoven approved.)

"Amongst the whirl and excitement of the bold and vigorous opening *presto*, the hymn-like second subject stands out in a marvellous way. Nothing is lost of the tenderness of the *andante* in the brilliant variations which follow it, and this is all the more wonderful because this piece is the most virtuoso-like of all Beethoven's chamber music. Tenderness with Beethoven was no maudlin sentiment, but the gentle sympathy of a strong man."

The aggressive impetus of the finale, *presto*, outdoes the energies of the first movement, inviting the applause of listeners.

Piano Sonatas

Earlier in these pages it has been mentioned that the 32 piano sonatas of Beethoven have been often referred to as the New Testament of pianists and

Verse copied by Beethoven in his own hand from an Egyptian inscription
**"I am all that is.
I am all that is, was and ever shall be.
No mortal has lifted my veil.
He alone is of Himself, and to Him alone
All things owe their origin."**

that Beethoven would have been ever remembered by these sonatas had he composed no other music. Strangely, the half dozen well-known sonatas (out of the 32) happen to be those with names attached to them, not given by Beethoven but by his publishers as marketing lures, and so we have them identified for us as "Pathétique", "Moonlight", "Waldstein", "Appassionata", "Tempest", "Les Adieux" and the "Hammerklavier".

It has been said, "Beethoven widened the scope of the piano sonatas to symphonic proportions with the 'Waldstein', and even more with the 'Appassionata' where he introduced new dynamic extremes, shattering the thoughtful calm of the opening with sudden fortissimo chords."

Sonata No. 2 in C-sharp Minor, Op. 27 – "Moonlight"

This sonata has been the subject of a great deal of romantic suppositions, mainly due to its dedication to the Countess Giulietta Guicciardi, for whom Beethoven had at one time nurtured a deep passion.

Contemporary accounts, however, suggest that Beethoven never intended this sonata to be a musical expression of love, unhappy or otherwise. Alexander Wheelock Thayer, Beethoven's greatest biographer, has pointed out that this sonata was based on the theologian Johann Gottfried Seume's poem *Die Beterin*, which describes a maiden kneeling at the high altar in prayer for the recovery of a sick father.

The best observation on this sonata, now generally accepted, is the statement of the poet and critic Ludwig Rellstab who simply declared that the first movement reminded him of moonlight on the Lake of Lucerne.

Sonata No. 21 in C Major, Op. 53 – "Waldstein"

This sonata was dedicated to Count von Waldstein, a close friend of Beethoven who was also himself a musician. From every standpoint it is a remarkable work, as revolutionary in the history of piano sonatas as the "Eroica" is among symphonies. The language is new from the very opening passage, a long strummed choral opening. This is not merely the introduction, it is the theme and it occupies a vast and spacious time scale.

The sonata is built out of unusual key relationships. The constant vacillation between major and minor becomes an integral part of the sonata's language.

The slow introduction of the second movement is a rather full-blooded romantic vision.

The finale is a piece full of high spirits and geniality. Its opening theme is a lyric song. Ensuing passages are stormy but the ending is bright.

Sonata No. 23 in F Minor, Op. 57 – "Appassionata"

This sonata was dedicated to Count Franz von Brunswick. The opening movement is built in the classic way out of strong contrasts: a rhythmically marked, motif opening theme and a flowing subsidiary theme. But the contrasts of mood, the sudden changes, the pauses followed by the torrents – all these give a new dimension of intensity to the classic form. The piano scoring is rich and sonorous with the second theme beautifully projected. Sonority is also at the heart of the slow movement: in the theme itself and in the way the simple, classic variations figure. The sonata's finale is an even sterner tragedy than the opening movement. At the end is a remarkable stroke of drama, a new theme in faster tempo for the coda. It is my favourite sonata.

Sonata No. 26 in E-flat Major, Op. 81 – "Les Adieux"

This sonata was dedicated to Archduke Rudolph, a musician of some talent who in earlier years was Beethoven's pupil. A strong friendship grew between the two men, and this sonata celebrates it. Beethoven himself gave the work its title "*Les adieux, l'absence et le retour*". This inscription has been misinterpreted by the romantic-minded but the sonata is no love poem. It is simply an expression of the sorrow at the parting of friends and the joy of reunion, and has been thus described: "The opening movement is dominated by a three-note motto. It forms the substance of the subsidiary theme, appears in a richly harmonised version in the development, and again forms the substance of the coda. The slow movement is rhapsodic and charged with a gentle melancholy. At the close there is an eruption. Suddenly, however,

British edition of Beethoven's sonatas
As the composer spoke of the British on his death-bed, he concluded, "God bless them"

the friend returns and is greeted with a whoop of joy. The finale follows immediately, a happy conclusion, replete with what almost sounds like hunting-horn figures. It is an extremely rich and subtle movement, with particularly complex contrapuntal passages in the development. At the end Beethoven, using one of his oldest tricks, slows down the thematic substance to a standstill, which is dispelled by another final whoop."

Piano Concertos

Beethoven composed five piano concertos. The first two – No. 1 in C Major, Op. 15 and No. 2 in B-flat Major, Op. 19 – show the influence of Haydn and Mozart.

With the third concerto, in C Minor, Op. 37, Beethoven visits a world of his own: "… a darker world that suggests an advance particularly in the sense of a specific and vivid human and musical presence. Thus the gestures of the lean, spare, sometimes severe first movement are those of tensely dramatic music, and Beethoven demands that it be fiery (con brio). But here he gives a dream episode in the development. Like Haydn, Beethoven sometimes liked setting slow movements in remote keys and the sound of the *largo*'s first hushed chord of E Major is a shock that does not lose its magic. After this feast of rapturous embellishment, Beethoven concludes with a vigorous *rondo*."

Concerto No. 4 in G Major, Op. 58

The concerto was dedicated to the Archduke Rudolph of Austria. From Beethoven's sketch books we have come to know that the serene motif at the beginning of this concerto grew out of the same thought that supplied the tempestuous opening of the Fifth Symphony – the motif that has been called "Fate knocking at the door".

Exploring brave new worlds
"He detonated such a profound charge of thought and passion that the world still vibrates with the shock," declared the cellist Robert Schauffler of Beethoven

But here it sounds gentle and ingratiating. One graceful phrase chases another across the melodious opening pages and despite the stormy grandeur with which they are all developed, it is supremely lyrical music from beginning to end.

The romantic dialogue of the second movement between the piano and orchestra was once compared by Franz Liszt to Orpheus taming the wild beasts. Beethoven's orchestra may not be exactly a wild beast but the harsh peremptory octaves in which it speaks, and the soft pleading phrases with which the piano replies might easily have been inspired by the thought of Orpheus supplicating the powers of the underworld. Gradually, the stern voice of the orchestra melts, the octaves dissolve into harmony and, at this movement's very end, the orchestra unites with the piano in a tragic little sigh of acquiescence.

The melancholy spell of the *andante* is broken by a whispering, vivacious theme, the refrain of the *rondo* finale. But after this discreet beginning, the *rondo* turns out to be rough in spirit as well as in form.

The finale is rich in contrasts. It charms, it blusters, it crackles, and after the grand flourish of the cadenza, it launches into a triumphant *presto* with the obstinate refrain still dominating the glorious orchestral frenzy.

Concerto No. 5 in E-flat Major, Op. 73 – "Emperor"

Also dedicated to Archduke Rudolph, this concerto fully lives up to its name, "Emperor". It is a magnificent work that, as is evident from the descriptions that follow, richly deserves its reputation as the foremost piano concerto.

"The first movement begins with a decisive chord of the full orchestra and the piano enters unconventionally with a sweeping cadenza – the kind of thing customarily reserved for the close of a movement. There are two such chords, the piano continuing its rhapsodic outburst after each, then the orchestra spreads the various themes of this movement – taken up by the piano alone and together with other instruments. The themes are developed stormily, restated and brought back again for a triumphant coda which replaces the conventional cadenza.

"The slow movement is romantic, personal and deeply thoughtful. The melody is sung mostly by the orchestra while the piano surrounds it with garlands of graceful figuration. Towards the end are hints of the principal theme of the finale, which follows without pause, in a joyous outburst. It is a *rondo* with a jaunty, vigorous refrain almost like a folk dance. There is a wealth of contrasting episodes, including a sort of hunting-call figure for the horns. The reckless drive of the movement appears to subside towards the end with a long series of descending chords for the piano, which underneath the tympani softly sustain the rhythm of the theme. But the whole is rounded off with one more burst of the exuberant refrain."

Symphonies

The nine symphonies of Beethoven truly rank among the highest creations of man's mind.

The first two symphonies carry the influence of Haydn and Mozart. The first truly Beethoven symphony is the Third Symphony, the "Eroica".

"The 'Eroica' was specifically designed as a tribute to Napoleon, the hero of the Revolution, and it is impossible not to perceive in the Fifth and the Seventh similar epic ideas, while the poetic basis of the Ninth is expressly displayed in the *Ode* by Schiller which Beethoven used for its finale.

"These three are all odd-numbered symphonies. Those bearing even numbers are more lyrical in mood. The Fourth is perhaps an expression of love and certainly the most human and happy of the series. The Sixth is a revelation of the composer's love of the Austrian countryside and the Eighth is the most lyrical and most nearly 'classical' of all. Each is a counterpart of the preceding odd-numbered symphony, and they are mostly written as pairs. For, each lyrical symphony is a perfect foil to the preceding epic. Only the Ninth has no companion and is a feast in itself, the most immense and expansive example of Beethoven's musical architecture in symphonic form."

Symphony No. 3 in E-flat Major, Op. 55 – "Eroica"

The music of this symphony is revolutionary, and not only in technique. Beethoven broadened the scope for emotional expression, giving voice to the revolutionary spirit of the age. Beethoven was a passionate democrat and admired the young Napoleon Bonaparte, whose name in fact originally appeared on the title page of the symphony and was later removed when Napolean declared himself Emperor and betrayed his democratic ideals. The new title page read: "In memory of a Great Man". In this symphony, Beethoven shattered the ground rules of symphonic writing for all time. "In the first movement Beethoven created a single span of uninterrupted music of unprecedented length in which a single broken-choral motif is constantly given a new treatment, enriched with a wealth of new ideas and propelled forward in a succession of great waves of heroic effort. The epic scale and inner conviction of the second movement, the Funeral March, and the intricate pent up rhythm of the third movement, the *scherzo*, are followed by the finale that takes the form of a highly unusual set of variations on two different themes."

Symphony No. 5 in C Minor, Op. 67 – "Fate"

As it has been said, "Here is the potent and concentrated and ultimate distillation of the genius that was Beethoven. This symphony is compounded of all that was the essential man and the essential music."

Beethoven's virtuosity inspired him to write for instruments beyond their accepted range. He powered music to reach undreamt of heights

After the first performance of the Fifth Symphony, Hector Berlioz, himself a composer of distinction, wrote in a newspaper an amusing satire. Berlioz pictured for his readers the concert hall in which this symphony had been played. After the public and the musicians had left the hall, the caretaker carefully locked up all the instruments of the orchestra in a room adjoining the stage. As soon as the caretaker left the room, the instruments of the orchestra came to life and held a heated discussion.

Almost every instrument complained that Beethoven had written for them the most difficult and tortuous passages.

The flute complained of almost having dislocated her neck taking certain high notes.

The horns complained that their lungs had been stretched to bursting point in holding over certain sustained notes as written by Beethoven.

The double basses growled angrily, having to play devilishly fast passages that made them feel as if they were giddy little violins.

And so, what with one complaint or the other, the instruments kicked up such a row that the caretaker resting in his room heard the uproar and hurried over to see what the matter was. The instruments gathered round him and told him what the rumpus was about.

After having listened to what all the instruments had to say, the caretaker admonished them severely for making all the noise and threatened that if they resumed their protests he would ask Beethoven to continue to write even more difficult music for them. On hearing this, all the instruments were terrified and lapsed into silence. The caretaker then left the room, locking it behind him and retired to his quarters for the night.

The four opening notes of this symphony have been characterised as "Fate knocking at the door". These four notes are especially portentous since some derivation of them is heard in nearly every bar of the first movement. (Incidentally, these four notes, comprising three short notes and one long note, were linked with the letter "V" in the Morse Code – represented by three dots and one dash – and during World War II the nations of the Free World started their daily radio programmes by playing the opening four bars of the symphony to depict "V for Victory".)

The first movement – *allegro con brio* – "is one savage onslaught of rhythm, the rhythm of the motif of Fate, sometimes in a whisper, sometimes in a roar, sometimes as an ominous throbbing in the depths of the orchestra. Even the relatively lyric second theme is built on it, and it brings the movement to a close with one final shout of defiance."

The second movement – *andante con moto* – is a series of variations on two alternating themes. The first is sung by the violas and cellos, in a smooth-flowing melody of feminine grace and charm. The second theme, square-shouldered and masculine, sounds in the orchestra.

The third movement – *allegro* in *scherzo* mode – "features the rather elephantine gambols of the double basses, with an atmosphere of terror that has seldom been equalled in music. In the midst of the suspense the motif of fate sounds softly in a slightly altered form. It is answered by the whispered plucking sounds of the strings, and the whole orchestra falls back, as if exhausted, onto a softly sustained chord of uncertain tonality. The music seems in a state of suspended animation, except for one muffled drum that throbs underneath it like a slow persistent heartbeat – beating

in the rhythm of the motif of fate. The suspense grows with the challenge of that rhythm, fragments of the *scherzo* theme weave through the orchestra, the uncertain harmonies shift more and more towards the C Major, which you feel is waiting there like the sun to burst out of the clouds. Just at the moment when the suspense seems absolutely unbearable the orchestra pulls itself together with a sudden tremendous crescendo and strides forth into the light with the magnificent heroic theme of the last movement."

The finale – *allegro* – has a surge and drive, with themes that are broad and massive and blunt. There are passing reminders of the *scherzo*, but only enough to point out that the terror of the *scherzo* has been banished. The final *presto* and the exultant chords at the end are confident and powerful, and shining with the promise of victory.

Symphony No. 6 in F Major, Op. 68 – "Pastoral"

Beethoven was always a lover of Nature. He often sought rural solitude as a means to soothe and refresh his turbulent spirit. He spent many hours in the Wienerwald, the woods then just outside Vienna, where the deafness that had robbed him of his hearing perhaps meant that he could sense and absorb the voice of Nature instead. He wrote to Baroness Droszdich: "It is as if the trees and rocks could understand my mute entreaties and respond to them."

Beethoven in his last years
Isolated from the world by his deafness, Beethoven sits composing the visionary last quartets. His piano seems to lie shattered by his efforts to hear the music he has written

The symphony is not actually the story in music of a journey into the woods. It is rather an expression, in music, of the spirit of Nature, and the feelings aroused in one by communication with Nature. To call this symphony "programme music" is to slight the music and belittle the composer. True, here and there we encounter more or less literal details – but these only in sufficient number and with sufficient emphasis to centre our attention on the sights and sounds that engendered the feelings expressed in the main body of the work.

In the first movement – *allegro ma non troppo,* "Awakening of Serene Impressions on arriving in the Countryside" – this feeling is apparent in the very opening phrase, expressing joyful contentment on reaching the countryside and the first four bars contain the germ of almost all that follows. Their varied rhythmic patterns are developed separately and together in a way that intensifies the music's emotional spirit, continuing through a spacious unhurried movement that ends in the same tranquil mood as it began.

The second movement – *andante molto,* "Scene by the Brook" – is evoked by the flow of murmuring strings which seems to run on even when not actually heard, as when the flute, oboe and clarinet are eased in with their short cadenzas, imitating the calls of the nightingale, quail and cuckoo, respectively.

The third movement – *allegro,* "Jolly Gathering of Country Folk" – opens with two lighthearted dance-like tunes. Both are repeated in different keys. A hunter's call is heard in the horns and bassoons, and repeated by the violins. The village band plays with ingenious syncopation. This section is very humorous as each rustic player tries to assert his own importance, especially the brass players

regardless of out-of-tune and defective valves on their instruments.

The fourth movement – *allegro,* "Thunderstorm, Tempest" – speaks with a distant rumbling on the drums that clouds over the merry-making of the previous movement. And then the storm breaks with violent outbursts from trombones and timpani, and a piccolo adding its shrill voice to whistle up a sharp squall of rain. Then the tempest roars out in its fury. The clouds open and there is thunder and lightning, and a screaming gale. The storm soon passes, the thunder dying away in the distance.

The fifth movement – *allegretto,* "Shepherds' Song; Gladsome and Thankful Feelings after the Storm" – sounds as if the last echo of the receding thunderstorm is answered by the piping of the shepherds' song of thanksgiving.

Beethoven conducting
Imperious and exacting, he used an endless variety of gesticulations to impress his will on the orchestra

The orchestra takes up from there to herald exultation in the miracle of the freshly washed sky and air, and return of the sun.

Symphony No. 7 in A Major, Op. 92

The symphony was dedicated to the Prince Regent (later George IV of England). Romain Rolland held up this symphony as an "orgy of rhythm". Beethoven himself is reported to have said: "I am a Bacchus pressing out delicious nectar for mankind." Wagner wrote: "I do not know whether Beethoven intended to portray a Dionysian feast in the finale, but nowhere will greater emancipation and power be found than in the Seventh Symphony. It is a mad extravagance of unbounded superhuman might, solely for pleasure – the pleasure which a river must experience when it bursts its banks." Elsewhere it was titled "Apotheosis of the Dance" – which it is!

The first movement – *poco sostenuto-vivace* – begins "with a magnificent introduction of the themes. The first comes at the very beginning, separating itself, in the thin voice of the oboe, from the mighty opening chord... Presently the strings intone ascending scales in crescendo, the basses alone holding aloof from these until the apex of their power is reached. Now the second theme follows, again in the penetrating voice of the oboe..."

Orchestral development follows and suddenly the main theme of the movement proper appears in the silken tones of the flute. At this point, it is clear why this symphony has been designated as the "dance symphony", for its quaint little theme is unmistakably imitative of a folk dance and is subjected to many different forms. Towards the end there is a new burst of revelry, culminating in fierce vehemence and power.

" Away from his home, Beethoven often sought peace by wandering in the beautiful countryside where he would sit for hours beneath trees with his precious sketch books into which he would scribble any musical ideas that came to him – ideas which he would use, months or even years later, in his compositions."

The second movement – *allegretto* – "happily falls short of being a funeral march. The suggestion is powerfully present: yet hear it through and you decide that Beethoven is now serious rather than sad, philosophical rather than pessimistic. The first theme, ushered in by a sombre chord in the horns and woodwind, is gloomy and ominous, but the counter theme, though still in the minor mode, lends a brightening touch of hopefulness. There is always a gleam of light in Beethoven's darkness.

"The movement is replete in amazing contrasts in colour, tonality and rhythms. As the movement draws to a close the original themes are glorified. A final daring touch in plucked notes near the end and at last an unexpected alternation in accent brings the movement to its conclusion."

The third movement – *presto-assai meno presto*. "The first theme opens the movement... Brilliant orchestral colour is freely applied... Superb climaxes develop with the ascending scales, and suddenly the swift scales are reversed to give a new effect. A most striking contrast is presented in the middle of the movement when the boisterous opening section is repeated in tones of ethereal delicacy, yet with every original detail of accent and phrasing perfectly imitated... The contrasting theme is much slower and rather solemn, and heard in a combination of clarinet, bassoon and horn with the last most prominent and against it is poised a long-sustained note of the violins... As the end is approached a prayerful spirit is breathed gently into the

music, only to be elbowed roughly aside by the violent chords in full orchestra that bring the movement to a close."

The fourth movement – *allegro con brio* – opens with a powerful chord in the string section and is duplicated even more powerfully by the remainder of the orchestra. The same figure is repeated and with scarcely a pause the wild dance-like first theme leaps into dynamic life – a bacchanal indeed.

At this point the "dance symphony" reaches its apotheosis. "Here the fundamental, the primal source of all music – rhythm – holds complete sway. There is an almost savage, primitive joy in these measures; a fierce exaltation of the purely physical that could be expressed only through rhythm, which more closely than any other element in music approaches and appeals to the physical. It is almost impossible for any human being to remain motionless through this movement... Here we become, whether we will it or not, a part of the rhythm created and driven along by the composer, conductor and orchestra; something involuntary, something deep within us, leaps and moves to the headlong abandoned onrush of this music...

"The second theme is almost as bacchanalian and contagious as the first and it leads to even wilder revels. But suddenly near the end there is a mysterious change, so subtly effected that we are scarcely conscious of the means employed. The original subject reappears, now in the tender, tremulous accents of the flute – infinitely gentle, pensive, yet still touched by joy. It is but a bit of byplay, an aside, a highlight, a momentary distraction, and the wild dance goes on until the end."

Symphony No. 9 in D Minor, Op. 125 – "Choral"

The symphony was dedicated to Friedrich Wilhelm III, King of Prussia. It was completed, after long delays, in 1824, and received its first performance in May of that year. The symphony towers high above Beethoven's other works of his last period, like Mount Blanc over its Alpine chain, and is indeed the masterpiece of his whole career. The symphony is best described in the words of British musicologist W.H. Hadow: "The first movement – *allegro ma non troppo* – begins with an ominous murmur, like the muttering of a distant storm, which suddenly bursts with a thunderbolt and rages with fierce elemental energy from horizon to horizon. Now and again there opens a space of quiet tender melody, as the sky may show through a rift in the tempest; now and again, by a miraculous effort of genius, Beethoven commands the whirlwind itself, bids it to be still, and so through stages of peace and conflict the great movement surges onward to its climax of sheer overwhelming passion."

The second movement – *scherzo; molto vivace* – which follows next "is the longest and greatest example of its kind, a wonderful outburst of rhythmic

> *" Beethoven was undoubtedly a great lover of liberty and felt deeply for the rights of the common man. "*

speed which sets the blood coursing and tingling. Its trio has one of Beethoven's happiest melodies, distributed between two different instrumental voices, and in both cases it gives a masterly example of the point to which the organisation of simple figures can be carried. Not less admirable is the contrast between its lightness of touch and the tremendous depth and earnestness of the *adagio*."

The third movement – *adagio; andante* – "opens with two bars of yearning prelude in which the very heart of Beethoven seems to burst; and there follows a lament which expresses and spiritualises the sorrows of all the world. It is answered by a second theme which, though grave, is of a serene cast, a responsive voice of comfort and resignation. And of these two, in varying converse, the entire movement consists. Complexity of plot would be out of keeping with the utterance of truths so mystic and so sublime."

The fourth movement – *finale* – is replete with changes of tempos: *Allegro assai, presto vivace; andante maestoso; adagio ma non troppo; allegro energico; allegro ma non tanto; sempre piu allegro, prestissimo.*

"It was on this finale that Beethoven expended his chief labour, and indeed, he may well have doubted how most fittingly to bring so great a drama to its triumphant conclusion. For a few moments the orchestra seems to share his anxieties; tragedy reaches its climax in crashing discords and passages of wild

unrest; themes of preceding movements are tried and rejected. At length there tentatively emerges the tune devised for Schiller's *Ode* which, with a shout of welcome, the music seizes and carries shoulder-high. When the chorus enters it is as though all the forces of humanity are gathered together; number by number the thought grows and widens until the very means of its expression are shattered, and we seem no more to be listening to music, but to be standing face to face with the living world."

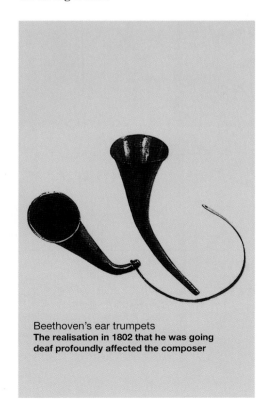

Beethoven's ear trumpets
The realisation in 1802 that he was going deaf profoundly affected the composer

FRANZ PETER
SCHUBERT

Born : Lichtenthal, Austria, January 31, 1797
Died : Vienna, Austria, November 19, 1828

Franz Schubert was one of 19 children born to a poor school master residing in a suburb of Vienna. Even in a family that had musical talents, Schubert showed an amazing precocity for music at an early age. Indeed, his instructor in music confessed later that whenever he set out to teach anything new to Schubert, he found, to his utter surprise, that the boy appeared to know it already.

Schubert started to compose music while still in school. Though these compositions were for the most part immature, his classmates thought they were marvellous. As he was too poor to buy the music notepaper needed for his compositions, his school fellows would purchase it for him from their pocket money. By the time he left school, Schubert had written many songs as well as instrumental and orchestral pieces.

His father wanted Schubert to become, like him, a school master, but the idea did not appeal to young Schubert for his soul was already wedded to music. Fate, however, did compel him to become a school teacher. Afraid of compulsory military service, he uneasily volunteered to teach the lowest class at his father's school at a yearly salary of 32 shillings. Schubert managed to combine his teaching duties with composing music and the years that followed were remarkable for the miraculous ease with which he produced his compositions.

Indeed, with the exception of Mozart, there is no one in the history of music to match the speed with which Schubert scrolled off one composition after another. Inspiration stood tirelessly at his elbow and he composed music as naturally as birds take to song.

Schubert's favoured field of composition was the song. In the songs composed up to that time, the words and music formed two distinct parts, and even when there was any connection between the two, it was of a superficial nature. With Schubert, and musicians thereafter, the song became an art form. The words and the music were now brought together and interwoven in such a way that the one could not be separated from the other without loss of purpose or expression or dramatic effect.

As re-created by Schubert, the German song, or lied, became the Romantic ideal of blending the various arts, and his lieder were the best examples of the marriage of music and poetry. To write songs in such satisfying and artistic form was in itself a singular achievement, but the astounding fact was the uncanny speed with which these songs were created. It was not unusual for Schubert to write as many as six songs a day. He went so far as to sleep with his spectacles so that directly he woke up in the morning he could start writing songs! Within his short life span he composed some 650 of them.

At one time Schubert shared a room with a poet named Mayrhofer and the two would often spend hours together, the one writing poetry and the other setting it to music. No sooner did Mayrhofer finish a poem than he would toss it across to Schubert who would read it through and immediately set it to music.

Inspiration came to Schubert at anytime, anywhere. He had merely to read through a poem for his mind to immediately suggest its appropriate musical setting. Once, he and a few friends stopped by at a tavern for a glass of wine after a long walk. Lying on their table was a book of Shakespearean verses. Idly flipping through its pages, Schubert's eyes caught the verse "Hark, hark the lark!" As he read this poem his mind started to fashion the appropriate melody.

Seizing a menu card he quickly scribbled the music as it flowed from him: it was "Horch, horch die lerch!" Many of his finest songs were composed this way.

During his lifetime, poverty constantly haunted Schubert. He was sometimes reduced to playing the violin in cafés and on the streets of Vienna to earn a few kreutzers. Indeed, Schubert was often so miserable and unhappy that he once said, "My music is the product of my genius and my suffering."

Schubert had no head for business, often parting with his songs for the price of a meal, while his avaricious publishers raked in hundreds of kreutzers. He usually received the equivalent of 10 pence for each song, and the highest sum he ever received for a single composition was £3. Schubert additionally wrote for various musical forms: operas, operettas, incidental (stage) music, church music, symphonies, chamber works: quartets and quintets, piano sonatas, impromptus, and three important song cycles. He died at the age of 31 – the youngest among the front-rank composers of the world. It is estimated that during his short life span Schubert must have consumed as much music notepaper as would have made a small fortune for a stationer.

Schubert's powers were actually growing when death intervened. It is the recognition of this fact – that Schubert died in the full flush of his genius – that inspired the following appropriate inscription on his tombstone:

"Music buried here a rich treasure
And yet fairer hopes."

Schubert's last request was to be buried close to Beethoven in Vienna's Währing cemetery.

> *"Schubert's favoured field of composition was the song. With him and musicians thereafter, the song became an art form."*

Notes on select works

The Erl King (Der Erlkönig) (D 328)

In German folk literature an Erl is a malicious spirit that lives in forests and is especially spiteful to children. The composition is based on a poem by Goethe.

The poem tells of a father carrying his child on horseback through a forest on a wild winter night. The terrified child imagines that it sees the Erl King and that he is calling out to him. The father tries to pacify the child, saying that it is only the howling wind. The child, however, refuses to be comforted and insists that he can distinctly hear the Erl King calling to come to him. As the child's terror rises, the despairing father urges his horse on to a faster gallop and holds the child closer to his breast. In vain, for when he arrives at his own door the child is dead.

Schubert has given the poem a musical setting of such dramatic power that no one on hearing this song can fail to be moved by it. It has been pointed out how, with great sensitivity, Schubert at first gives "...the impression of the wild elements and the headlong ride through the night; the terror of the child; the anxiety of the father; the mocking summons of the Erl King; and combines it all in sounds that rush with ever-increasing turmoil, till, with their arrival at the door of their house, the music, like their mad ride, stops suddenly, and in a stillness of despair the father's horror at finding his child dead in his arms is told simply in seven quiet words."

Piano Trio in B-flat (D 898)

Schubert's serious involvement with the Piano Trio composition came only towards the end of his short life.

Major compositions

Music scholar and Schubert specialist Otto Erich Deutsch had prepared a thematic catalogue of all Schubert's works in 1951 (revised in 1978), giving them "D" (for Deutsch) numbers which replaced the unsystematic earlier Opus listings.

Incidental Music
Rosamunde (D 797)
  Ballet I
  Ballet II
  Entr'acte III

Song Cycles
Die schöne Müllerin (20 songs) (D 795)
Winterreise (24 songs) (D 911)

Songs (over 650)
An Sylvia (Shakespeare) (D 891)
Aufenthalt (Rellstab)
Ave Maria (Storck) (D 839)
Der Doppelgänger (Heine)
Der Erlkönig (Goethe) (D 328)
Die Forelle (Schubert) (D 550)
Frühlingstraum (Muller)
Gretchen am Spinnrade (Goethe) (D 118)
Der Hirt auf dem Felsen
  (w. clarinet obbligato) (D 965)
Nacht und Träume (Collin) (D 827)
Die Post (Müller)
Ständchen (Horch, horch, die lerche)
  (Shakespeare – Grillparzer)
Die Stadt (Heine)
Der Tod und das Mädchen
  (Claudius) (D 531)
Der Wanderer (Lübeck) (D 493)
Der Wanderer an den Mond (Solde) (D 870)
Wanderers Nachtlied (Goethe) (D 768)
Wiegenlied (Anon.) (D 498)
Wiegenlied (Seidl) (D 867)

Symphonies (9)
No. 5, B-flat Major (D 485)
No. 8, B Minor "Unfinished"
  (D 759) – two movements only
No. 9, C Major "Great" (D 944)

Chamber Music
(including 15 String Quartets)
Octet, F Major (D 803)
Quintet for Piano and Strings,
  A Major "Trout" (D 667)
Quintet for Strings, C Major, (D 956)
String Quartet No. 13, A Minor (D 804)
String Quartet No. 14, D Minor
  "Death and the Maiden" (D 810)

Masses
Deutsche Messe (German Mass) (D 872)
Die Nacht, male choir
Ständchen (D 920) alto and female voices

The great master of the German "lied"
Schubert had an incomparable lyric gift and a wealth of beautiful melodies

Piano Music
Impromptus (D 899)
  No. 2, E-flat Major
  No. 3, G Major
  No. 4, A-flat Major
Impromptus (D 935)
  No. 2, A-flat Major
  No. 3, B-flat Major
    "Andante con variazioni"
  No. 4, F Minor
Twelve Ländler (D 790)
Moments Musicaux (6) (D 780)
  No. 3, F Minor "Air Russe"
  No. 6, A-flat Major
Fantasia, C Major "Wanderer" (D 760)

Waltzes
"Valses Nobles" (D 969)
12 Waltzes (D 145)
36 Waltzes (D 365)

Piano Sonatas
No. 16 in G Major (D 894)
No. 17 in C Minor (D 958)
No. 18 in A Major (D 959)
Allegretto in C Minor (D 915)

Piano Trios
No. 1 B-flat Major (D 898)
No. 2 E-flat Major (D 929)

Violin and Piano
Sonata, A Major (D 574)
Sonatina, No. 1, D Major (D 384)
Sonatina, No. 3, G Minor (D 408)
Arpeggione and Piano Sonata,
  A Minor (D 821)

Piano duet
Andantino Varie, B Minor
3 Marches Militaires (D 733)

The nature lover
The most spontaneous of composers, Schubert transformed his impressions of nature into music

The B-flat trio was composed in early 1827, soon after the death of Beethoven and in the light of the spiritual attachment that existed between the two composers, the older man's influence may be taken for granted. Schubert did not carry the piano trio beyond the peak the form had reached with Beethoven, but even without the drama and grandeur of Beethoven's compositions, this Schubert Trio is a work of symphonic proportions – and one of the most beloved pieces in chamber music literature.

"Death and the Maiden" ("Der Tod und das Mädchen") (D 810)

This String Quartet, No. 14, in D Minor was composed in 1824-25 and the theme of the second movement was taken from part of Schubert's famous song of the same title. This work has been adjudged one of the most inspired quartets ever written, both in form and in content. Its spiritual theme is supposed to be "Fate and Life" according to musicologist Laura Stanfield Prichard. On the other hand, music historian Homer Ulrich has said that no attempt should be made to read a programme into the music.

The first movement is characterised by gloomy melancholy which has been interpreted as "a struggle with Death". The second movement, *andante con moto*, is in strong contrast to the passionate first movement. Here Schubert did not make use of the first part of his song, which depicts the maiden's terror, but the peaceful song of Death.

The third movement, *allegro molto*, is marked by strong rhythms. The finale is an example of the combined *rondo* and sonata forms. The movement contains a clear quotation from the Erl King (the child's final cry) as Schubert's cry of distress to Death.

Quintet in A (for piano and strings) "The Trout Quintet" (D 667)

Its movements are *allegro vivace, andante, scherzo, andantino* (theme and variations), *finale allegro giusto*. The quintet is one of the liveliest compositions created by Schubert. It expresses the carefree spirit of summer and the Hungarian rhythms of the finale bubble over with joie de vivre.

Rosamunde (D 797)

This composition consists of overture, ballet and incidental music by Schubert written for Helmina von Chézy's play *Rosamunde, Princess of Cyprus*.

The play itself was a relatively unimportant and undramatic concoction of Romantic ideas, and it was only the wonderful music that saved it. Schubert wrote this composition in five days. The most outstanding portions are the soprano song "The Full Moon is Shining" and the music for the entr'actes and the ballets.

Symphonies

Symphony No. 8 in B Minor – "Unfinished"

To call this the "Unfinished" symphony is somewhat misleading. It is, as a symphony in conventional form, incomplete, for there are two movements instead of the usual four. In that sense it is "unfinished". But in a larger sense, it is utterly perfect in its compositional form.

The symphony has been thus described: "It leaves nothing unsaid. It explores the most mysterious regions of the human soul and heart. In language of inexpressible beauty it communicates from composer to hearer an intensity of passionate emotion, a degree of spiritual exaltation, a completely satisfying and wholly expressive message…"

In the first movement, melody sings through the very first note. The marvellous succession of melodies and the varied versions of them flow in a smooth stream. But there are passionate outbursts too, and intense dramatic utterances shouted forth in the orchestra's full and powerful voice. There is gentleness, however, in the constant recurrence of the chief song of the movement. Mighty chords, given in full orchestra, close the movement.

In the second movement the essential beauty and contrast is achieved through modulations – mysterious, unexpected, unconventional – but always beautiful. Modulation is, in simple terms, a radical change of musical effect, caused by a change of tonality or "key". To select the key to which the modulation is to be made, then to make it by logical musical processes, requires skill of no mean order. However, the best way to appreciate this movement is to abandon yourself to its recurrent beauty.

"The mood of the symphony does change as this second movement begins. The bass strings intone a descending passage in pizzicato, portentous like the footsteps of an advancing fate. This melancholy figure persists and then gives way to a pensive dialogue in the woodwind, the violins singing softly in the background. Later, the heavy footfalls of destiny draw closer; the gentle plaint uttered by flutes and violins and clarinets appears again and again.

"Towards the close of the movement the final version of the early woodwind melody appears in an augmented state, and again comes the ominous progression of bass notes like the restless pacing of some giant creature, shadowing the bright orchestral colours that tint every measure of the symphony. There follows what Schumann names as the best discourse upon music – 'silence'."

Symphony No. 9 in C Major – "Great" (D 944)

This symphony was Schubert's last and generally regarded as his greatest work.

"The symphony begins with a romantic little passage on the horns. The theme is taken up by the woodwind, violas and cellos. It bursts out like a fanfare from the bassoons, and its romantic spirit is well developed before the *andante* gives way to the *allegro*. The rhythmically punctuated main theme is hammered out by the full orchestra, before it is relieved by a quick but gracious minor theme on the woodwind.

"The second movement, *andante con moto*, has the characteristics of a slow march. One tune grows out of the other. In the middle of the movement comes one of the best-known passages for horn – only a few simple notes, but indescribably effective.

"The third movement is a *scherzo, allegro vivace*, but having the same grand proportions as the other movements. The main part is in sonata form and opens with the strings playing staccato and two graceful 'Ländler' melodies follow. The trio sounds very like a Viennese waltz.

"The *finale, allegro vivace*, is like an endless ride over rough ground. New whims and diversions are continually introduced. A new theme – dominated by four repeated notes – is used to build up a coda which is just as overwhelming as some of those created by Beethoven."

Bound for the Vienna Woods
Schubert and his friends are seen setting out on an excursion. The composer's life was greatly lightened by his loyal circle of friends who were among the poets, painters and musicians of Vienna

NICCOLÒ
PAGANINI

Born: Genoa, Italy, October 27, 1782
Died: Nice, France, May 27, 1840

Niccolò Paganini began to play the violin with his father at the tender age of 6. Paganini senior decided to use his son's talent to generate an income and to that end left no stone unturned to make the boy a precocious virtuoso.

The result was that young Paganini made great progress in an astonishingly short time. He composed his first violin sonata when he was 8 years old and he played in public for the first time when he was 9.

If his father had been harsh with him and driven him to practise for hours in the initial stages of learning the violin, his mother was a gentle, pious lady who gave him spiritual support and encouragement. In her dreams she saw an angel predicting a great career for her son. He remained tenderly attached to his mother throughout her life.

When Paganini outgrew parental teaching, he became a student, first of the violinist Cervetto who encouraged him to give private performances. Those performances soon aroused the interest of Giacomo Costa, Genoa's leading violinist. Costa was proud of Paganini and in 1794, when the boy was 11, presented him at a very successful public concert. His progress thereafter was so prodigious that he was taken to Parma to study under Alessandro Rollo.

When father and son reached Parma, they found Rollo ill in bed. As they were waiting there, Niccolò noticed a manuscript of Rollo's latest violin concerto. He casually picked up a violin and sight-read the music to such perfection that Rollo, rushing out of his bed, exclaimed: "I can teach you nothing. In God's name, go and see Paer. Here you would be wasting your time." Ferdinando Paer had been Rollo's own teacher.

During his year-long stay in Parma, Paganini gave several concerts and also played for the royal family. In 1796, he returned to Genoa and lived there till 1799. Prominent violinists from all over Italy, having heard of Paganini's fame, visited him in Genoa. At about that time he also suddenly became interested in the guitar and mastered it completely.

A great influence in Paganini's life was the discovery of the half-forgotten "*L'arte del violino*" by the Italian composer Pietro Locatelli, published half a century earlier. Locatelli's volume contained 24 caprices for solo violin which, in Paganini's words, "opened up a world of new ideas and devices that never had the success they deserved because of excessive difficulties". Paganini paid tribute to the earlier master by quoting Locatelli's Caprice No. 7 in his own Caprice No. 1.

In 1801, aged 19, Paganini moved to Lucca, also in Italy, where he remained for the next eight years. Lucca became the base of his operations. He was appointed leader of the new National Orchestra and gave many successful concerts in northern Italy. However, he gambled away most of the money he earned, even going so far as to pawn his violin.

On one occasion when Paganini appeared for a concert in Livorno without his instrument, a wealthy amateur lent him a Guarnerius, and refused to take it back after the concert, declaring, "I do not want to profane the instrument after Paganini has played on it."

Conditions in Lucca changed drastically in 1805 when Princess Elise was installed as the ruling sovereign. The princess was young, art-loving and attractive. Before long she discovered Paganini's talent and made him solo violinist at her court. There were strong indications that Paganini was romantically linked with her.

As time went on, Paganini grew tired of being a courtier. In 1808, when the court moved to Florence, its orchestra was dissolved and Paganini then left Lucca to embark on the career of a travelling virtuoso.

In 1813, Paganini made his debut in Milan, the cultural centre of Italy. For that occasion he wrote a new piece which was to become a favourite in his repertoire – "Le Streghe" ("Witches Dance"), variations on a popular ballet tune of the day. His first concert at La Scala was a great triumph and within the next two months, he performed 11 more times.

A very favourable review appeared in a Leipzig musical journal: "In a sense Paganini is without question the foremost and greatest violinist in the world. His playing is truly inexplicable. He performs certain passages, leaps and double stops that have never been heard from any violinist."

In 1824, when Paganini was playing in concerts in Northern Italy, he met Antonia Bianchi, a young singer. They had a liaison that lasted until 1828. She bore him a son to whom Paganini was deeply devoted. Antonia was also the assisting artist in all of Paganini's concerts, except the last.

Paganini did not venture out of Italy until he was 45 years old. In 1828 he set out to conquer Northern Europe. And conquer it he did. Vienna, Berlin, Paris, London were all at his feet. His series of concerts in Vienna caused a sensation; the public went wild with excitement. Clothes, sweets and special dishes were named after him. His likeness was engraved on walking sticks and snuff boxes. When Paganini visited Paris three years later, the enthusiasm of the public there was even greater. In London, too, Paganini got standing ovations. Records show that Paganini gave 14 concerts in Vienna, 11 in Berlin, 12 in Paris and 15 in London.

Veneration of Paganini was not confined only to the top violinists of the day. The Classical masters Schumann and Schubert, and the Romantic, Liszt, were also affected by his superb, inexplicable talent. The sensitive Schubert, after hearing Paganini, declared, "I heard an angel sing in the Adagio." Liszt was so overwhelmed by Paganini's technique that he took a sabbatical and subjected his own already fantastic piano technique to intense scrutiny, declaring that his aim was to be known hereafter as "the Paganini of the Piano".

Paganini reached the dizzy heights of his profession not only by his technical wizardry but also by the magnetism of his personal appearance. The French critic Castil-Blaze described him thus: "Five feet five inches in height, built on long sinuous lines, a long pale face with strong lineaments, a protruding nose, an eagle eye, curly hair flowing to his shoulders and hiding an extremely thin neck. Two lines were engraved on his cheeks by his profession, one might say, for they resembled the S-shaped sound holes of the violin."

Such was Paganini's appearance and magical mastery of his instrument that superstitious persons felt there must be something supernatural about him. It was whispered that he was in league with the Evil One; popular belief credited him with being the son of the Devil. Some people swore that they saw the "faint person of the Devil standing close to Paganini's elbow" and guiding the bow arm.

> " *Extolled as the 'Wizard of the Violin', Paganini was the prototype of the Romantic virtuoso. He achieved limitless mastery of his instrument. He exacted every possible secret from the violin, which he loved beyond anything else.* "

Major compositions

Violin and Orchestra
Concerto No. 1, E-flat Major, Op. 6
Concerto No. 2, B Minor,
 Op. 7 "La Campanella"
Fantasia on the G-string
 (after Rossini's Mosè in Egitto)
Moto Perpetuo, Op. 11

Violin and Piano
Carnival of Venice
Sonata No.12, E Minor, Op. 3 No. 6
Sonatina "Grande"
Variations on "Dal tuo stellato soglio"
 (after Rossini's Mosè in Egitto)
Nel cor più mi sento

Violin
24 Caprices, Op. 1
No. 5, A Minor
No. 9, E Major "La Chasse"
No. 13, B-flat Major "Le Pire du Diable"
No. 17, E-flat Major
 "Andantino Capriccioso"
No. 20, D Major
No. 24, A Minor "Tema con variazioni"

Violin and Piano Pieces
Le Streghe
1 Palpiti
Non più mesta

Violin Concertos
No. 1, D-dur Major, Op. 6
No. 2, h-möll, Op. 7 "La Campanella"
No. 0 (orchestrated by F. Mompellio)

Paganini was shrewd enough to realise the value of all manner of publicity and encouraged the aura of mystery surrounding him. He refused to publish his compositions – except for the 24th Caprice – so that others would not be able to copy his technique. It is said that so powerful was this aura of demonic subterfuge he had cultivated that people often crossed themselves whenever he passed by.

Paganini amassed much money from the concerts and recitals that he performed over the years but lost most of it in gambling, to which he was addicted. He was imprisoned when a casino he owned failed and he was unable to pay his debts. In prison he asked for his violin and it was handed to him. It is said that because of the dampness in his cell, the strings on his violin snapped one by one until only the G-string remained. But such was Paganini's skill that he would spend hours playing on the G-string with great inventiveness. His famous "Air on the G-string" corroborates this story.

The rigours of intensive concertising all over Europe began to slowly affect Paganini's health. His playing began to falter. From 1834, increasing illness put an end to his playing career. Yet he maintained his interest in the violin till his death in 1840 from cancer of the larynx.

Paganini's place in music history

*P*aganini represents the turning point of virtuosity," wrote Schumann, meaning that Paganini's technique was not mere effect but an integral artistic ingredient. Extolled as "the Wizard of the Violin", Paganini was the prototype of the Romantic virtuoso. He achieved limitless mastery of his instrument. He exacted every possible secret from the violin, which he loved beyond anything else. It has truly been said of him: "By his technical wizardry and personal magnetism Paganini dominated the history of the violin as its foremost virtuoso. His impact was so overpowering that an entire generation of Romantic musicians became aware of the significance of virtuosity as an important element in art."

Among Paganini's most striking effects were left hand pizzicato and totally innovative double stops. His writing for harmonics caused an entire generation of violinists to devote much of their time to that technique.

His technique has been described thus: "Paganini often used unusual fingerings by stretching rather than by the more conventional shifting. The build of his hand was peculiar and enabled him to reach four 'A's on four strings without moving his hand. In other words, he could reach from the lowest to the highest notes on the fingerboard by sheer stretch.

"Another particular hallmark of Paganini's violin style was his ability to perform entire pieces on the G-string, which demanded almost acrobatic control of the fingerboard – a kind of daredevil technique for moving with lightning speed from the lowest to the highest positions."

Of his bowing it was observed that he took "up-beat" phrases with a downbow and accentuated phrases with an upbow. Paganini manipulated his bow exclusively with forearm and wrist while holding the upper arm close to his body. His arms were unusually long, which enabled him to immobilise the upper parts. Yet another innovation was Paganini's reliance on the bouncing bow.

During his life Paganini published only his path-breaking Caprice No. 24. This was deliberate. It was his intuitive approach and hard practice that enabled him to exploit to the hilt all the technical possibilities of the violin. He amazed and captivated his listeners and at the same time teased and baffled his colleagues by his stunning control over the instrument. Since he made his original score unavailable, before all his recitals and concerts copies of the score were distributed to the accompanying musicians and gathered back at the end.

Notes on select works
Concerto No. 1, E-flat Major, Op. 6

Andrea Amati of Cremona
Inventor of the modern violin

"This concerto, written in 1817-18 reveals Paganini's technical wizardry already fully-fledged. Contemporary audiences must have gasped at the quite extended passage of double-stop thirds, chromatic in some places but also sometimes in harmonics. Apart from that, the concerto also shows how greatly Paganini's melodic style was influenced by the Italian opera of his time, especially Rossini. The theme with which the soloist enters in the first movement, with its large leaps, brings the coloratura aria to mind, and there are recitative-like elements in the development section in the first movement and in the *adagio*.

"Although the work comes under the general heading of the 'virtuoso concerto', it can uphold some more substantial claims: the first movement testifies to the composer's serious intentions, in its 94-bar-long orchestral exposition, constructed according to the book, and in the motivic associations set up between individual themes. On the other hand, it is also made clear in the first movement, by the soloist's opening statement that this is the work of an instrumental virtuoso whose purpose it is to display the full extent of his skills. Sections of thematic elaboration are placed directly next to passages where the emphasis is wholly on virtuoso technique, without the slightest attempt to integrate, or even mediate, between the compositional principles involved. The development section, finally, takes the form of a succession of variously constructed segments, designed to show off alternately the executants' cantabile playing and his prowess in multiple stopping.

"The second movement, an expressive *adagio*, is like a great operatic 'scena' with some scope for the tragic tone.

"The *rondo*, finale, owes its 'airy' character to the delicate combination of 'ricochet' bowing and staccato."

Concerto No. 2, B Minor, Op. 7 – "La Campanella"

This concerto was composed in 1826 and its fame is mainly due to the theme of the third movement which is stated by a triangle.

"The first movement, *allegro maestoso*, includes the usual orchestral introduction preceding the statement of the first and second theme by the soloist. In this case, too, Paganini develops them according to the sonata form interpreted in a rigorous way, but with some liberties.

"In the second movement, *adagio*, the horns announce the entrance of the soloist, who states an initially simple melody underlined by the punctuations of the plucked strings which is gradually enriched by embellishments, so that its almost vocal initial singability acquires a more specifically violinistic character.

"The third movement, the *rondo (andantino, allegretto moderato)* represents the strong point of the whole concerto. The *rondo* shows a shorter structure and presents a Trio in the central part. The famous motif of the campanella (little bell) is left to the hammered notes of the triangle. In the various recurrences typical of the *rondo* formula, the motif comes up in various forms following Paganini's creativity, naturally assisted by a long series of virtuosic technical solutions. Among other things, the pizzicato with the left hand which the musician kept for his Variazioni makes its first appearance in the movement."

Concerto No. O
(Orchestrated by F. Mompellio)

"This concerto was discovered in 1972 in an antique dealer's shop in London and is now held at the Instituto di Studi Paganiniani in Genoa which edited the critical edition. The work was discovered in two separate unsigned manuscripts, the first containing the solo part and the second an accompaniment for guitar on the basis of which the musicologist Federico Mompellio developed the

" Such was Paganini's appearance and his magical mastery of his instrument that superstitious persons felt there must be something supernatural about him. "

orchestral part. It appears that this concerto was probably sketched out before the Concerto No. 1 in D Major.

"The first movement *risoluto* is characterised by the two-theme *allegro* preceded by an introduction played by tutti which is over extended. The discussion of the two themes and their development comply with the canons of the sonata form interpreted with a certain degree of flexibility while still maintaining their expressive identity according to the law of contrast. Within this practice Paganini uses dexterity passages, two-note chords, chromatic embellishments, repetitions in the higher octave and wide intervals, pouring out these effects with a considerable flourish until the usual coda puts an end to such profusion.

"The *rondo* is characterised by the rhythm of the Polonaise, going back to the French tradition of the violin concerto (Rode and Kreutzer). Like the initial *allegro*, in the *rondo* the artist must come to terms with a 'pre-established' formula which goes against his artistic nature, more inclined towards the close form of the opera air. In the various recurrences of the episodes and ritornelli, Paganini manages to avoid the typical repetitiveness of the *rondo*, making use of dexterity passages and timbre contrasts to give variety to a form which in itself is monotonous and repetitive. This is done by relying on virtuosity with the violin to compensate for the lack of inventiveness."

Sweet strings
This instrument of circa 1600 was crafted by the famous Italian school of violin-makers at Cremona (Amati, Guarneri and Stradivari)

FELIX
MENDELSSOHN
BARTHOLDY

Born : Hamburg, Germany, February 3, 1809
Died : Leipzig, Germany, November 4, 1847

Felix Mendelssohn was fortunate to be born into a highly cultured and prosperous Jewish family. At the age of 6, he was taught to play the piano by his mother and subsequently had good teachers to further his precocious talent.

Together with his brother and two sisters, Mendelssohn grew up in a happy home. All the children received an excellent education. He was especially close to his older sister Fanny, a competent amateur pianist who became a noted composer in her own right.

In 1812, the family moved from Hamburg to Berlin. It was in Berlin that Mendelssohn gave his first piano concert at the age of 9. He composed prolifically from the age of 10, and was ever ready to conduct the Sunday morning musicales that were the delight of friends, neighbours and musicians gathered in the Mendelssohn home.

He studied at the best school of music in Berlin. In one year alone, 1822-23, Mendelssohn composed six symphonies, five concertos, two quartets and many other works. His outstanding overture to Shakespeare's *A Midsummer Night's Dream* was written when he was just 17 years old.

In 1829, at the age of 20, Mendelssohn undertook the gigantic task of studying and producing Bach's "St. Matthew Passion" – a practically forgotten work that had not been performed since Bach's death about 80 years earlier. His efforts to revive this and other great works by Bach led to a renaissance of Bach's music which was to have tremendous significance not only in Mendelssohn's time but for later generations, right down to the 21st century.

In fact, had Mendelssohn himself composed no music whatever, his success in reviving Bach's music would have assured him a firm place in history.

Mendelssohn travelled extensively through Germany, Austria, Switzerland, Italy and France, as well as made several visits to England and Scotland. His impressions of their peoples were reflected in his compositions.

In 1833, Mendelssohn was appointed to supervise the entire musical life of Düsseldorf and in 1835 he took over the direction of the Gewandhaus ("Clothworkers' Hall") concerts in Leipzig. His own tastes reflected his studies of Baroque and early Classical music. He built up the Gewandhaus Orchestra as the best in Europe and laid the foundation of the world famous Leipzig Conservatoire. Leipzig soon came to be recognised as the anti-radical musical centre of Europe.

Good-natured and amiable, Mendelssohn made friends everywhere. Musically conservative, he nevertheless became deeply attached to the Romantics – Schumann, Chopin and Liszt. He also came in contact with Berlioz. His home became a meeting place for some outstanding personalities of the cultured society of his day. In 1837 he married Cécile Jeanrenaud and had five children with her which completed his happiness.

Amongst Mendelssohn's prodigious output of compositions, those that stand out prominently are his Violin Concerto (in E Minor) – universally beloved of masters of the violin; his music to Shakespeare's *A Midsummer Night's Dream,* regarded as the highest consummation of his youthful precocity; "The Hebrides" Overture ("Fingal's Cave") written after his visit to the islands off the west coast of Scotland – a masterpiece of romantic imagination and tone painting; the "Italian" and "Scottish" Symphonies

and the oratorio "Elijah" which ranks second only to Handel's "Messiah".

Mendelssohn's frequent travels all over Germany and the strain of incessant composing soon began to affect his health. The Mendelssohn family was not fated to lead long lives. He had mourned in 1835 the death of his father, followed a few years later by his mother's demise. The death of his youngest son dealt him a severe blow. And the death in 1847 of his favourite sister Fanny came as an added shock. A few months later he followed her on November 4, 1847, aged just 38.

Mendelssohn's place in music history

Mendelssohn had no difficulty giving clear form to his musical expression. From his early years he oriented himself towards the favoured Classical techniques of composition. He respected the fugue technique of Bach and the instrumental techniques of Handel. He was further influenced by Mozart and Beethoven's instrumental approaches. But the towering achievement of the teenaged prodigy was to have developed his own unmistakable style based on earlier Classical models. Mendelssohn made use of almost every musical form, and his sureness of touch and good taste ensured that nothing he wrote was mediocre.

Commenting on Mendelssohn, German musicologist Curt Sachs said: "His works were born of a loving, not a bleeding heart. They were neither gigantic nor violent, but sunny, happy and pure."

Violinist Jascha Heifetz declared: "If it is conceivable that the music of Mendelssohn can die, then all music can die."

Mendelssohn's wife
The composer once wrote: "The best part of every pleasure is gone if Cécile is not there"

Major compositions

3 Oratorios (including "Elijah")
Opera: Lorelei (unfinished)

Concertos
Violin Concerto in E Minor, Op. 64 (1844)
Piano Concerto No. 1 in G Minor,
  Op. 25 (1832)
Piano Concerto No. 2 in D Minor,
  Op. 40 (1837)
Capriccio brillant, B Minor, Op. 22
  (piano and orch.)
Rondo brillant in E-flat, Op. 29 (1834)
  (piano and orch.)

Overtures
Fingal's Cave (Hebrides),
  Op. 26 (1830/1832)
Calm Sea and Prosperous Voyage,
  Op. 27 (1832)
A Midsummer Night's Dream, Op. 21 (1826)
Ruy Blas, Op. 95 (1839)
Scherzo arr. from Op. 20 Octet

Songs and Part-songs
On Wings of Song, Op. 34, No. 2
Grüss (Eichendorff), Op. 63, No. 3

Stage Music
A Midsummer Night's Dream, Op. 61 (1842)
Wedding March from
  Midsummer Night's Dream

Symphonies
No. 3, A Minor, Op. 56 (1842) "Scottish"
No. 4, A Major, Op. 90 (1833) "Italian"
No. 5, D Major, Op. 107 (1830)
  "Reformation"

Chamber Music
7 String Quartets
Octet, E-flat, Op. 20
  (for double string quartet)

Cello and Piano
Song without Words,
  D Major, Op. 109 (1845)

Piano
Songs without Words (8 Books)
No. 25, G Major, Op. 62, No. 1
  "May Breezes"
No. 30, A Major, Op. 62, No. 6
  "Spring Song"
No. 34, C Major, Op. 67, No. 4
  "Bee's Wedding"
Rondo Capriccioso, E Major, Op. 14

Renaissance of Bach's music
Had Mendelssohn himself composed no music
whatever, his success in reviving Bach's music
would have assured him a firm place in history

Notes on select works

Violin Concerto in E Minor, Op. 64
It is arguably the most enjoyable violin concerto ever written – serene, beautiful, without a single bar of harshness, a work that is today a popular classic. It has been said that this is written as if from the very soul of the violin.

English composer and pianist William Sterndale Bennett was rhapsodic when he heard it and said to Mendelssohn: "There seems to me something essentially and exquisitely feminine about it, just as in the Beethoven Concerto there is something essentially and heroically masculine. Beethoven had made the Adam of Concerto, and you have mated it with the Eve."

Indeed, such is the intrinsic appeal of the music that it has been the favourite choice of many violinists when making their concert debuts. This concerto was first performed by Ferdinand David in 1845 with the Gewandhaus Orchestra.

The very beginning of the concerto is unconventional. The solo violin, instead of the orchestra, announces the passionate principal theme – a long, boldly arching melody, which works up to quite a climax before the orchestra interrupts with the transmission to the second theme that itself is a drooping little melodic figure with a slight touch of melancholy. The cadenza for the violin alone, instead of coming as it usually does at the close of a movement, is very effectively placed just before the return of the first theme which enters in the orchestra while the violin is still spinning out the rapid arpeggios of the cadenza. The impression one gains is that of the violin accompanying the orchestra, instead of the other way round. All three movements of the concerto are meant to be played without pause. There is a mysteriously quiet transition to the second movement which has a broad melodic flow and an atmosphere of almost religious dignity. The last movement is light-hearted, capricious and brilliant.

Piano Concerto No.1, G Minor, Op. 25

Mendelssohn himself gave the first performance of this concerto in 1813 at a concert where his overture to *Midsummer Night's Dream* and his "Symphony in C Minor" were also played.

It is said that the success of this concerto in the heyday of Mendelssohn's popularity was so great as to provoke Hector Berlioz to write a satire. In the satire, the concerto became such a rage that people hummed its melodies in the streets; great virtuosos performed it at their concerts; students at the Musical Academy diligently practised it; all amateur pianists enthusiastically thumped it out. The concerto was soon so often performed that in the end the piano at the Academy came to know the whole work by heart and would commence to play it, all by itself, at the mere approach of a student!

In the satire such independent and persistent performances of this concerto by the Academy's piano so exasperated everyone, that eventually the director of the Academy chopped up the piano into fragments. Still the pieces continued to play the concerto among themselves. Finally, in sheer desperation, the director rushed out into the street and seizing the still-tinkling pieces threw them all,

> **"** *Mendelssohn's works were born of a loving, not a bleeding heart. They were neither gigantic nor violent, but sunny, happy and pure.* **"**

with a curse, into a nearby stream, and thus at last rid himself and the whole neighbourhood of a musical curse that had almost driven everyone crazy.

Orchestral

"The Hebrides" or "Fingal's Cave" Overture, Op. 26

On touring Scotland in 1829, Mendelssohn was greatly impressed with the Hebrides, particularly with his visit to Fingal's Cave, a famously beautiful spot on the island of Staffa. It has been said of the music of this overture that in hearing it one can imagine oneself on a ship, gliding over rocking waves, sensing about one a vast expanse of sea and sky, of light breezes blowing. "Indeed, such is the suggestion of the music, with its sudden contrasts of loud and soft, staccato and legato, of long sustained notes with restlessly moving parts that, knowing the title, one has to stretch one's imagination very little to hear the birds scream, the winds whistle, and smell the salt seaweed on the rocks," writes music critic and writer W.F. Apthorp.

Richard Wagner, on the strength of this work, had praised Mendelssohn as "a landscape painter of the first order".

A Midsummer Night's Dream, Op. 21

This overture was composed when Mendelssohn was only 17 (in 1826) – a most remarkable event testifying to his prodigious talent.

"The first quiet chords of the overture remind one of 'Once upon a time'. Then the gossamer-winged fairies lead one into the rich world of fancy and the enchantment is not broken until the last

quiet chords seem to say 'and they all lived happily ever after'."

It was only 17 years later that Mendelssohn composed the rest of the music for the play of which the best-known pieces are often added to the overture to form a five-part suite.

There are four parts to the music.

The Scherzo, played at the end of Act I is a whirling joyful movement which dances off like a *perpetuum mobile*.

The Intermezzo is placed at the end of Act II.

The Nocturne III accompanies the scene in the forest, after Puck's teasing, the lovers at length fall asleep.

The Wedding March IV, which opens Act V, is concerned with the wedding between Prince Theseus of Athens and the Amazon Queen Hippolyta. This march is still played at weddings to this day.

Symphonies

Mendelssohn wrote five symphonies, besides a series of 12 early symphonies for strings completed by the age of 14.

Symphony No. 3 in A Minor, Op. 56 – "Scottish"

Mendelssohn visited Scotland in 1829 and was much fascinated by its music and history. This symphony has been thus described: "The first movement has a grave introduction. There is a 'motto' theme, heard at the beginning, and recurring at periods through the work. The movement proper is in somewhat more vigorous, but not less Romantic style than the introduction. There are typical Mendelssohn melodies, gently melancholy, and a return to the sombreness of the introduction.

"The second, rather than the third, is the *scherzo* movement of this symphony. A transitional passage for horn and woodwind precedes the establishment of the graceful rhythm, which however seldom becomes boisterous. The spirit of the music is light and gay; there is none of the robust vigour associated with a Highland 'fling'.

"The third movement may have been suggested by Mendelssohn's reflections on Holyrood Castle where he had visited the very room where the unfortunate Queen (Mary Stuart) had lived. It has gravity, even majesty, with a reflective and somewhat melancholy note that could be a remembrance of the tragic events that came to pass. But the music can as well suggest the wild hills and forests of Scotland, or the overbearing sadness of the plains and lonely moors.

"The fourth movement is, in a musical sense, definitely Scotch. Here the wild Highlander, claymore in hand, sweeps down from his rugged hills joyously to do battle. Here is the impetuous, the vigorous dance of the North and a retelling in suggestive musical terms the glorious deeds of Scotland's heroes. There is a contrasting section, somewhat more restrained, yet even more suggestive of Scottish music."

Symphony No. 4 in A Major, Op. 90 – "Italian"

Mendelssohn travelled extensively all over Europe and it was his stay for several months in Italy which later inspired him to write this symphony. He was fascinated and charmed by the Italian festivals with their colour and dances. He happened to be in Rome for the coronation of Pope Gregory XVI and was impressed with the

" The composer William Sterndale Bennett said, when he heard Mendelssohn's Violin Concerto in E Minor: 'There seems something exquisitely feminine about it, as in the Beethoven Concerto there is something heroically masculine. Beethoven had made the Adam of Concerto and you have mated it with the Eve.' "

magnificent rites that accompanied it. These elements were woven into the symphony.

Here is a description of it: "The violins are entrusted with the principal theme, the woodwind and horns supplying a richly coloured accompaniment. An interlude, in which the introductory motive of the movement is heard again in woodwind against a crisply staccato counter figure in the strings, precedes the more powerfully scored representation of the chief musical idea." Mendelssohn was a Romantic but he was also a man who loved fine workmanship of the Classical style. And so, as a part of the development of this vigorous, free and beautifully fashioned movement, there is an ingenious fugato in the strings which leads to a general interweaving of previous thematic material which persists to the close of the movement.

"There is something song-like in almost everything that Mendelssohn wrote... The second movement is a song so lovely and so simple and moving... The introductory figure is heard in woodwind and the upper strings. This is followed by the chief theme of the movement which you will hear in the mellifluous combination of oboe, bassoon and viola to an accompaniment by low strings and woodwind...

"The third movement is sprightly and vigorous music in its *scherzo*. Melodically and rhythmically it is one of the pleasant things in symphonic form which Mendelssohn has left us. Violins have a graceful and lively tune. Bassoons and horns, contrasted both in timbre and

in melodic figure with violins and flutes, give a highly effective trio, and a combination of strings against bassoons, brass and timpani supply interesting colour and rhythm..."

The fourth movement: Mendelssohn having been in Rome during the festival periods must have seen the saltarello – a typical Italian peasant dance – many times, and he did capture in this symphony the bounding vitality and spirit of it. If the saltarello is a dance of quite vigorous and abandoned character, towards the end the music even adopts the mad rhythm of the tarantella – a wildly exciting and vigorous dance, supposed anciently to drive from the body the poison of the tarantula's bite. Both dance rhythms, saltarello and tarantella, are employed with brilliant effect, the original impulse of the saltarello becoming dominant at the end of the movement.

The Leipzig Gewandhaus Orchestra

Founded in 1781, this orchestra was given a home in the Gewandhaus. The second Gewandhaus Hall built between 1881 and 1884 was completely destroyed when Leipzig was bombed on February 20, 1944. The new hall was not dedicated until long afterwards, on the orchestra's 200th anniversary in 1981. In earlier years, when Mendelssohn was its conductor, it was indisputably the best orchestra in Europe. With other great orchestras coming up since then, it remains one of the finest in Europe.

Hector Berlioz
Leipzig 6 Décembre 1853

HECTOR **BERLIOZ**

Born : La Côte-Saint-André, France,
December 11, 1803
Died : Paris, France, March 8, 1869

Hector Berlioz was born in a typical French middle-class family. His father, a doctor, supervised his education at home and Berlioz did not go to school until he was 18. His many early years at home were spent in wide reading which included Virgil, Shakespeare and Goethe. Those years also gave him time to develop originality of thought, which later was to mark his music. It made him a rebel against traditional rules as well.

His introduction to the world of music when still young, happened one day when he found a flageolet – a high pitched recorder-like instrument – in a bureau drawer at home. Fascinated by it, he soon taught himself to play it so well that his father allowed him to take singing, flute and guitar lessons.

In the early 1800s, very few households had pianos at home. The Berlioz home was no exception; so young Hector never got around to playing one. Years later, when he approached the Paris Music Conservatoire for the post of teacher in harmony, his application was rejected because he did not know how to play the piano!

Berlioz's father was keen that his son should have a medical career, but Hector expressed his preference for a career in music. His father then offered him a silver flute as a bribe if he studied medicine in Paris. This ruse worked and Hector agreed to go to Paris.

At the Medical School in Paris, Berlioz's first sight of the dissection room so filled him with horror and revulsion that he jumped out of the window into the street outside. However, not to displease his father he did attend medical lectures for a year and at the same time managed to attend every concert or opera performed in the city. A temporary closing of the Medical School came as an excellent opportunity for Berlioz to escape the hated dissection room forever.

Back home, Berlioz communicated his firm resolve to become a composer and the family expressed their total disapproval. His father withheld any financial help. Returning to Paris, this time as a student at the Conservatoire, Berlioz attended every musical programme and studied the scores before and after each performance.

At the Conservatoire he upset the director, Luigi Cherubini, by spreading his own subversive ideas on harmony. So strongly did the director come to dislike Berlioz that for three consecutive years he voted against Berlioz for the prestigious Prix de Rome, the scholarship given by the French government to study the arts in Rome.

Berlioz, with his fiery red hair and equally fiery blue eyes, was a romantic figure. But the Shakespearean English actress Harriet Smithson, with whom he fell madly in love, did not find him so. When Berlioz threw himself at her feet

An army of sound
Berlioz's huge orchestras and extravagant sound effects inspired caricaturists

at the entrance to the stage door and threatened to take poison if she did not marry him, she thought him quite mad.

In 1830, Berlioz won the Prix de Rome and went to Italy, staying there for two years. Returning to Paris, he gave his first concert at which his prize-winning Cantata and the "Symphonie Fantastique" were performed.

It happened that Harriet, who lived in England, was in Paris at this time and so Berlioz invited her to the concert. The written narrative that Berlioz had supplied with the symphony clearly mentioned that the music, though having appealing melodies, was meant to express also his disappointment and rage at unrequited love.

The stormy orchestration of the symphony, powered particularly by the brasses and tympani, was music the like of which had never been heard before. Overpowered by this ocean of sound, Harriet consented to marry Berlioz. They lived together as man and wife for 10 years before they drifted apart and led separate lives.

At about the time Berlioz gave his first concert, the French Government commissioned a Requiem for an official ceremony. Berlioz composed a most impressive work for soloists, chorus, organ and an enlarged orchestra of 16 brasses (instead of the normal four) leading to an overwhelming volume of sound, dramatic rather than religious. The concert almost bankrupted Berlioz, for he paid out of his own pocket for the extra instruments.

Berlioz's compositions, strangely, did not meet with much success in Paris itself – except for his oratorio "The Infancy of Christ" – but they were a great success in other countries, especially in Germany and Russia, where they were hailed as works of genius.

Mendelssohn, Schumann and Liszt spoke up for him in Germany, while in Russia, Mussorgsky, a well-known composer himself, who thought the world of Berlioz, went somewhat overboard in lavishing praise: "In music there are two great giants, the thinker Beethoven and the super-thinker Berlioz."

In 1864, when he had stopped composing and became morose, Berlioz had the romantic idea of going to Dauphiné to see Estelle Duboeuf whom he had adored as a 12-year-old boy, but whom he had never seen since. The meeting took place and made a deep impression on him; his correspondence with her and visits to her home were a great comfort in his last years.

Up to now life for Berlioz had been reasonably good. There were the usual upsets when some of his compositions were not received as well as expected. But soon a series of disasters were to cloud his life. His second wife Marie Recio died in 1862. His opera "The Trojans in Carthage" was hissed at on its first performance in Paris. The death of his son Louis in 1867 was the final blow.

He tried to forget his miseries by going on a tour to Russia, the scene of his greatest early triumphs, and thence to Monaco, but this failed to revive his spirits. He returned to Paris, where he died on March 8, 1869.

Berlioz's place in music history

Berlioz was a great musical Romantic. He had a genius for orchestration. He understood not only the full tonal resources of the symphony orchestra, but also the latent scope for development of its standard instruments. Indeed, his *Treatise on Orchestration and Instrumentation* is regarded as a classic. The fact that he was also a musical megalomaniac cannot be overlooked. He once suggested that an orchestra should have 460 instruments to be used with a chorus of 360 voices, four chorus masters and two assistant conductors, one for woodwinds and one for percussion, who were to take their cues from the conductor-in-chief, Hector Berlioz! He drew censure for promoting and experimenting with such grandiloquent ideas.

Berlioz's greatest contribution was his opening a new avenue in the kingdom of music. In composing his "Symphonie Fantastique" he gave music a programmatic overlay and became the father of programme music – "instrumental music which tells a story, illustrates literary ideas, or evokes pictorial scenes" – according to Michael Kennedy in the *Oxford Dictionary of Music*. "In doing this Berlioz did not realise what richness he was sowing, for not only Liszt, but later also Richard Strauss, Rimsky-Korsakov, Lalo and Saint-Saëns garnered the harvest."

Berlioz had another talent that needs to be mentioned. At a certain stage in his life, when his financial state was causing him anxiety, Berlioz turned to journalism. He wrote with an elegant and effective pen. His memoirs give good and revealing information on music and musicians of his time. Berlioz was full of puckish humour and his several satires provided much laughter and entertainment.

Notes on select works
Symphonie Fantastique (Episode in the Life of an Artist), Op. 14

The symphony was written when Berlioz was besotted with the celebrated Shakespearean actress Harriet Smithson. "The ambiguous suggestions of the final movement can be accounted for by Berlioz's bitter and almost insane grief when calumnious stories as to the character of Miss Smithson came to his ears. He revised this movement, but the music remains. The composer made handsome apologies for crediting evil reports about his lady and three years after the symphony was first performed, they were married."

Programme of the Symphony

"A young musician of unhealthily sensitive nature and endowed with vivid imagination has poisoned himself with opium in a paroxysm of lovesick despair. The narcotic dose he had taken was too weak to cause death, but it has thrown him into a long sleep accompanied by the most extraordinary visions. In this condition his sensations, his feelings, and his memories find utterance in his sick brain in the form of musical imagery. Even the Beloved One takes the form of a melody in his mind, like a fixed idea which is ever returning and which he hears everywhere.

First movement: Dreams, Passions

"At first he thinks of the uneasy and nervous condition of his mind, of sombre longings, of depression, and joyous elation without any recognisable cause, which he experienced before the Beloved One had appeared to him. Then he remembers the ardent love with which she suddenly inspired him; he thinks of his almost insane anxiety of mind, of his raging jealousy, of his reawakening love, of his religious consolation.

Major compositions

Operas
Benvenuto Cellini (2 Acts), Op. 23
Damnation of Faust (4 Acts), Op. 24
Les Troyens (5 Acts)
Béatrice et Bénédict

Orchestral Works
Symphonie Fantastique, Op. 14
Harold in Italy, Op. 16
Romeo and Juliet, Op. 17 (Dramatic symphony with soloists and chorus)
Carnaval Romain, Op. 9
Benvenuto Cellini – Overture
Rákóczy March

Oratorio
L'Enfance du Christ
Requiem, Op. 5

Song Cycle
Summer Nights ("Les Nuits d'Été") for mezzo-soprano and piano

"The incarnation of Romantic genius"

Second Movement: A Ball

"In a ballroom, amidst the confusion of a brilliant festival, he finds the Beloved One again.

Third Movement: Scene in the Fields

"It is a summer evening. He is in the country, musing, when he hears two shepherd lads who play, in alternation, the tune used by the Swiss shepherds, to call their flocks. This pastoral duet, the quiet scene, the soft whisperings of the trees stirred by the zephyr wind, some prospects of hope recently made known to him, all these sensations unite to impart a long unknown repose in his heart, and to lend a smiling colour to his imagination.

"And then She appears once more. His heart stops beating, painful forebodings fill his soul. 'Should she prove false to him!' One of the shepherds resumes the melody, but the other answers him no more. Sunset... distant rolling of thunder... loneliness... silence.

Fourth Movement: March to the Scaffold

"He dreams that he has murdered his Beloved, that he has been condemned to death, and is being led to execution. A march that is alternately sombre and wild, brilliant and solemn, accompanies the procession. The tumultuous outbursts are followed without modulation by measured steps. At last the fixed idea returns, for a moment a last thought of love is revived – which is cut short by the death blow.

" In composing his Symphonie Fantastique, Berlioz gave music a programmatic overlay to become the father of programme music. "

Fifth Movement: Witches' Sabbath

"He dreams that he is present at a witches' revel, surrounded by horrible spirits, amidst sorcerers and monsters in many fearful forms, who have come together for his funeral. Strange sounds, groans, shrill laughter, distant yells, which other cries seem to answer. The Beloved melody is heard again, but it has lost its shy and noble character; it has become a vulgar, trivial and grotesque dance tune. She it is who comes to attend the witches' meeting. Riotous howls and shouts greet her arrival. She joins the funeral orgy... bells toll for the dead... a burlesque parody of the Dies Irae... the witches' round dance and the Dies Irae are heard together."

Harold in Italy, Op. 16

This is a symphony in four movements, with solo viola. In 1834, Berlioz was commissioned by Paganini to write a viola concerto and chose as his programme an episode from Byron's epic poem *Childe Harold*. Identifying himself with the hero of the poem, Berlioz based his symphony on his own experiences in the Abruzzi Mountains. The viola was meant to interpret Harold's (and Berlioz's) joie de vivre and melancholy, while the orchestra describes the Italian landscape and the colourful life of the people.

The four movements are very different in character, but the viola has a repeated motif which gives unity to the work. The programme is indicated in the titles of the movements: Harold in the Mountains, March and Evening Prayer of Pilgrims, Serenade of the Abruzzi Mountaineer to his Beloved, Orgy of Brigands.

Romeo and Juliet, Op. 17

It is a dramatic symphony with soloists and choir. It was dedicated to the violinist Paganini in gratitude for a gift of 20,000 francs.

The orchestra was very large (160 players) and the choir numbered 98.

The Queen Mab *scherzo* at the beginning of the third movement was particularly well received and has since remained a favourite orchestral piece on concert programmes.

The symphony comprises an orchestral introduction, a sung prologue and four movements, each of which describes several scenes from Shakespeare's play of the same name.

"Orchestral introduction. Riot in the marketplace in Verona, and fight between the Capulet and Montague families. The Prince intervenes.

"Prologue. Choir recitative with stanzas, following (contralto solo), Recitative and Scherzetto (tenor solo and choir).

"I (Orchestra only) Romeo alone and sorrowful. In the distance noise from a ball in Capulet's house.

"II (Orchestra only) Night of romance. The Capulet's garden silent and deserted. The younger members of the Capulet family leave the feast; as they pass by they hum the evening's melodies. The love scene, Juliet on the balcony and Romeo in the shadow.

"III (Orchestra only) Queen Mab, the fairy of dreams. Juliet's funeral procession. A march in fugal form, first in

orchestra alone and then with a simple psalm tune in the choir; afterwards the choir sings the march, while the orchestra plays the psalm. Romeo in the Capulet family vault. He calls on Juliet, Juliet awakens. Transport of joy, destroyed by the first effect of the poison. The lovers' last agony and death (Orch. only).

"IV The crowd streams to the churchyard. Fight between the two families. Recitative and Friar Laurence's song. Oath and reconciliation."

Carnaval Romain, Op. 9

This delightfully exciting music was written originally as the introduction to the second act of Berlioz's opera "Benvenuto Cellini".

"There is an introduction, beginning with fiery and energetic rhythm which relaxes for the presentation, by cor anglais, of the melody of Benvenuto's love song in the first act. The music grows in swiftness and in excitement, and the saltarello, of impetuous rhythm and highly elaborated figuration, is delivered with glowing brilliance. The two chief subjects are developed together, the dance figure finally becoming dominant, urging the music onward to the powerful concluding measures."

Rákóczy March

This is arguably Berlioz's best-known music. It was originally written as a "Marche hongroise", the theme being a characteristic Hungarian tune of great antiquity. Berlioz in his autobiography gives a description of the music and of its electrifying effect: "First the trumpets gave out the rhythm, then the flutes and clarinets softly outlining the theme, with a pizzicato accompaniment of the strings. Then there came a long crescendo, broken by dull beats of the bass drum, like the sound of distant cannon, strange restless movement was heard before the orchestra finally let itself go in a cataclysm of sweeping fury and thunder."

Benvenuto Cellini – Overture

Berlioz, famous as a critic and musical humourist as well as composer, did not hesitate to turn his wit upon his own music occasionally.

Commenting upon the first performance of his opera "Benvenuto Cellini", he remarked: "The overture received exaggerated applause, but the rest was hissed with admirable energy and unanimity."

The opera has not survived, but the rather flamboyant overture is in the repertoire of most symphony orchestras.

Like all good overtures, it embodies thematic material taken from the opera, but, unlike the best overtures, does not condense and synthesise the drama itself. It is notable for its inexhaustible vigour and fulsome elaboration for the genuinely lovely melody (sung in the opera by the philandering Cellini to his love) for flute, oboe and clarinet. Indications of Berlioz's yearning for orchestras of prodigious size

and effect can be observed near the end, where the entire brass choir is enlisted in a theme intimated near the beginning, while three kettle drums, tuned to a major chord, are mercilessly pounded.

Béatrice et Bénédict – Overture

Berlioz was a great lover of Shakespeare and in 1862 he adopted the shortened version of the comedy *Much Ado About Nothing* as a two-act opera which he called "Béatrice et Bénédict". In this the sinister intrigue of the villainous Don John against the virtuous Hero is omitted and full use made of the story of Béatrice, the beautiful and sharp-tongued man-hater, and Bénédict, the witty gallant who is equally opposed to thoughts of love and marriage.

By an ingenious hoax this oddly assorted pair is induced to leave their antagonistic repartee and walk the earth together as unusually fond lovers. The overture is an epitome of the comedy, and the bustling puckish little phrase by which it opens, and which recurs throughout the overture, may well be intended to represent the sparkling raillery of Béatrice and Bénédict before the miracle overtakes them.

Following the lively opening there is a tender melody (with an effective pizzicato bass) which one takes to be the lovers in their more melting moments. The gay and the tender interweave and there are boisterous passages with fine work from the trombones.

Later, a melody of almost Mendelssohnian ease and grace makes its appearance, after which the original themes make further interplay and run on to a merry finish.

FRANZ **LISZT**

Born : Raiding, Hungary, October 22, 1811
Died : Bayreuth, Germany, July 31, 1886

When Franz Liszt was a few weeks old he was so puny that his father had him measured for a coffin, expecting him to die in infancy. But Liszt lived to become a superb pianist, an excellent composer and a great lover. Success in life came to him without the usual struggle that was the fate of many other great composers.

His father Adam, a steward on the estate of Count Esterházy in Raiding, gave him his early training on the piano from the age of 6. When Liszt was 9 years old, Adam Liszt took him to a neighbouring town to play a concert. Several noblemen who were present were so impressed with his talent that they offered to finance his musical education for the next six years. The family soon after moved to Vienna where Franz Liszt, now 11, studied with Carl Czerny who was amazed enough by his talent to refuse to charge Liszt his usual tuition fees.

Czerny himself was a pupil of Beethoven and he requested his teacher to hear Liszt play the piano. At first Beethoven parried the request but Czerny persisted till Beethoven finally agreed. Liszt played a Bach fugue. Beethoven, now very interested, asked Liszt whether he could transpose that fugue into another key. Liszt agreed and, in fact, transposed the fugue in several other keys in succession, to Beethoven's surprise and delight. Liszt next played the first movement of Beethoven's C Major Piano Concerto. Beethoven was completely won over. He kissed Liszt on the forehead and said prophetically: "You are one of the fortunate ones, for you will give joy and happiness to many people."

In 1823, when he was 12 years old, Liszt went to Paris. He gave private lessons with conspicuous success. He studied and taught music, performed concerts and lived his life to the full. The artistic and literary climate of Paris, of Chopin, George Sand and Berlioz, of Balzac, Flaubert, Lamartine and Victor Hugo suited his temperament.

"Liszt's Triumph"
Liszt's frontal attack overwhelms General Bass – a caricature of 1842 illustrating the victory of Liszt's lighter, Romantic pianistic style

electrifyingly fast passages or in beautiful cantabiles in the dreamier ones. This Paganini recital was to be of great significance in Liszt's further development as a pianist.

Liszt now set about practising intensively, four to five hours every day. He played exercises in thirds, sixths, eighths, tremolos, cadenzas, etc. As a result of these tremendously taxing efforts he developed an outstanding piano technique. Liszt set himself to become "the Paganini of the Piano", a master performer for whom all difficulties were mere child's play, developing also the rare skill of playing by sight any piece of new music placed before him.

By the time he was 23, Liszt had had a number of love affairs. In Chopin's salon he met the great love of his life. She was the Countess Marie d'Agoult, who wrote novels under the pseudonym of David Stern and fancied herself as the second George Sand – minus the cigar. The Countess left her husband who was 20 years her senior, and her children, and went with Liszt to Geneva where they made their home for six years. They had three children in the 20 years of their romance.

During his years with Marie d'Agoult, Liszt frequently went on concert tours all over Europe. He sought publicity by every possible means. When he came on stage he wore gloves which he removed with great deliberation while the audience waited. He then seated himself at the piano, not facing the audience, but with his handsome profile turned to its most favourable angle. He also wore his hair longer than most musicians did at that time. At one recital he even appeared in full Magyar costume, complete with jewelled sword!

Liszt gave his first public concert the following year, aged just 13, in the Paris Opera House. Newspaper reports of that concert read like a fairytale. Members of the orchestra were so enthralled by his playing that they forgot to attend to their own parts. "Le petit Liszt" was the sensation of Paris. Later, in London too, Liszt met with equal success. Thereafter he toured the South of France and Switzerland, being acclaimed everywhere as a pianist beyond compare, prodigious at such a young age.

But Liszt's pleasure in performing in public strangely diminished. He experienced a deep feeling of loneliness and turned to religion for comfort. He informed his father of his desire to become a priest. "You belong to Art and not to the Church," his father replied.

Nevertheless, Liszt immersed himself in the Bible and other religious books, reading day and night. He was 16 when his father died. On his death-bed, Adam Liszt expressed the fear that women would play a disturbing part in his son's life. Before he was 17, Liszt discovered the truth of his father's words.

In 1831, the great violinist and composer Niccolò Paganini gave his first performance in Paris. Liszt was present at that recital. By the end of the recital Liszt was simply overwhelmed by Paganini's stunningly astounding technique, whether it was in

> **"** *Liszt the composer was overshadowed by Liszt the pianist. He achieved the goal he had set himself – to become the 'Paganini of the Piano'.* **"**

In 1843, Liszt became visiting Court Artist in Weimar, Germany, and five years later was director of the Weimar Opera. By this time he had broken off with Marie d'Agoult and took with him to Weimar a new love – the cigar-smoking Polish princess, Carolyne von Sayn-Wittgenstein, whom he had first met in Russia. Their lavish household in Weimar became the Mecca of musicians. It was during this time that Liszt raised enormous sums at benefit concerts for various causes – for the relief of flood sufferers, for the publication of Scarlatti's works and for the erection in Bonn of a statue of Beethoven. Composers flocked to present their scores before him and he championed their music as "the music of the future".

As director of the orchestra at Weimar, Liszt conducted the works of many composers, such as Berlioz's "Benvenuto Cellini" and Weber's "Euryanthe". As his second daughter, Cosima, had married the German opera composer Richard Wagner, Liszt naturally conducted many of Wagner's compositions such as the "Flying Dutchman", "Tannhäuser" and "Lohengrin".

From 1849 onwards Liszt's working time was divided between Weimar, Budapest and Rome. During this time he also made peace with the Church which had refused permission for him to marry his divorced Polish princess, but permitted him to become an abbé.

As abbé, Liszt wore the picturesque flowing robes of his office and composed requiems for the salvation of his soul. He remained with the princess until she died, though this did not deter him from other amorous adventures.

Liszt was visiting his daughter Cosima, Wagner's widow, when he caught a severe cold which led to pneumonia. After a brief illness he died on July 31, 1886.

Liszt's place in music history

The keyboard virtuoso beyond compare", as he was acknowledged, Liszt made a tremendous impact as the most phenomenal pianist of his time. Indeed, Liszt the composer was overshadowed by Liszt the pianist. He achieved the goal he had set himself – to become the "Paganini of the Piano". Audiences were overwhelmed by his stunning playing and charming personality. And women particularly adored him.

Many factors prevented Liszt from receiving proper recognition as a composer. Several of his piano pieces are virtuoso works whose value can only be rated as astounding. Although he did not invent the symphonic poem, he perfected it. His one-movement programme pieces such as "Mazeppa", "Les Préludes" and "Tasso" are prominent musical examples.

Liszt recognised the importance of the national schools of music in Europe and supported the composers Borodin, Rimsky-Korsakov, César Franck, Saint-Saëns, Grieg and Albéniz – all of whom went on to found the new national schools of Russia, France, Italy, Norway, Bohemia, and Spain. It was Liszt's strong commitment to the national schools that affected and overturned Germany's musical supremacy.

Liszt in his old age
Honoured and revered all over Europe, he devoted the last years of his life to teaching

Notes on select works

Piano Concerto No. 1, E-flat Major

This work is a perfect example of a virtuoso concerto. It is not only brilliant music to show off technique but a special type of music which has to be played boldly and recklessly, with a sort of swashbuckling nobility and a lordly disregard of the limitations of 10 fingers! It is written in one continuous whole, uniting the several movements of the traditional concerto, much as Liszt and his Romantic contemporaries tended to unify the sonata and symphony into one movement.

The concerto opens with the main theme which has an imperious commanding rhythmic figure given out by the strings, and punctuated by chords of the woodwind and brass instruments. It is an exultant theme to which Liszt used to sing as he played it. There is a slow second theme sung by the cellos and basses which corresponds roughly to the traditional melodic slow movement.

This concerto was for a long time ridiculed as the "triangle concerto", because of the triangle which introduces the sparkling *scherzo* section. (This was quite enough to disturb the equanimity of the Viennese pundits; and for several years it became impossible to perform it in Vienna.) The motto theme of the beginning keeps bobbing up through the final martial *allegro* that quickens into a headlong, flashing *presto*.

Symphonic Poems

Although Liszt's fame rests chiefly on his music for solo piano, his achievements in the field of purely orchestral music are considerable as he perfected the symphonic poem form with his one-movement programme pieces. He wrote no less than 12 between 1848

and 1857 while he was living with Princess Carolyne in Weimar where he held the post of musical director. The titles of his symphonic poems are relevant only in a loose way because they do not tell a detailed story as did the later tone poems of Richard Strauss. The purely musical aspect was paramount for Liszt. An interesting feature of each of these pieces is Liszt's use of a basic theme which recurs throughout in a variety of innovative transformations or disguises.

"Les Préludes" No. 3

The programme written on its score quotes lines by Alphonse de Lamartine, the French writer and poet, describing the composer's life as a series of events – love,

Liszt and Wagner
Liszt was Wagner's father-in-law.
The king of the piano and the great master of the orchestra were united in their artistic ideals

storms and pastoral quietude – leading up to "that unknown song of death". Its main theme, first heard on the strings and in longer notes on the trombones, is subjected to various transformations suggesting tender, pastoral and martial moods. There is a contrasting theme

introduced on horns and violas, and this melody too is richly orchestrated.

"Mazeppa" No. 6

It is a more descriptive piece based on the Victor Hugo poem concerning the Polish nobleman tied to a wild horse which was driven into the Ukraine. The music begins with a shriek on woodwind and brass, followed by a rushing string passage with the Mazeppa theme on trombones and lower strings. The fury increases until we hear Mazeppa's fall (a chord for full orchestra with timpani strokes) followed by his rescue by Cossacks who make him their leader. The final section is a march of triumph featuring an Oriental theme.

"Tasso, Lamento e Trionfo" No. 2

Its theme is a song which Liszt heard sung by a Venetian gondolier to one of the 16th-century Italian poet Tasso's verses. The gloomy opening leads to a faster section suggesting the poet's sufferings; a central episode portrays a festive court scene with a minuet begun by two solo cellos; the triumphant final section indicates Tasso's posthumous fame.

"Orpheus" No. 4

Poetry and music are celebrated here, though it does not refer to the Greek myth of Eurydice, but simply presents Orpheus taming the wild beasts by the beauty of his singing with his lyre. A work of orchestral impressionism, this was held by Wagner to be Liszt's finest composition.

Hungarian Fantasia (for pianoforte and orchestra)

This work is composed of Magyar folk melodies strung together after the fashion of the Rhapsodies. These works are

Major compositions

Choral Works
Ave Maria (choir and organ)
Faust
Prometheus
Christus (Dante)
  No. 3, Tu es Petrus
  No. 4, Christus vincit
The Legend of St. Elizabeth
Missa Chorales in A Minor (choir and organ)

Piano Concertos (2)
No. 1 in E-flat Major
No. 2 in A Major
Hungarian Fantasia

Songs
O, quand je dors (Hugo)
Es muss ein Wunderbares sein (Redwitz)
O Lieb, so lang du lieben kannst (Freilligrath)
Die Lorelei

Symphonic Poems
Les Préludes
Tasso
Mazeppa
Orpheus
Prometheus
Hamlet
Totentanz (Dance of Death)
Malediction (pianoforte and strings)

Piano
Mephisto Waltz
Spanish Rhapsody
Hungarian Rhapsodies
  No. 2 in C-sharp Minor
  No. 6 in D-flat
  No. 12 in C-sharp Minor
  No. 15 in A Minor "Rákóczy March"
Liebestraum, Op. 62
Polonaise, E Major
Valses oubliées No. 1
Paganini étude, "La Campanella"
Frühlingsnacht
St. Francis walking on the water
Soirées de Vienne

Transcriptions by Liszt
(Transcription for piano of works of other
great composers)
Bach: Fantasia and Fugue in G Minor
Prelude and Fugue in A Minor
Beethoven: Fantasia on Ruins of Athens
  (with orch.)
Chopin: Polish Songs
The Maiden's Wish, Op. 74, No. 1
My Joys, Op. 74, No. 12
Gounod: Faust Waltz (with chorus and orch.)
Paganini: Andantino Capriccioso,
  E-flat Major
La Campanella (Rondo de la Clochette)
La Chasse, E Major
Schubert: Fantasia – The Wanderer,
  Op. 15 (with orch.)
Hungarian March No. 4
  (pianoforte for 4 hands, orch.)
Soirées de Vienne
Hark, hark, the lark
Der Lindenbaum
Schumann: Widmung
Verdi: Rigoletto Paraphrase de concert
  (with quartet)
Wagner: Spinning Chorus
Tannhäuser Overture

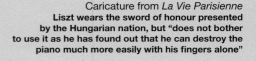

Caricature from *La Vie Parisienne*
**Liszt wears the sword of honour presented
by the Hungarian nation, but "does not bother
to use it as he has found out that he can destroy the
piano much more easily with his fingers alone"**

characterised by the distinctly national atmosphere of the Hungarian Csárdas, which consists of two movements: a lassan or slow movement of contemplative nature, followed by a friss, full of wild exuberance and abandon.

Liszt had apparently gathered together a large quantity of Hungarian melodies, which he had learnt from the gypsies, and conceived the idea of uniting them in the creation of what he called "Gypsy Epics".

"Hungarian Fantasia" is a brilliant piece of work throughout and thoroughly in keeping with the best traditions of Liszt.

Hungarian Rhapsodies

Liszt composed 20 Hungarian Rhapsodies, all based on authentic folk tunes. The rhapsodies follow the Magyar tradition of a slow strain (lassan or lassú) leading to a fast and brilliant finale (friska or friss) and this arrangement of material adds to the dramatic effect.

Rhapsody No. 2 is the general favourite and serves as an excellent representation of the entire series. The 6th and 12th are frequently played, the 15th contains Liszt's version of the Rákoczy March and the 14th makes use of the most famous of all Hungarian folk songs – "the Heron" – which appears also as the chief theme of the Hungarian Fantasia, with orchestra.

Rhapsody No. 2 consists of the usual slow and a fast section (lassú and friska respectively). The first subject, stated by the trumpets, is like a battle-call, and is followed by a noble tune decidedly rhapsodic in character. A third theme is allotted to the oboe. The quick section is in G Major. The melodies become more popular in style and the pace increases; it is as though we had passed from the presence of the Magyar nobility to the wild merrymaking of the peasantry. There is a slackening of this impetuous mood when we come to a section marked *allegretto*. The work ends with a showy coda based on one of the themes of the friska.

The climax of the work (by far the most popular part) is reached in the well-known fast tune. From there to the end it continues to introduce spectacular effects of great melodic and rhythmic variety, finishing with a *cadenza, prestissimo,* which never fails to draw the desired applause.

The Hungarian
Although he spent most of his life outside his native country, Liszt's Magyar origin appears recurringly in his music

RICHARD **WAGNER**

Born: Leipzig, Germany, May 22, 1813
Died: Venice, Italy, February 13, 1883

Richard Wagner's father died when he was only a six-month-old baby. It was his stepfather, a talented actor, who introduced the young Wagner to the fascinating world behind the floodlights. Richard soon came to love and understand the full potential of the stage.

When he was 11 years old, Wagner heard Weber's opera "Der Freischütz". Its extreme romanticism, much like the literature he was devouring, struck a responsive chord. Beethoven's "Fidelio", with which he fell in love at the age of 16, set him well on his visionary way to becoming an opera composer.

Wagner's days as a student at Leipzig University were brief but wild, enlivened by passionate gambling and love affairs. He continued to read Shakespeare and Schiller, and studied composition seriously with Theodor Weinlig.

In 1836, at the age of 23, Wagner married Minna Planer, a singer and actress. Initially, she had plenty to complain about – Wagner was a penniless composer, heavily in debt, who could not hold the conducting job she found for him. Soon, he openly turned unfaithful, adding much to Minna's unhappiness. The Wagners went together to Russia in 1837, she to sing, he to conduct in the opera house at Riga. But here too he quarrelled with the management and left Russia.

Their next trip was to London. It was made by boat instead of coach for the sake of their Saint Bernard dog, but was so stormy a sea voyage that it took a month instead of a week to reach England. They left for Paris shortly after where they lived for three years.

During the voyage to England, Wagner spent much of the time on deck listening to the yarns of the sailors. One of the stories was of a Dutchman condemned for a crime he had committed to sail the seas until redeemed by the love of a pure young girl. The story so interested Wagner that he took it as the plot of his opera "Der fliegende Holländer"

Wagner in his home
In a room that proclaims his love for the luxurious, the master discusses plans for the creation and performance of his works with his wife Cosima and his father-in-law Liszt seated in the window

(The Flying Dutchman). The performance in Dresden of "The Flying Dutchman" and of "Rienzi" – which he had composed earlier in Paris – led to a well-paid appointment at the Court of Saxony. But this appointment, too, was terminated when the politically vocal Wagner threw in his lot with the socialist nationalist revolutionaries of 1848 (the May Uprising in Dresden). He was outlawed and with the long suffering Minna fled to Switzerland.

It was to be a 12-year exile. There he wrote books on subjects such as race (he was notorious for his anti-Semitic views enunciated in *Judaism in Music,* holding that the Jews' music was shallow and artificial), vegetarianism and hygiene, as well as two influential volumes on music and art. He returned to Germany in 1862.

Minna died in 1866, after 30 years of marriage, though they had separated for several years before her death. Soon after, Wagner met Cosima, the daughter of Countess Marie d'Agoult by Franz Liszt, and wife of the conductor Hans von Bülow. She bore Wagner three children before they were legally married in 1870. As a birthday surprise for Cosima,

Wagner composed the "Siegfried Idyll", one of his most agreeable compositions.

Wagner's compositions witnessed many ups and downs. "Tannhäuser" was hissed off the stage in Paris because Wagner had not thought it fit to introduce a ballet into the second act, as was customary. Even "Tristan und Isolde", which many consider his greatest opera, had to struggle for recognition.

It was in "Der Ring des Nibelungen", the "Ring Cycle", that Wagner's personality was most triumphantly assertive. The libretto that he himself wrote, deals with supermen and superwomen, gods and goddesses. The music weaves themes for each of the characters into a continuous thread of narrative melody. The orchestra gives expression to the conflicting loves and hates of the characters.

It took Wagner 20 years to complete the four operas (which take 18 hours to perform). Though overlong, repetitious and romantic to the point of absurdity, they remain among the high points of 19th-century opera.

Ludwig II of Bavaria ("Mad Ludwig") became a passionate admirer of the composer and his music, so much so that he financed Wagner's performances and debts. On Wagner's 59th birthday, the cornerstone of the Festival Theatre in Bayreuth (the Bayreuth Festspielhaus) was laid and a home, Wahnfried, was presented to him. The world had at last accepted him at his own high valuation. Festivals of Wagner and only Wagner

Stupendous sound Frenchmen considered Wagner's deep sonorities and vivid orchestral effects too violent an assault on their ears

operas were held in Bayreuth every year after the triumphant 1882 premiere of "Parsifal": first by Cosima, then son Siegfried and Siegfried's widow Winifred. The concerts were interrupted by World War II, but annually resumed under the direction of Wieland and Wolfgang Wagner, Richard's grandsons.

Wagner witnessed the "Parsifal" premiere, though he was ill. After the performance he went with his family to Venice to rest and there a final heart attack brought his turbulent life to a peaceful end on February 13, 1883. He was 69 years old. He is buried in the garden of the Villa Wahnfried in Bayreuth.

Wagner's placec in music history

Utterly possessed by his grandiose conceptions, Wagner forgot that there are limits to human endurance and pushed his singers to outrageous lengths. As he usually wrote for the full power of the orchestra, Wagnerian singers were expected to let

their voices be heard not only above the orchestral sounds but also the full length of the auditorium. These singers were, therefore, subjected to more than the usual physical fitness and in their persona were quite different from the singers of the operas of other composers.

"The Ring" exemplifies Wagner's revolutionary approach to opera which dispensed with recitative and individual numbers in favour of long stretches of continuous music. Also distinctive was Wagner's use of leitmotifs – tunes or phrases that represented a character or an idea and were used to evoke some development in the thing thus represented.

A great innovator, Wagner introduced bass clarinets and English horns into the orchestra, brought the brasses to prominence, divided the string choirs and combined tones in harmonies of unusual sensuousness.

After Bayreuth had become a reality, the art of Wagner began to dominate musical life all over the world. A reaction was inevitable. It arose immediately after the turn of the century, first with the French Impressionists led by Debussy, and later with other composers who had an anti-romantic, practical attitude to music.

Joseph Deems Taylor, the American music composer and critic, wrote about Wagner: "He was one of the world's greatest dramatists; he was a great thinker; he was one of the most stupendous musical geniuses that, upto now, the world has ever seen. The world did owe him a living. What if he was faithless to his friends and to his wives? He had just one mistress to whom he was faithful to the day of his death: Music. There is not a line of his music that could have been conceived by a little mind. There is greatness about his worst

Major compositions

Operas
The Flying Dutchman, 3 Acts (1841)
Rienzi, 5 Acts (1842)
Tannhäuser, 3 Acts (1845)
Lohengrin, 3 Acts (1850)
The Ring of the Nibelung,
 4 parts (1853-74)
 i. The Rhinegold, 1 Act
 ii. The Valkyrie (Die Walküre), 3 Acts
 iii. Siegfried, 3 Acts
 iv. The Twilight of the Gods
  (Götterdämmerung), 3 Acts (1869-74)
Tristan und Isolde, 3 Acts (1865)
(The) Mastersingers of Nuremberg,
 3 Acts (1868)
Parsifal, 3 Acts (1882)

Orchestral
Eine Faust Overture (1840 rev. 1851)
Siegfried Idyll (1870)
Trauermusik (on Weber's "Euryanthe")

Piano
Ein Albumblatt, C Major (1861) (Several arr.)

Songs
Seven Songs from Goethe's "Faust"
Der Tannenbaum
Fünf Gedichte von Mathilde Wesendonck

mistakes. The miracle is that what he did in the little space of 70 years could not have been done at all, even by a great genius."

Notes on select works

Overture to "The Flying Dutchman"

The legend of the unfortunate mariner condemned to sail the seas in his spectral ship to the end of time is one of the old and familiar superstitions connected with the sailor's life. Wagner made use of it in this early opera, modifying it to permit the inclusion of an idea that seems always to have obsessed him – the power and certainty of redemption by love.

"A curiously wild yet harmonically unsatisfying chord in strings, colourless yet strong and fierce as a stormy wind, opens the overture. The motif of the unfortunate Dutchman immediately follows, projected in tones of horn and bassoon, then begins one of the most brilliant storm pictures in music. The wind whistles through the rigging and tears at the tattered sails. Crested green seas come crashing over the side, and the seamen's hoarse cries sound in the midst of the gale as they rush about the decks and struggle with ice-crusted rope and spar. The storm spent, we hear calm passages, based upon the air known as 'Senta's Ballad', the heroine's song extracted from the second act of the opera. There is a jolly sailor's dance, and with daylight and fair weather, we have more strongly the beautiful phrase from 'Senta's Ballad', which is also to be the motif of redemption by love.

> " *Utterly possessed by his grandiose conceptions, Wagner forgot that there are limits to human endurance and pushed his singers to outrageous lengths.* "

It is delivered several times, finally by the full orchestra; derivations of it appear in the final fading and peaceful orchestral light in which the overture closes."

Siegfried Idyll

This was not only Wagner's birthday gift to his wife Cosima, but a reward for giving him their son Siegfried.

"On Christmas morning, 1870, as she lay with her little son in that mysterious region that lies halfway between sleeping and waking, Cosima, thinking, we may believe, that she was still dreaming, heard such music as might have comforted another Mother, eighteen hundred and seventy years before. On the stairs before her door stood Wagner and his little orchestra, playing with their skill and with all their hearts this beautiful and intolerably poignant serenade."

Tristan und Isolde

Wagner made of the music of "Tristan und Isolde" the mightiest paean of love and passion, of suffering and death through love that mortal ears have ever heard. The legend of the Irish princess, Isolde of the White Hands, and Tristan, knight of ancient Cornwall, antedates the Wagnerian opera by several centuries. Stripped of detail and the circumstances of time and place, it is ageless as humanity. "Tristan is a rather long opera, with the faults and virtues inherent in that hybrid form of art. Yet its music, quite apart from the action and reduced to its fiery distillate, becomes the mightiest and saddest and fiercest utterance of human passion that music can pronounce.

"On symphony programmes, two excerpts are commonly played – the

Prelude and Isolde's 'Song of Love and Death'. They are usually performed without pause. However, the 'symphonic synthesis' arranged by Leopold Stokowski includes not only the Prelude and 'Liebestod', but also the indescribable love music from the second act, together with passages taken from the first and third acts. The music is presented as a symphonic poem, a single, unified rhapsodic utterance. It is not to be regarded as 'excerpts' from the opera, but as a distinct musical work with a climactic scheme of its own, built of the synthesised elements of the music without regard to their sequence in the stage performance. In this form, and according to its mood, the music can be roughly

Parsifal at the Castle of the Grail
Only Wagner operas were held in Bayreuth every year after the triumphant 1882 premiere of "Parsifal"

Cosima Wagner
The composer's second wife devoted her life to his art

divided into three sections, the Prelude, the Liebesnacht (Night of Love) and the Liebestod (Isolde's Death through Love)."

Prelude to Lohengrin

"Unearthly harmonies, like pale blue aromatic vapours ascending, steal to our enchanted ears as this strange music begins. They rise from strings and faintly blown woodwinds; they are warmed and coloured more deeply as the string choir presently descends from ethereal harmonies into richer and stronger tones. Almost imperceptibly a crescendo begins, growing to an impassioned climax, drawing upon the sonorities of the mightiest brazen voices, and culminating in one majestic golden phrase – the solemn motif of the Holy Grail.

"In the few minutes of this serenely beautiful music Wagner presents to us a miracle, and withdrawing it again, leaves us lost in contemplation. This music was written to suggest the apparition of the Holy Grail, long lost to sinful men, yet again vouchsafed to him in momentary vision as it moved across heaven's illimitable blue.

"Escorted by crowds of angels, the vision moves closer to the earth, the contours and glowing reflection of the Grail ever more clear and wonderful, until its blazing glory enfolds the enchanted beholder and strikes him blind and numb with worship and with awe.

"Away into the vast spaces of the heavens moves the incredible beauty of the vision, followed by its celestial choirs, trailing after them, like disembodied voices, the strange pale harmonies that announced their coming."

Prelude to Act III of Lohengrin

"This is one of Wagner's briefest and most brilliant operatic preludes – a small but intense preparatory utterance preceding the moment in the opera when Lohengrin, the strange and powerful knight whom Elsa has loved and wed, and Elsa herself, are escorted to the nuptial chamber. Here is an epithalamium of riotous exuberance. Strings and woodwinds and brass join in high-hearted outpourings; the masculine strength of the trombones, the little accents of timidity in the lovely woodwind passage in the middle section and the exalted concluding measures magnificently portray the moment of supreme happiness which presently is to be revealed in the following scene in the opera."

Ride of the Valkyries (Die Walküre)

"The stormiest music we know, the wildest and fiercest and most vividly picturesque, is this music from the third act of "Die Walküre". Much has been set down in notes to illustrate the swift rhythm and leapings of ridden horses, but nothing, before or since, has had the superb and detailed suggestiveness, the incredible power of this marvellous tone picture. The Valkyries in ancient Scandinavian mythology were fierce war-like daughters of Odin (Wotan), whose duty it was to snatch up the fallen in battle and to bear them to Valhalla. They were themselves warrior maidens and rode through the upper airs upon great steeds, accompanied by thunder clouds and lightning.

"The music is taken from the scene wherein the Valkyries are gathering on the top of a mountain, after having descended to earth to recover the bodies of heroes to be enlisted in the hosts of Wotan. Their wild cry and the rumour of their steeds' swift hooves are heard, and closer and closer the thundering band approaches. Now the orchestra's mightiest forces are summoned; the leaping rhythm of mighty chargers sways and moves and compels the band. There is even the gigantic neigh of these swift steeds in the woodwind; the upward-leaping rhythm roars through the brass and detonates in the timpani. Swiftly the marvellous spectacle courses on, and fades from view along a steep mountain pass, the echoing hoof beats lingering briefly behind."

Wagnerian "Swan Song"
The bird from Wagner's tale of the Swan Knight, "Lohengrin", is shown here teaching the composer the proper use of the right foot!

MODEST
MUSSORGSKY

Born : Karevo, Russia, March 21, 1839
Died : St. Petersburg, Russia,
March 28, 1881

The son of a landowner, Modest Mussorgsky spent the first 10 years of his life on his father's estate. Here, he heard folk songs and stories from the Russian *moujik* peasants and listened with childish sympathy to their grievances. When he was 13 years old he was sent to a school for cadets in St. Petersburg, to be shaped into an officer and a gentleman. After he graduated he became a uniformed dandy in a crack Russian regiment.

All this time Mussorgsky knew music only as an amateur. Then he met the composer Aleksandr Dargomyzhsky, who introduced him in turn to Balakirev, Cui and Rimsky-Korsakov. Balakirev taught him the fundamentals of composition, but Mussorgsky was instinctively unwilling to discipline his wild talent and fit into the conventional pattern.

At 19, Mussorgsky resigned his commission and started work as a government clerk upon joining the Russian civil service. The salary was very small and he lived on the edge of starvation. Since his father had lost his fortune when the serfs were liberated in 1861, Mussorgsky could look for no help from his family.

A giant of a man, Mussorgsky's rugged strength and individuality set him apart from the other four composers of the group known as "The Five". These composers – Aleksandr Borodin, Mily Balakirev, César Cui and Nikolai Rimsky-Korsakov – were dedicated to the nationalist objective of promoting Russian music, taking inspiration from folk songs and folk melodies. (As matters turned out, both Mussorgsky and Rimsky-Korsakov gradually drifted away from the other members of the Big Five.)

Mussorgsky's output consisted of songs, piano pieces, dramatic and orchestral works, all of which bear the stamp of his crude and unique genius.

" The first musical realist in Russia, Mussorgsky raised his voice against Tsarist iniquities and composed music that stirred the masses. His music was unconventional. "

Mussorgsky's birthplace
A quiet, cheerful child, he showed an early disposition for music, especially for the piano

Mussorgsky's place in music history

The first musical realist in Russia, Mussorgsky raised his voice against Tsarist iniquities and composed music that stirred the masses. His music was unconventional. He avoided the influence of other composers and previous musical traditions, seeking instead to distill the basic elements of music and use them to express his ideas in his own way.

The bulk of Mussorgsky's compositions were published posthumously. His executors were taken aback to notice the volume of his unpublished works. Among the mass of dusty manuscripts they found the original scores of "Boris Godunov" and "Night on Bald Mountain". It was decided that Rimsky-Korsakov, who was one of the executors of Mussorgsky's estate, should revise the scores of both operas. But Rimsky-Korsakov overdid the editing, which took away the essence of Mussorgsky from the music. Many purists and musicologists in the 20th century decided to undo this damage and now the original scores, bearing Mussorgsky's unmistakable innovative genius, are being performed all over the world.

The memorial exhibition of the works of the painter and architect Victor Hartmann, in 1874, inspired Mussorgsky to compose his "Pictures at an Exhibition" as a collection of piano pieces, which were later orchestrated by several composers, most notably Ravel.

Had Mussorgsky composed nothing but the opera "Boris Godunov", he would have earned his place among the great composers. Just as "Carmen" is the perfect French opera, so is "Boris" its perfect Russian counterpart. Mussorgsky minced no musical words in its powerful tonal blasts against tyranny. In crashing chords and ringing arias he cried out for justice for the masses, charity for the poor and punishment for evil-doers. The opera had some 20 performances before it was withdrawn because the Tsar deemed it a subversive utterance.

Mussorgsky's other great opera was "Khovanshchina", which told of the conflict between the old order and the new under the Tsar, Peter the Great. The opera boils with nationalistic feeling aided by native folk songs and melodies typical of the Russia of its time and after.

As a song writer Mussorgsky achieved distinction. His children's cycle "The Nursery" was a deeply felt work which sensitively projected an understanding of children as people in their own little world.

Mussorgsky lived mostly a lonely life. He turned to vodka and narcotics to relieve his depression and the feeling that he was a failure. When his money gave out and a fatal illness attacked him, he became a charity patient in the Saint Nicholas Military Hospital in St. Petersburg where he died, at just 42 – a neglected, forlorn figure.

Notes on select works

A Night on Bald Mountain

Mussorgsky was so vacillating in his original conception of this music, and at times thought of inserting such fantastically unreasonable ideas, that the suspicion arises he may have been under the influence of drugs (as he often was) when he wrote it. Certainly the orgiastic celebrations suggested in this piece have never been witnessed by mortal eyes, but materialise in the music like the wild and terrifying illusions of a nightmare. It would be more realistic to suggest that the composer's friend, Rimsky-Korsakov, had something to do with the extraordinarily descriptive and colourful music, for he revised, re-orchestrated and put it into playable form.

" Mussorgsky avoided the influence of other composers and previous musical traditions, seeking instead to distill the basic elements of music and use them to express his ideas in his own way."

"A detailed description of the music is scarcely necessary, considering the programme which is printed in the published score. Subterranean sounds of unearthly voices; appearance of the spirits of darkness, followed by that of the god Chernobog; Chernobog's glorification of the Black Mass; the revels; at the height of the revels there is heard from afar the bell of a little church which causes the spirits to disperse; dawn."

Prelude and Entr'acte from "Khovanshchina"

"For the plot of his opera, Mussorgsky chose the stirring incidents of the end of the 17th century, when, as his friend Vladimir Stassov suggested in his *Life*, the passing of the old and the birth of the new Russia 'afforded a rich subject'. There were at times such disagreements on matters of national policy that serious struggles between opposing factions kept the country in a state of ferment. One of the prominent figures in these struggles was that of Prince Khovantsky, and from his name is derived the name of the opera.

"The Prelude is highly atmospheric, descriptive and moving. It paints the pale and wintry skies as day breaks over the Kremlin in Moscow, and establishes a mood superbly in keeping with the highly dramatic scenes that follow upon its conclusion. The Entr'acte usually played on symphonic programmes is extracted from Scene II, Act IV. Here, one of the figures in the drama – a victim of the uprising of the New Russia – begins his long journey into exile. There is a gloomy and terribly persistent figure in the bass, compounded of the low strings and bassoons; this, with the melancholy song that appears above it, produces an atmosphere of desolation almost without parallel in orchestral music."

Pictures at an Exhibition

Composed in 1874 as a suite for piano, it was inspired by a memorial exhibition of the works of Viktor Hartmann, who had been a friend of the composer. Mussorgsky paid homage to his friend by describing 10 of his pictures in music. They are connected by an interlude (Promenade) repeated four times in varied forms.

(i) The Gnome: A waddling barrel-legged dwarf. By changing the tempo from 5/4 to 6/4, Mussorgsky gave the impression of the ungainly and heavy gait of the bulky figure.

(ii) The Old Castle: A minstrel singing in front of a medieval castle.

(iii) In the Tuileries: Children quarrelling at play. A swarm of children and their nurses under an avenue of trees in the Tuileries Gardens, Paris.

(iv) A Polish Chariot: An ox-drawn dray and its driver.

(v) Ballet of Chickens in their Shells: Hartmann's sketch for the décor of a scene in the ballet "Trilby" in which the pupils of the dramatic school were to perform as unhatched chickens.

(vi) Samuel Goldenberg and Schmuÿle: Two Jews of the Warsaw ghetto, one rich and the other poor.

(vii) The Market at Limoges: Chattering and bickering market-women.

(viii) In the Catacombs: A self-portrait of Hartmann carrying a lantern through the catacombs of Paris.

(ix) The House supported by Hens' Legs (or the Hut of Baba-Yaga): Hartmann's picture represented a clock in the shape of a witch's cottage. Baba-Yaga was a witch in Russian legend. The music represents a witch's ride.

(x) The Great Gate of Kiev: Hartmann's sketch of an ornamental gate in ancient Russian style, with a dome shaped like a Slav helmet, inspired this piece.

Several of these compositions are masterpieces of character portrayed in music, e.g. the clamouring children in the Tuileries, the market-women, and the gesticulating Jews. Others are distinctively Slav in character

e.g. the drover's melancholy tune in the fantastic house of the witch, and the majestic music for the gate at Kiev. This last is reminiscent of the coronation scene in 'Boris Godunov'.

The suite is not specifically pianistic, and there have been many arrangements of it for orchestra, the best and most frequently played being Ravel's.

The Nursery

A cycle of seven songs composed in 1868-72 with words and music by Mussorgsky. He loved children and while playing and singing with them, he was always studying their reactions. Every little story they told was a source of inspiration to him.

Song No. 1: "With Nanny"

The child asks Nanya (his nurse) to tell him a story perhaps about the "wicked wolf" that eats up the children who do not obey their parents, or about the Prince who limps and the Princess who sneezed so hard that she broke all the window panes. The music strongly emphasises each episode – the wolf eating, the Prince limping and the Princess sneezing.

Song No. 2: "Stand in the Corner"

The child has been naughty and is put in the corner, from which its voice is heard: "I haven't done anything wrong, Nanny, it was the cat's fault. Nanny's nose is always dirty – Nanny's bonnet is always crooked – don't love Nanny anymore."

Song No. 3: "The Cockchafer"

The child tells how once he built a sand castle, and a big fat cockchafer with huge feelers came and sat on the roof. Suddenly it flew towards him and bumped against his forehead so hard that it was stunned and fell to the ground. Is it dead?

Song No. 4: "Dolly's Cradle Song"

A child's lullaby for her doll.

Song No. 5: "The Evening Prayer"

The child prays: "Dear God, take care of Mother and Father, my brothers and Grandmama," and then adds a long list of aunts and uncles. She goes faster and faster, mechanically and without expression, until she forgets where she has got to and the nurse has to prompt her to finish by praying for herself.

Song No. 6: "The Hobby Horse"

The child is galloping all over the garden. A sudden powerful chord indicates that he has fallen and hurt himself.

His mother, trying to attract his attention to something else, says, "Can you see that sweet little bird on the bush over there?" Then everything is forgotten and the child goes on riding his hobby horse.

Song No. 7: "The Cat and the Bird Cage" (Mimi the Brigand)

The child describes the cat creeping up to the bird cage. "The bullfinch trembles and chirps with fright. The cat is about to stretch its paw into the cage, when it receives a hard slap from the small hand of the child, which also happens to hit against the side of the cage. 'Mama, how hard the cage is!'"

Major compositions

Operas
Boris Godunov, Prologue and 4 Acts (1874)
Khovanshchina, 5 Acts (1873)

Orchestral tone poem
Night on Bald Mountain (1872)
(popularised in the Disney film *Fantasia*)

Piano
Pictures at an Exhibition (1874)

Songs
Ballade
Hopak
The Little Star
(The) Nursery cycle (1868-72)
Songs of the Flea (Goethe), orch. (1879)
Songs and Dances of Death, cycle (1875-77)

ROBERT ALEXANDER
SCHUMANN

Born : Zwickau, Germany, June 8, 1810
Died : Endenich, Germany, July 29, 1856

As the son of an editor and bookseller, Robert Alexander Schumann's boyhood was spent amidst literary influences, and much of the music he later composed was written as the direct result of literary stimuli. Schumann's father was just as pleased to note his son's love of great literature as he was to perceive the unusual musical talent the boy had started to manifest from an early age.

Schumann spent most of his boyhood either dreaming at the piano or poring over the writings of Jean-Paul Richter, whom he idolised and whose romantic style he imitated in his own writings.

His father who had encouraged both his literary and musical leanings died unfortunately early and his mother prevailed upon Schumann to study law. For a short time Schumann made some pretence of studying law, but soon gave up. With the help of his piano teacher Friedrich Wieck, he finally convinced his mother that music was his forte.

Resolving to become a great pianist, but impatient with his slow progress during the first two years, Schumann devised a special mechanical contrivance to exercise the fourth finger, which is not as supple as other fingers of the hand. The invention recoiled badly on him. In striving to exercise his fourth finger with this mechanism, he strained it so badly that nothing could be done to restore it to normal. Schumann was compelled to abandon his dream of becoming a great concert pianist.

For the world of music this proved to be a fortunate accident, for it caused Schumann to turn from piano playing to composing music.

Schumann's marriage to Clara Wieck, the daughter of his piano teacher, has been the subject of considerable comment among his biographers.

Schumann's childhood home
The son of a prosperous publisher and bookseller, he had a tranquil childhood

Neue Zeitschrift für Musik (*The New Music Journal*) which he founded and edited for nearly 10 years.

At the time Schumann started this journal, music criticism had degenerated into mere stereotyped flattery. Under Schumann's editorship, *The New Music Journal* raised the standard of music criticism from the depths into which it had descended.

Schumann showed musical balance when discriminating between the good and the bad: whenever a young, unknown composer or a new composition deserved praise, Schumann saw to it that this was given.

He was, with equal fairness, critical of anything that was mediocre, or just superficially pleasing. Schumann's straightforward and scholarly comments on the musical matters of his time soon came to attract attention everywhere.

What is really remarkable is that Schumann had the knack of estimating the true worth of any new music that came to his notice, as well as of the many young composers he came in contact with. It speaks very highly of Schumann's special abilities in this direction to recall that after listening to only one of Chopin's early variations, he immediately wrote in his paper a glowing tribute to Chopin that contained the now famous sentence: "Hats off, gentlemen – a genius!" Again, when Brahms first came to him with a letter of introduction from the violinist Joseph Joachim, Schumann carefully studied Brahms's compositions and praised him as "the young eagle" and wrote appreciatively of the "deep song-melody" of Brahms's music.

> " *Composition for Schumann was not a matter of building a structure in musical notes, but of finding an outlet for personality. The emotional content is the important element in his music.* "

To understand the tragic circumstances under which Schumann died, it is necessary to say something about him as a man. He had an extremely sensitive nature – being highly strung, moody and melancholic. He was often so self-absorbed in his thoughts that he became completely detached from his surroundings.

The chaotic state of Schumann's mind was reflected in the letters addressed to his intimate friends. In some of these he tells them ominously that "the music is silent" and "night is falling".

Indeed, the night was descending for Schumann, as his mind was gradually deteriorating. He complained at first of the note 'A' constantly sounding in his head and later of hearing voices and entire chords of music.

When in the last few years of his life it became apparent to Schumann that he would have to earn a more steady living if he was to support his wife and seven children in a reasonable manner, he found that he could not adjust his extremely introverted nature to so practical a necessity. Though he did take up appointments as conductor, he had to give them up sooner or later. Orchestras found it difficult to follow or understand a man who was so absent-minded that he forgot to beat time, and would suddenly go silent for minutes on end during rehearsals and stand there completely absorbed in his thoughts.

The stress of composition often brought on bouts of feverish excitement, which were followed by moods of profound gloom when his compositions were not well received by the public. It is not surprising that towards the end of his life Schumann headed for a complete

The marriage was one of the most romantic in the history of music. Although very much in love, the couple had to wait four years before her father gave his consent to their marriage, which was in all respects a happy one. Besides raising a fine crop of children, his wife, who was an accomplished pianist, also became the official interpreter of his music. As a matter of fact, Clara Schumann the pianist was far better known in society than her husband Robert Schumann the composer. At one public function, on being introduced by Clara, Robert was asked: "And tell me, Mr Schumann, are you musical too?"

Schumann is remembered today as much for the music he composed as for the innumerable articles he wrote on musical matters in the periodical nervous breakdown. In 1854, Schumann tried to commit suicide by throwing himself into the River Rhine. He was rescued by some boatmen and spent the last two years of his life in a mental home, where he eventually died in his loving wife's arms.

Schumann's place in music history

Schumann is generally considered the most near-perfect incarnation of the Romantic spirit. Most of his Romantic qualities were derived from and nourished by literary sources. Among the writers and poets who influenced him most were Jean Paul Richter, Heinrich Heine, Joseph Freiherr von Eichendorff and E.T.A. Hoffmann. His music "contains all the carefree and exuberant enthusiasm, dreamy, weak melancholy and deep despair of youth".

In Schumann's view, music's only function was to express what a composer feels. Composition for him was not a matter of building a structure in musical notes, but of finding an outlet for personality. The emotional content is the most important element in Schumann's music and is of strong expressive power.

Schumann's most characteristic compositions are his superb piano works. He was at his best and happiest when writing for the piano. Next to his piano compositions, Schumann is remembered for his songs, the majority of which are touching in their purity and sincerity. Schumann shares with Schubert the title of founder of the German lied form of song.

Orchestral music was second in importance to his music for the piano and lieder. He wrote four symphonies of which the finely wrought No. 1 in B-flat Major ("Spring") and No. 3 in E-flat Major ("the Rhenish") are the most appealing. His incidental music set to Byron's poem *Manfred*, especially its Overture, is highly listenable. In chamber music, his E-flat Major piano quartet and brilliant Op. 44 piano quintet stand out as very fine compositions.

Notes on select works

Piano Music

Starting with "Études Symphoniques", a set of 12 variations on a theme, Schumann showed a strong penchant to string together a whole lot of individual pieces under one title. For example, his "Kinderscenen" (Scenes of Childhood) contained 13 pieces with appropriate names like "Of Foreign Lands and Peoples", "Playing Tag", "Child's Petition", "At the Fireside", "Child falling Asleep", "Knight of the Hobby Horse" and "Träumerei" (Reverie). The last named became famous for its lovely and touching melody. His "Papillons" (Butterflies) strung together 12 pieces, "Carnaval" 21 pieces, "Kreisleriana" eight pieces and "Davidsbündlertänze" (the League of David Dances) 18 pieces.

Fantasy in C, Op. 17

This is one of the three major pieces of piano music from the Romantic period (the other two being Chopin's Sonata in B-flat Minor and Liszt's Sonata in B Minor). In 1838, Schumann wrote about it to Clara Wieck: "I have just finished a Fantasy in three movements. I do not think I have ever written anything more impassioned than the first

Major compositions

Chorus and Orchestra
"Paradise and the Peri", Op. 50
Requiem for Mignon, Op. 98b
2 Masses

Opera
"Genoveva"

150 Songs
(Including 6 song cycles
covering 83 songs)
Individual songs such as:
 "Ich grolle nicht" (Heine)
 "Mondnacht" (Eichendorff)
 "Wanderlust" (Kerner)
 "Widmung" (Ruckert)
 "Wiegenlied" (Hebbel) Cradle Song
 "Die Nüssbaum" (Mosen) The Nut Tree

Symphonies (4)
No. 1 in B-flat Major, Op. 38 – "Spring"
No. 3 in E-flat Major, Op. 97 – "Rhenish"

Concertos
Piano Concerto in A Minor, Op. 54
Cello Concerto in A Minor, Op. 129
Violin Concerto in D Minor, Op. posth.

Piano Music
Arabesque in C, Op. 18
Carnaval, Op. 9
Davidsbündlertänze, Op. 6
Études Symphoniques, Op. 13
Fantasy in C, Op. 17
Fantasiestücke, Op. 111
Kinderscenen, "Scenes of Childhood",
 Op. 15 (incl. Träumerei)
Kreisleriana, Op. 16
Papillons, Op. 2
Sonata No. 3, F Minor, Op. 14
Toccata, C Major, Op. 7
Waldscenen, Op. 82

movement. It is a profound lament about you. You can understand the fantasy only if you transport yourself back to the unhappy summer of 1836 when I had to give you up. Now I have no reason to compose in so miserable and melancholy a way!"

In Part I, the opening theme begins *fortissimo* accompanied by quick figures in the bass. There is an interlude, somewhat quieter, but still sombre. Part II, *maestoso*, introduces a glorious theme in rich chords. Part III brings the work to a peaceful and logical conclusion.

Quintet for Piano and Strings, E-flat Major, Op. 44

This "paradise of beauty" has been put down as superior to anything in chamber music since Beethoven's day, praised as "certainly the finest composition extant employing the particular combination of instruments it embraces. Its claim to this position is due chiefly to its originality and brilliance, and to the beauty of the balance between piano and strings."

The first movement – *allegro brilliante* – is actually woven out of two harmonic motives and developed from these simplest of materials. The two middle movements – the slow movement in *modo d'un marcia* and the third movement *scherzo molto vivace* – have greater meaning and breath. The finale – *allegro ma non troppo* – is equally significant and a worthy ending to the work. This is achieved by a rising climax formed by the combination of the first motives of the first and last movements.

Piano Concerto in A Minor, Op. 54

This is one of the most popular piano concertos by reason of its abundant melody, vivacity of contrasting rhythms, beautifully balanced form, perfect writing for the solo instrument and piquant orchestration. This is no virtuoso bravura, but a romantic poetical work.

The first movement – *allegro affetuoso* – as in Beethoven's last two concertos, breaks with Classical tradition with the piano beginning the work and without waiting for an orchestral introduction of thematic material. The concerto follows the sonata form and has been described as follows: "After energetic piano chords the theme is introduced by the wind instruments, then the piano. The first bar of the theme forms the basis of the development of the coda, while the second bar forms the germ of the theme of the second and third movements."

The second movement – *intermezzo, andantino grazioso* – begins with a dialogue between piano and strings. The middle section contains a striking melody on the cello. After a repetition of the dialogue, soloist and orchestra pass over abruptly to the lively third movement.

The third movement – *allegro vivace* – "has the piano spinning a glittering web round the orchestra's melodies".

Symphony No 3, E-flat Major, Op. 97 – "Rhenish"

The name "Rhenish" for this symphony was authorised by Schumann himself who said that he wished to convey through it some of the spiritual atmosphere of the Rhineland. He was particularly inspired to write the fourth movement after witnessing the installation of a cardinal in Cologne Cathedral.

The first movement begins with the full orchestra stating the opening theme, essentially the vitalising principle that can be almost always felt through its elaborations. The movement's concluding passages rise to a climax of tremendous power.

The second movement approaches the form and character of the conventional *scherzo*. Its lightness and engaging rhythms are of special interest.

The third movement is vintage Schumann – quiet, romantic and full of tenderness and restrained passion.

The music of the fourth movement has often been called "the cathedral scene". The rites attendant upon the elevation of a cardinal, which took place in Cologne's magnificent cathedral, and which Schumann witnessed, impressed him deeply and inspired this sonorous and dignified music. The movement is intimately connected thematically with the fifth movement into which the music passes without pause. This section represents the festivities of the people in honour of the installation of their exalted cardinal. A climax of great brilliance and majesty is developed with the movement ending in a festive mood.

Clara Wieck
Schumann's wife and the great love of his life, she gave him understanding and inspiration

FREDERIC **CHOPIN**

Born : Zelazowa Wola, Poland,
March 1, 1810
Died : Paris, France, October 17, 1849

*F*rederic Chopin was fortunate in being born in an environment that was kind to the growth of artistic talent. His father numbered many intellectuals among his circle of intimates, and young Chopin grew up in an atmosphere of culture and refinement.

It is recorded that even as an infant the sound of music made him weep and before he could read or write, Chopin had already begun to take piano lessons from a Bohemian musician. Soon after this Chopin started composing music. His music master would write down his efforts and correct them for him. By the time he was 9 years old, Chopin's talent for music was being discussed beyond the family circle.

He got invitations to play for almost all the princely houses in Warsaw. At the age of 15, Chopin entered the Warsaw Conservatoire to study composition under Professor Joseph Elsner, his teacher and lifelong friend.

In the course of his weekend excursions to the countryside around Warsaw, Chopin became interested in the local music and folklore. He was fascinated especially by the rhythms and simple melodies of folk songs. Upon his return from the countryside he would often spend hours at his piano improvising mazurkas and polonaises and making experiments in touch and in the fingering of broken chords. These experiments were later to crystallise into a technique inseparable from his art, a technique that was to revolutionise the whole art of piano music.

This deep interest in folk music and the exchange of opinions he had with the intensely national-minded literary men of the day, bred in Chopin a love for his country which was to remain with him all his life.

It is recorded that at a farewell party before Chopin left Warsaw for Paris, some of his friends presented him a silver goblet filled with Polish earth,

" For sheer beauty of pianistic sound
Chopin had no equal.
No other composer has written so much
dreamy and poetic music for the
piano as he has. "

with these words: "May you never forget your native land wherever you may go. May you never cease to love it with a warm and faithful heart." Chopin kept this goblet and the earth in it by his side for the rest of his life.

In Paris, Chopin met such eminent musicians as Cherubini, Rossini, Mendelssohn, Schumann and Liszt. He soon had the entrée to Parisian society and moved in the best artistic and aristocratic circles. His life became the life of the Paris salon. According to one observer, "He began to display a fastidiousness in his choice of clothes, and in the arrangement and decoration of his rooms, which was matched only by his fastidiousness in composing."

Much has been written about the women in Chopin's life. His liaison with the novelist who wrote under the pseudonym George Sand, in particular, is probably the most publicised love affair in the history of music. The reason for the wide publicity given to this affair may well be because all writers have found George Sand to be very attractive material for their pens. Sand undoubtedly cut a very unusual and colourful figure in the society of her time and was much written about. She was mistress to many famous artists and poets before she met Chopin, and her view of free association in man-woman relationships was unusual to say the least.

Mme Aurore Dudevant – or George Sand as she preferred to call herself – was a brilliantly intellectual woman, a great writer, a political activist, opposed to monarchy, tradition and convention. She wore trousers, drank strong drinks, smoked vigorously, swore

Chopin's birthplace at Zelazowa Wola
In his youth he would often wander into the country to listen to the fiddling and singing of the peasants

like a trooper and moved about freely in a man's world with an insouciance and poise that appealed to men just as much as it shocked them. One of Chopin's biographers, in rather hyperbolic terms, described George Sand as "a voluptuary without vice" and as "a woman in whom qualities of compassion, of hypocrisy, of pure motherliness and of the vampire were grotesquely mixed. Through her veins coursed the blood of kings and courtesans. Generations of unsanctified unions had brought her into being."

Many conflicting opinions have been voiced by Chopin's biographers about the propriety of his love affair with George Sand, but all of them have unanimously declared that under the spell of passion for this extraordinary woman Chopin composed some of his finest music. Their affair lasted for 10 years. They lived in neighbouring apartments in Paris in the winter and spent summers together at her chateau in Nohant. Chopin was often ill and she nursed him very devotedly. While in Majorca with her and her two children, Chopin composed the marvellous 24 preludes which are among his best-loved works.

In 1846, George Sand's son, who hated Chopin, maliciously created a quarrel which broke the liaison. Chopin left her, never to return. He even refused to see her on his death-bed, three years later. After their parting, Chopin composed no more. But to the last he kept hidden in his journal a lock of George Sand's hair in an envelope with the initials G-F (George-Frederic) on it.

Modern research has shown that if Chopin's liaison with George Sand was of an intimate nature, his affair with the beautiful and talented Countess Delphine Potocka was just as intimate, if not more so. It is even generally believed that Chopin fathered a child as a result of his affair with the Countess. Whatever the truth in that respect, the fact remains that it was Countess Delphine Potocka who comforted Chopin during his last few days on earth.

His health, which had been bad, deteriorated rapidly. To complicate matters his financial position caused him considerable anxiety. In order to earn some money Chopin decided to give a recital. But though he played exquisitely and the recital was well received, the exertion of it all proved too much for him and he almost fainted after the last number.

A brief visit to England only aggravated his poor condition and he returned to Paris with his health completely broken. The end was now very near. Confined to bed, Chopin's last few days were brightened by the frequent visits of Delphine Potocka. Many years ago, when they had first met, Chopin had been captivated by the thrilling quality of her voice. And now, once more, his last moments were enchanted by the many songs that the Countess sang to him.

As the end approached, Chopin was tormented by the fear of being buried alive and one of his final requests was for his body to be cut open before burial. His last words were: "When I am gone play me some music and I know that I will hear you from beyond."

In an agony of intense pain, a victim of tuberculosis, Chopin finally closed his eyes to the light of day on October 17, 1849. Present at his funeral were all the great figures in the world of society and art. They buried with him the silver goblet filled with Polish earth which his friends had presented to him almost 20 years ago when he left his native soil to settle in France. But his heart they cut out and sent to his beloved Poland.

Chopin's place in music history

Chopin has been called – and not without reason – "the Poet of the Piano" and "the Keyboard King". For sheer beauty of pianistic sound Chopin had no equal. No other composer has written so much dreamy and poetic music for the piano as he has. His music abounds in lovely little snatches of song. It is, as admirers have put it, music that constantly seems to be exploring new intensities of sentiment, new wonders in delicacy. It is music that "says things in a way that chokes one; simplicity is passionately simple; when the music is hot, it is red hot". Chopin excels in use of colour. His music "is melody conceived in terms of colour, of constantly changing colour, of colour in motion, in flow".

In all the music that Chopin wrote there is the stamp of artistic sincerity. He wrote music as he felt it, and every bar that he wrote had obviously made his own nerves tingle. There is the story of how Chopin was once playing by himself a certain section of his A-flat Polonaise when he worked himself up to such a pitch of musical terror and excitement that finally, in panic, he fled from the piano!

How does Chopin's music affect its listeners? Let his biographer J.D.M. Rorke, speak to us: "After the final chord of a typical Chopin composition has been struck one can still vividly recall the wonder of it all. Together with the composer we have walked by still waters and in green pastures; we have burned with love and longing; have struggled and fought; have dallied in lotus-covered isles and galloped through the wild dark; in a place of prayer we have had moments of mystic vision; we have wept; we have dreamed; we have triumphed, we have feared. We have been through, at any rate, some of these experiences, and each of them superlative in its kind, the flowers the fairest, the tears the bitterest, the prayers the solemnest, the love the blindest, the wrath the fiercest that could be conceived."

Chopin was a master of the small form. The piano pieces he composed were ballades, études, fantasies, impromptus, mazurkas, nocturnes, préludes, scherzos and waltzes. He wrote virtually nothing but piano music – no symphonies, no operas or oratorios, and very little orchestral work. Even his two piano concertos are centred on the piano, with the orchestra treated as unavoidable background.

The music he composed in the small forms is intense, poetic and filled with feeling. Many pieces are delicate

Major compositions

Concertos
Concerto No. 1 in E Minor, Op. 11
Concerto No. 2 in F Minor, Op. 21
Andante Spianato and Grande Polonaise, Op. 22 (piano and orchestra)
Introduction and Polonaise Brillante, Op. 3 (piano and cello)

Piano Sonatas
No. 2, B-flat Minor, Op. 35 "Funeral March"
No. 3, B Minor, Op. 58

Other Piano Works
Ballades (4)
Barcarolle, F-sharp Major, Op. 60
Berceuse, D-flat, Op. 57
Écossaises, Op. 72, No. 3
4 Scherzos
12 Études, Op. 10
Tarantelle in A-flat Major, Op. 43
Impromptus (4)
  (including "Fantaisie Impromptu")
58 Mazurkas
20 Nocturnes
13 Polonaises
24 Préludes, Op. 28
14 Waltzes
17 Polish songs, Op. 74
Rondo, C Major, Op. 73 (two pianos)

George Sand
The passionate woman who deeply influenced Chopin's life

and some are fervently patriotic. His Sonata No. 2 in B-flat Minor, Op. 35 stands out as his most famous large work. The sonata contains one of music's three most famous funeral marches (the others being in Beethoven's Third Symphony, the "Eroica", and Wagner's "Götterdämmerung").

Notes on select works

Ballades

Chopin often took long walks in the countryside of Warsaw and was attracted and moved by the rhythm and the simplicity of the folk songs that were the inspiration for the ballades. However, it is also known that Chopin told Schumann that some of his ballades were inspired by the poetry of his countryman Adam Mickiewicz. As a result, many attempts were made to find connections between individual ballades and Mickiewicz's poems, but nothing definite was established. It is more reasonable to assume that Chopin only attempted to re-create the spirit of the poetry and not attach the music to any particular poems.

Ballade No. 1 in G Minor, Op. 23

It is the most frequently played of the group of four. Its introduction, two secondary themes, their development and the coda are clearly identified.

Ballade No. 2 in F, Op. 38

Of this ballade, Schumann wrote that Chopin had said that he had been inspired to compose it by a poem of Mickiewicz, but Schumann was of the opinion that music like this was more likely to inspire a poet to write words to it. The pianist Arthur Rubinstein saw in this ballade a picture of the wind playing with a flower, caressing it and ending by breaking it.

Ballade No. 3 in A-flat, Op. 47

This ballade is in a lighter mood but said to have the same source of inspiration. Schumann saw in it "the intellectual Pole, accustomed to move in distinguished circles of the French capital".

Ballade No. 4 in F Minor, Op. 52

Herbert Weinstock, co-author of the *Men of Music* compendium (1939), calls this ballade the most difficult of them all and comments on its unity despite its three separate themes. Chopin himself considered it the most poetic ballade. It has a deeper emotional content than any of the others.

Études

Op. 10 (12) & Op. 25 (12)

Chopin's études were youthful works, written between 1828 and 1833. Liszt wrote about them: "These compositions, which have been given such a modest name, are none the less perfect in their genre, which Chopin himself created and gave his mark to, as he stamped all his works with his poetic genius."

Several of the études were later given names such as the "Black Keys" (Op. 10, No. 5), the "Revolutionary" (Op. 10, No. 12), the "Butterfly Wings" (Op. 25, No. 9), and the "Winter Wind" (Op. 25, No. 11).

Op. 10, No. 3 in E Major

This is probably the most beautiful étude ever written. The German pianist and composer Theodor Kullak called it "a wondrously beautiful tone poem, more of a nocturne than an étude". According to his pupil Adolph Gutmann, Chopin himself said that he had never created a more beautiful melody.

Op. 25, No. 7 in C-sharp Minor

This étude has the title "Duo" and has been interpreted as a dramatic scene. Many literary explanations of it have been offered.

Op. 25, Nos. 11 & 12

These études are called the "Winter Wind" and the "Ocean". Both names indicate the elemental strength of the études, but the descriptive element must not be allowed to conceal their perfection as absolute music.

Weinstock describes these last études of Op. 25 as mighty tone poems and notes their masculinity. In his opinion, they alone would have sufficed to establish Chopin as a great composer.

Mazurkas

These are based on the old Polish dance, the mazur, from Mazovia. Chopin often introduced characteristic features from folk music into them. It is said that

Chopin never played a mazurka twice in the same way. A music critic who heard Chopin play in London said: "The mazurkas lose half their meaning if they are played without a certain freedom and capriciousness. They are impossible to imitate, but they are irresistible if the pianist is at one with the music." Professor Kenneth Kleszynski wrote that all 58 mazurkas are almost without exception masterpieces. Listen to Op. 41-2 & 3/ Op. 50-2/ Op. 56-1/ Op. 63 – 1 & 2/ Op. 67– 1 & 4/ Op. 68 – 1, 2, 3.

Nocturnes

In the early part of the 18th century, "notorno" was already known as a title of instrumental pieces played in the evenings in the open air.

Chopin took for his model the nocturnes of the Irish composer John Field, who had created what we mean today by a nocturne – a slow piece with a simple melodic line, often richly ornamented. The melody is often repeated after a more developed middle section.

Chopin retained Field's form, but furnished his melodies with refined ornamentation and surprising harmonies which raise his compositions well above those of his predecessor. Indeed, Chopin's 20 nocturnes had seemed completely revolutionary to some of his contemporaries.

Nocturne Op. 9, No. 2 in E-flat
Chopin often played this work and it has always been one of the most popular nocturnes.

Nocturne Op. 15, No. 2 in F-sharp
This is notable for its poetic mood, its original melody and its Italian cantabile ornamentation.

Nocturne Op. 27, No. 1 in C-sharp Minor
This is considered by many to be Chopin's finest nocturne – even as his greatest composition.

Nocturne Op. 27, No. 2 in D-flat
One of the most frequently played nocturnes, this is excellently suited for displaying a virtuoso technique.

Nocturne Op. 38, No. 1 in C Minor
One of Chopin's most important compositions, it is described by James Huneker, the American music writer and critic, as "a miniature music drama". Huneker also pointed out its heroic quality and that it is free from mawkishness, being "Chopin of the mode masculine".

Polonaises
Among 13 of these was one with orchestra with the title "Andante Spianato", Op. 22.

Polonaise, Op. 40, No. 1 in A – "Military"
There is the story that one evening Chopin was so moved when he was playing this that he imagined he saw a procession of Polish noblemen and ladies advance into the room to the rhythm of the polonaise. The vision was so life-like that he ran from the apartment in terror and dared not return that night.

Polonaise, Op. 53, No. 6 in A-flat – "Heroic"
It is more often referred to as the "Heroic" polonaise. Chopin's pupil Adolph Gutmann made the point that "Chopin did not thunder this polonaise in the way we are used to hearing it played. In the famous passage in octaves he began pianissimo and continued without much increasing the volume. Chopin never hammered."

Préludes, Op. 28
Chopin intended to create in his préludes something corresponding to Bach's "Well-Tempered Clavier", a series of piano pieces in all keys. Though many of these 24 pieces are very slight, they cover a wide range of feelings. Rubinstein called them "the pearls among Chopin's works" and biographer James Huneker said: "If all of Chopin were to be destroyed, I would pray to keep the préludes."

The best known of the préludes is No. 15 in D-flat ("the Raindrop"). The last prélude, No. 24 in D Minor, is fiercely passionate and in some ways a pendant to the Revolutionary Étude.

Rhythm of the polonaise

Scherzos

The 4 scherzos are among Chopin's finest compositions. Huneker claimed that from them alone the real Chopin, the inner Chopin, could be re-constructed. Unlike most scherzos, they are not jocular or humorous, but intensely dramatic.

Scherzo No. 1 in B Minor, Op. 20

It begins with a couple of dissonant chords. The middle portion is based on a Polish Christmas carol "Sleep child Jesus".

Scherzo No. 2 in B-flat Minor, Op. 31

This is the most frequently played scherzo. The beginning, according to Chopin represents a question and answer. It is more perfect in form than the B Minor and just as passionate. As a critic declared, "Chopin never loses his equilibrium; he never allows passion to decay into realism."

Scherzo No. 3 in C-sharp Minor, Op. 39

This one is in keeping with the spirit of the earlier two scherzos. A chord for the left hand in the sixth bar stands out "like a prize-fighter's fist which could knock a hole in a table"!

Scherzo No. 4 in E, Op. 54

It is more truly a scherzo than the three earlier ones. "It has tripping lightness and there is sunshine imprisoned behind its bars," according to one description.

Waltzes

Some of Chopin's waltzes were composed under personal impulse. For example, Waltz Op. 70, No. 3 in D-flat was composed by Chopin on a morning in October 1829 "while thinking of Constantia Gladkowska". Another Waltz, Op. 69, No. 2 in B Minor was presented on September 24, 1835 as a parting gift to Maria Wodzinska, to whom Chopin had been engaged but whose family opposed the marriage. Of the 14 waltzes, the three forming Op. 34 have been given the title "Valses Brillantes", and one, Op. 18, the title "Grande Valse Brillante". The last is pure dance music and clearly intended to make people want to dance. Huneker calls Op. 64, No. 2 in C-sharp Minor "the most poetic of them all".

Sonata No. 2 in B-flat Minor, Op. 35

This sonata is Chopin's outstanding large work. It contains one of music's most famous funeral marches.

It is said that the starting point of the composition was apparently the "Funeral March" and that the other three movements were written by Chopin to accompany it. This explains the relationship between the elegiac sostenuto (a sustained elegy) and the *scherzo*'s *più lento* on the one hand and the trio section of the "Funeral March" on the other. At the end there comes the quick, spectral last movement – "night wind over graves" as Rubinstein called it.

> " *In all the music that Chopin wrote there is the stamp of artistic sincerity. He wrote music as he felt it, and every bar had obviously made his own nerves tingle.* "

Piano Concertos

No. 1 in E Minor, Op. 11

This concerto is really No. 2, but was published first. It was composed in 1830 and performed for the first time, with Chopin at the piano, in the same year in Warsaw. The performance was a great

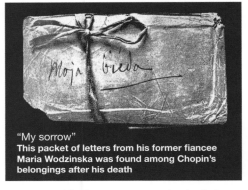

"My sorrow"
This packet of letters from his former fiancee Maria Wodzinska was found among Chopin's belongings after his death

success, with the composer-pianist being called back four times.

In the letter that Chopin wrote to a friend, he particularly mentioned the slow movement which has a romantically dreamy and melancholy character. It was meant to reproduce one's impressions when gazing out over a landscape that evokes beautiful memories – like a glorious moonlit night in the spring.

No. 2 in F Minor, Op. 21

This was really Chopin's first concerto composed in 1829. The concerto is not Chopin at his best, but it is still considered superior to the E Minor.

The first movement is vigorous, rich in melody and ideas, while the second movement is based mainly on a very poetic nocturne theme, embroidered with arabesques in the solo parts. While composing the *larghetto*, Chopin's thoughts were on Constantia Gladkowska with whom he was in love for several years. But he never dared to confess his love. The concerto was later dedicated to Countess Delphine Potocka, Chopin's other love.

JOHANN
STRAUSS II

Born : Vienna, Austria, October 25, 1825
Died : Vienna, Austria, June 3, 1899

*J*ohann Strauss II ("the Younger") was popularly known as the "Waltz King". But Johann's father (1804-49), also named Johann, was no less a waltz king of his time. A whole generation had danced to his melodies and applauded his band when he toured Europe. His three sons (Johann, Josef and Eduard) were all intensely musical and wrote very many waltzes, polkas, galops and marches, not forgetting some highly regarded operettas. The developing talent and initiation of his eldest son, Johann – who composed his first waltz at the age of 6 – however, aroused his jealousy.

In 1844, when Johann was 19, matters came to a head. The young man had quit his father's dance band and been engaged by Dommayer's Casino in Vienna to play for its fashionable patrons. All Vienna turned out to see, hear and dance to the heady music of Johann Strauss Junior.

Papa Strauss, having done everything in his power to prevent his son from getting the job, sent a faithful friend to the ballroom at Dommayer's on Johann's opening night, with instructions to hiss. But when the handsome young man appeared, leading the band gracefully not only in his own waltzes but also his father's, and when the cheering crowd hoisted him on their shoulders and carried him in triumph around the room, what could the faithful friend do but join in the applause! Father and son were later reconciled.

Johann (Junior) formed his own band. He played the violin facing the audience, while the band played his dreamy waltzes for the court balls. The waltzes "Blue Danube", "Artist's Life", "Vienna Woods", "Roses from the South", "Wine, Women and Song" were all written to be danced to, but they also made delectable listening. Those few who had not been swept off their feet by the waltz craze found themselves waltzing internally to the vivacious rhythms and lilting melodies of those Strauss pieces.

Major compositions

Operettas (16)
Die Fledermaus (The Bat), 3 Acts (1874)
Der Zigeunerbaron
 (The Gypsy Baron) (1885)

Instrumental
Perpetuum Mobile

Orchestral
(Over 480 waltzes, polkas, galops, marches)

Polkas
Annen Polka, Op. 117
Pizzicato Polka, Op. 449
Tik-Tak Polka, Op. 365
Tritsch-Tratsch Polka, Op. 214

Waltzes
Tales from the Vienna Woods, Op. 325
Wine, Women and Song, Op. 333
Roses from the South, Op. 388
Accelerationen, Op. 234
Blue Danube, Op. 312
Voices of Spring, Op. 470
Morning Papers, Op. 279
Emperor Waltz, Op. 437
Artist's Life, Op. 316

It has been said of Johann Strauss II that he elevated music from a ballroom dance to the status of a virtual symphonic poem. The Waltz King, with his unquestioned fame, was naturally expected to tour. For 30 years, beginning in 1856, Strauss not only successfully travelled all over Europe but also enjoyed conspicuous success in England and the United States. He was a great favourite in Russia too where all his concerts were attended by the Tsar (Alexandr II) who hailed him as Austria's most successful ambassador. Strauss's Golden Jubilee in 1875 was celebrated in Vienna with tributes from all over the world.

Strauss married three times. His first wife died young and the second relationship ended in a divorce on grounds of musical incompatibility. His third marriage, in 1887, was to Adele Deutsch, who encouraged his talent. They were together until his death when he was 74 years young, his heart beating in three-quarter time until the very end.

"When he died," said music critic and author Louis Biancolli, "something of Vienna died with him. For in all his music he hymned the enchantments of his immortal city for all time."

Strauss with Brahms
Though a composer of light music, Strauss won the admiration and friendship of several serious composers for his melodic genius and great musical intelligence

Adele Strauss, Brahms inscribed the opening measures of the "Blue Danube Waltz", and underneath added the words: "Unfortunately not composed by Johannes Brahms."

Like Franz Schubert, Strauss the Younger composed music with incredible ease. Melodies poured out of him as from an inexhaustible spring.

All Strauss waltzes fit a basic pattern, a slow introduction followed usually by five waltz sections, and finish with a coda that re-introduces the main waltz tunes in a continuous sequence, creating a sense of quickening musical pace. It was a format that every composer would use to good effect but Strauss's best waltzes were more poised and better orchestrated by finely balanced rhythmic combinations, and his melodies simply more graceful than those of anyone else. They captured the particular mood of 19th-century Vienna with its gaiety, sophistication and hedonism.

Strauss's place in music history

Strauss lifted light music, and the waltz in particular, to an incomparably higher plane. His music was still "light music", but so elegant in form, so charmingly melodious, so lively, fresh and at the same time simple and fine in rhythm and harmony, that he not only captured the general public, but also won the ungrudging admiration of serious composers.

Johann the Younger had his rivals too: the waltz composers Ziehrer, Waldteufel and the operatic Jacques Offenbach in France.

Wagner called Strauss "the most musical brain I have ever met". The great Brahms was an equally staunch admirer of Strauss. Asked for an autograph by

JOHANNES
BRAHMS

Born : Hamburg, Germany, May 7, 1833
Died : Vienna, Austria, April 3, 1897

Brahms's father Johann Jakob, although earning a meagre livelihood as horn player and double bassist with the Hamburg State Theatre Orchestra, made it a point to educate his son in music from his earliest years. The young Johannes Brahms learnt everything that his father could teach him about the violin and cello, and also took lessons separately in piano and composition from other teachers.

He took his instruction in music seriously, practised diligently and covered reams of paper in exercises in harmony and counterpoint. Bach and Beethoven were the two composers on whom he sought to model his ongoing course in music.

When he was 14, Brahms appeared in a public concert where he played compositions by Bach and Beethoven, as also a set of variations of his own.

A happy opening in Brahms's life was his decision to go on tour in 1853 as an accompanist to Eduard Reményi, a renowned Hungarian violinist. With Reményi, Brahms wandered from town to town in Germany. In the course of their tours Reményi took Brahms to visit the famous violinist Joseph Joachim in Hanover. Joachim so strongly approved of Brahms's compositions that, unasked, he gave him letters of recommendation to Franz Liszt in Weimar and to Robert Schumann in Düsseldorf.

Brahms was warmly received by Schumann, who was captivated by the novelty of Brahms's music. Schumann called him "the coming man" and "the young eagle" and wrote a long article titled *Neue Bahnen* (New Paths), about Brahms in the magazine *Neue Zeitschrift für Musik*, which made the young performer and composer known all over Germany.

Brahms's meeting with Schumann was a major turning point in his life. It heralded the foundation of a three-way mutual admiration society consisting of Schumann, his wife Clara and Brahms.

Schumann hailed Brahms as a musical prophet, the like of whom he had never heard before. Clara, one of the finest pianists of the day, played Brahms's piano works better than he did himself and brought them to public notice in the many cities she visited on her extensive tours. When Schumann died in July 1856, it was the 23-year-old Brahms that Clara turned to for comfort. They remained lifelong friends. So close was the relationship between Clara and Brahms, 14 years her junior, that biographers believe Brahms remained a bachelor because of it.

From 1854 to 1858, Brahms lived in Detmold, in the principality of Lippe, where he was court music teacher and conductor. At 29, he went to Vienna to conduct the Singakademie. He wrote some fine choral works for this group, but resigned after a year. Next, he took up an engagement with the Gesellschaft der Musikfreunde (Society of Friends of Music) in Vienna for three years.

Brahms knew he was at his best when he was working alone at a leisurely pace in his simple bachelor quarters. He was a painstaking composer who reworked his pieces again and again before he pronounced them satisfactory.

His years in Vienna from 1874 to 1897 were marked by great compositions. His output comprised four symphonies, works for orchestra including the "Academic Festival Overture" and the "Tragic Overture", choral works including the "German Requiem", numerous motets, canons and vocal ensembles, 230 songs of unique beauty, two concertos for piano, a concerto for violin and a double concerto for violin and cello, much chamber music and pieces for a variety of instruments, especially the piano.

Brahms was awed by the symphonic masterpieces of Beethoven and uncertain about producing examples of his own.

He took five years over his first piano concerto. In 1876 he completed his First Symphony, 14 years after he began it. With its broad, abstract Classical form, its emotional progression from tragedy to triumph and the nobility of its hymn-like finale theme, it was quickly dubbed "Beethoven's Tenth" by the famed German conductor Hans von Bülow.

As he stood bare-headed and grief stricken at the funeral of his dear friend Clara Schumann, Brahms, then suffering from cancer, caught a chill. A few months after, on April 3, 1897, he followed her to the grave.

Brahms's place in music history

Brahms has often been spoken of as the Third Big "B" of Classical Music, the other two being Bach and Beethoven. That classification is certainly not without merit for his works are among the most consistent of any composer. His meticulous, self-critical approach never allowed publication of any of his works which he deemed less than excellent.

Brahms created Classical music structures in a Romantic age. Form was no handicap to him. He is the best proof of the truth of Schumann's saying that form really gives freedom – it is a restriction that inspires.

In contrast to the tendency of the age, Brahms loved polyphony and used all its possibilities in masterly fashion. He refused to dazzle listeners with fine orchestral sounds in the way contemporary taste demanded. In spite of all this, Brahms was not anti-Romantic. The underlying spirit of his music is Romantic. His compositions are noted

Brahms's birthplace at Hamburg
A reserved boy living in a world of his own imagination, Brahms had a childhood shadowed by poverty. At an early age he had to earn his living by playing dance music at cheap cafés

Major compositions

Orchestral
Serenade No. 1 in D Major, Op. 11
Serenade No. 2 in A Major, Op. 16

Symphonies (4)
No. 1, C Minor, Op. 68 (1876)
No. 2, D Major, Op. 73 (1877)
No. 3, F Major, Op. 90 (1883)
No. 4, E Minor, Op. 98 (1884-85)

Piano
3 Sonatas
2 Ballades
17 Intermezzos
3 Rhapsodies
2 Variations
16 Waltzes
21 Hungarian Dances (for four hands)
Capriccio in B Minor, Op. 76, No. 2

Overtures
Academic Festival, Op. 80
Tragic, Op. 81

Piano Concertos (2)
No. 1, D Minor, Op. 15
No. 2, B-flat Major, Op. 83

Violin Concertos
D Major, Op. 77
Double Concerto for violin,
  cello and orchestra in A Minor, Op. 102

Chamber Music
Quintet for clarinet and strings
  in B Minor, Op. 115
Quintet for piano and strings
  in F Minor, Op. 34
3 Quartets for piano and strings
3 Trios for pianoforte, violin and cello
Trio for piano, violin and horn, Op. 40
Trio for piano, clarinet and cello
  in A Minor, Op. 114

Strings
Sextet, No. 2, G Major, Op. 36 (1864-65)
2 Quintets (1882-90)
3 Quartets (1859-75)

Violin and Piano Sonatas
No. 1, G Major, Op. 78 (1878-79)
No. 2, A Major, Op. 100 (1886)
No. 3, D Minor, Op. 108 (1886-88)
Sonatensatz, C Minor (1853)

Cello and Piano Sonata
No. 1, E Minor, Op. 38 (1862-65)

Vocal
Alto Rhapsody, Op. 53
  (alto, male choir and orch.) 1869
German Requiem, Op. 45 (1861-67)
Liebeslieder Walzer (Op. 52)
  (pianoforte duet, vocal quartet) (1868-69)
Wiegenlied, Op. 49, No. 4 ("The Lullaby")
Gypsy Songs (Zigeunerlieder),
  Op. 103 (1887)

for their rich textures resulting from a dense fabric of interwoven melodies. This gives his music an emotional depth quite different from the passionate intensity of Tchaikovsky. For example, in the Clarinet Quintet he beautifully conveys a sense of autumnal melancholy. Apart from his great orchestral music, his concertos for various instruments, his heart-felt chamber music and masses of works for the piano, Brahms also wrote over 250 songs, many of which were deeply poetic, simple and inspired by folk verses.

Notes on select works
Symphony No. 1, C Minor, Op. 68

Brahms's contemporary, the iconic conductor Hans von Bülow, is said to have called this symphony "the Tenth", regarding it as a continuation and development of Beethoven's Ninth. It is the broad cantabile theme of the finale that approaches the "Freude" theme in Beethoven's Ninth.

The first movement, *allegro,* opens with a slow and intense introduction, with a rhythmic throbbing pulse and a harmonic flight. This is the germ of the musical material on which the whole movement is based.

The second movement, *andante sostenuto,* is a perfectly lyrical movement which reminds one of the poetic song writer Brahms. The beautiful instrumentation is peculiar as Brahms for once uses the solo violin.

The third movement, *un poco allegretto e grazioso,* is a graceful and subtle movement in which the chief motifs are borne along by the woodwind and constantly spun round by delicate string figures.

The fourth movement, *adagio, più andante non troppo ma con brio,* has the same tragic note as the introduction to the first movement, but dark clouds are swept away by the entry of the broad cantabile theme. Like Beethoven's C Minor, Brahms also ends with a brilliant C-sharp finale.

Symphony No. 3, F Major, Op. 90

Composed in 1883, its first performance in Vienna was an enormous success. Clara Schumann thought that the symphony was a forest idyll.

The first movement, *allegro con brio,* is introduced by three chords from the wind instruments, which occur again and again through the movement. The top notes of the chords are F - A - F which is the motto and the theme of the symphony – the letters are meant to stand for Brahms's maxim "*Frei aber froh*" (free but happy). The clouds pass over to a violin melody, which is the main theme of the symphony.

The second movement, *andante,* begins with a dialogue between clarinets and deep strings and the lyrical meditative theme seems to have the character of a folk song. The choral contribution of the brasses gives a solemn character to the movement.

The third movement, *poco allegretto,* has an orchestration so sensitive and delicate that it has been called the lightest of all Brahms's symphonic movements. It takes the place of a *scherzo* in the symphony but it is more properly a melancholy romance. The refined rhythm gives the movement a character of its own.

The fourth movement, *allegro,* is dramatic and is based on short themes and constantly changing romantic moods. The main theme, introduced in unison by the strings, is constantly worked up into new rhythmical changes in the course of the movement.

Symphony No. 4, E Minor, Op. 98

At its first performance in 1885 this symphony was a great success. The *scherzo* was repeated and the whole audience rose and paid homage to the composer.

The symphony has been called an "elegiac symphony", a "character symphony" and also "tragic". The composer Walter Niemann said that it was an expression of Brahms's "own tragic perception that as a composer he can never be placed by the side of Beethoven".

In the opinion of Peter Latham, Brahms's English biographer, few movements in sonata form are so closely organised as the first *allegro* of this symphony. The ordering of the diverse

Brahms with Schumann's daughters
He dedicated several songs to his friend's daughters; their mother Clara was the great love of his life

elements so that each fulfils its appointed function in the grand and intricate design is done with such unerring skill that the piece becomes a veritable tour de force of formal construction. "From beginning to end the logic is inexorable, and the amazing knot of imitations, canons and inversions in the development is only the supreme example of an intellectual pressure that never relaxes."

The second movement, *andante moderato,* was compared by the music critic Max Kalbeck to "a plain which had been laid waste like the Campagna in Rome".

The third movement, *allegro giocoso,* is thus described by Latham: "In this *scherzo* the gaiety is of superhuman dimensions, but it also includes other shades of mood."

The fourth movement, *allegro energico e passionato* "occupies a special place in symphonic literature with respect to form as it is written as a passacaglia, that is, a variation movement with 30 variations on an 8-measure bass theme". Musicologist D.F. Tovey has the final word on these wonderful variations by declaring that "one of the greatest orchestral works since Beethoven rushes onward to its tragic close".

Piano Concerto No. 1, D Minor, Op. 15

Composed in 1859, this was Brahms's first instrumental concerto. In respect of the piano technique, this concerto is one of the most difficult in the whole of piano literature. The form is Classical with the usual three movements, but the relationship between the orchestra and the piano is quite novel. The concertos written so far were for the most part compositions designed for virtuoso and bravura performances, in which the orchestra merely accompanied the player. In Brahms's concertos most of the bravura element disappeared and the solo instrument became a part of a symphonic whole. And to such an extent, that this concerto may well be called a "symphony for piano and orchestra".

In the first movement, *maestoso,* the main theme is introduced by the orchestra and then worked up symphonically with the piano. The development goes beyond the framework of a normal concerto movement, but is elevated and powerful.

The second movement, *adagio,* is based on a religious choral theme. According to the theoretician Rudolf Breithaupt, "It is like a suffering, comfort-seeking soul crying to heaven and losing itself in the mysticism of eternity."

The third movement, *allegro non troppo,* with its ardent, rhythmically exact opening theme is not only a pleasing task for a pianist but also a passage full of humour and life.

Piano Concerto No. 2, B-flat Major, Op. 83

This concerto was performed for the first time in November 1881 with Brahms at the piano and Alexander Erkel as conductor. German music critic Eduard Hanslick called it a "symphony with piano obbligato", but others affirmed it is also a "symphony for piano and orchestra". It has four movements and the soloist's part calls for an unusually powerful pianist to keep up with the orchestra.

The first movement, *allegro non troppo,* has the piano begin just after a single horn statement.

The second movement, *allegro appassionato,* has a piano cadenza after

which the orchestra takes up both the themes following a long and detailed development.

The third movement, *andante,* has a peaceful introduction for solo cello and forms a happy contrast to the storm in the second movement.

Alfred von Ehrmann, Brahms's biographer, has described the fourth movement, *allegretto grazioso –* "as gracious as a ballet, as witty as a comedy, as sensitive as a pastoral play, as intoxicating as champagne". Latham avers that "for the sustained lightness and brilliance of this music there is only one model – Mozart".

> " *Brahms created Classical music structures in a Romantic age. His compositions are noted for their rich textures resulting from a dense fabric of interwoven melodies. This gives his music an emotional depth quite different from the passionate intensity of Tchaikovsky.* "

Violin Concerto in D Major, Op. 77

Written in 1878, after detailed consultation with Joseph Joachim, it was performed for the first time in 1879 at the Gewandhaus in Leipzig, with Joachim as soloist and Brahms as conductor. The concerto is considered to be the second greatest violin concerto after that of Beethoven. It has also the unique distinction of having attracted as many as 19 leading violinists, Jascha Heifetz foremost among them, to write their own cadenzas for it.

The main theme of the first movement, *allegro non troppo,* is almost pastoral in mood. It is interrupted by a more energetic and rhythmical figure, which prepares the way for the soloist, who glides into the main theme. Later, the soloist and the orchestra join forces to build up a completely symphonic form.

The second movement, *adagio,* has the woodwind, with the oboe taking up the melody of the very beautiful main theme. This is taken up later by the

solo violin, and developed into freely improvised and richly figured variations.

The third movement, *allegro giocoso, ma non troppo vivace,* is in *rondo* form, permitting the soloist to show his skill. The main theme is marked by folk dance and gypsy rhythms.

Concerto for Violin and Cello in A Minor, Op. 102

The concerto was composed at Lake Thun in Switzerland during the summer of 1887. Brahms took as his model earlier forms of the concerto in which two or more instruments were used in conjunction with an orchestra – such works as Bach's "Concerto for Two Violins", Mozart's "Sinfonia Concertante" and Beethoven's "Triple Concerto for Violin, Cello and Piano". Brahms's choice of solo violin and cello, however, was completely original. The tonal extremes and inherent technical problems involved intrigued Brahms who took it on as a challenge.

The first movement, *allegro,* opens with the bold, tersely stated skeleton

Brahms at the piano
"His piano playing was so tender, so full of fancy, so free, so fiery, that it held me enthralled!" declared violinist Joseph Joachim

Brahms in the garden
of Johann Strauss's home

" *Apart from his great
orchestral music, his concertos
for various instruments, his
heart-felt chamber music and
masses of works for the piano,
Brahms also wrote over 250
songs, many of which were
deeply poetic, simple and
inspired by folk verses.*"

Hungarian Dances

These are compositions for the piano. In four books, they are totally 21 in number and were all written for four hands.

Brahms had always been keenly interested in folk music, especially Hungarian, and typical Magyar features mark several of the *rondo*s in his instrumental concertos and in his chamber music works. It is entirely due to Brahms that these melodies have become "common property". The technical simplicity of the editions for four hands contributed to their popularity. The later editions for two hands were considerably more difficult.

However, in using the title "Hungarian Dances", Brahms was guilty of the same mistake as Liszt. Both confused gypsy melodies with Hungarian melodies.

Brahms's dances are pure gypsy music. True Hungarian folk music was brought to light for the first time in the 20th century by Béla Bartók and Zoltán Kodály.

themes continue to provide material for dialogue between soloists and orchestra.

In the second movement, *andante,* sentiment is unconcealed, which Niemann called "a grand ballade steeped in the rich mysterious tone of a northern evening atmosphere". It opens with a two-note motif before introducing the broad main melody in the two solo parts and the orchestral strings. The middle section contains two new melodies: the first for the woodwinds, the second a dialogue between the soloists.

The final movement, *vivace non troppo,* is one of Brahms's Hungarian-flavoured *rondo*s, filled with earthy good humour and almost demoniacal vigour. The basic *rondo* theme is stated first by the cello and then by the violin. Later, by way of contrast, are pages of tenderness and great warmth. The concerto concludes with a "disguised" version of the opening theme.

of the main subject before the cello inaugurates its own vigorous role with an impassioned and unaccompanied recitative. The woodwinds follow with a second subject, leading to a brief violin recitative. The solo cello then re-enters, building an unaccompanied duet with the violin to a powerful and sonorous climax. Throughout the course of the movement the bold rhythms and dark colours of the

EDVARD **GRIEG**

Born : Bergen, Norway, June 15, 1843
Died : Bergen, Norway, September 4, 1907

Edvard Grieg was fortunate in having a mother who was an accomplished pianist and who started teaching her son the piano when he was 6 years old. From his early years Edvard listened with interest to his mother playing Mozart and Chopin, among other composers.

He was 15 years old when Ole Bull, a famous Norwegian violinist and a family friend, visited the family. Grieg's parents showed him some of their son's efforts at composition. Ole Bull was impressed and strongly advised Grieg's parents to permit their son to become a musician.

Grieg joined the Conservatory at Leipzig in Germany and worked so hard that he suffered a nervous breakdown. This, complicated by pleurisy, left him with only one functioning lung.

In 1862, Grieg returned from Leipzig to Norway and in the following year travelled to Copenhagen in Denmark, to begin his career as a pianist. There he met his cousin and future wife, Nina Hagerup.

In Copenhagen, where he lived for three years, Grieg met many musicians, among them the Dane, Nils Gade, and his nationalist compatriot Rikard Nordraak. From Nordraak, especially, Grieg learned to think in terms of national music based on folk songs. With him, Grieg founded the Euterpe Society, whose members were pledged to promote Norwegian music.

Grieg's married life was happy and Nina, who had a beautiful voice, sang his songs enchantingly in the many concert tours which she made with her husband all over Europe. Grieg's wonderful range of pieces for the piano, which he himself played, also made their concerts a delight for audiences. He was 23 years old and flushed with happiness in his first year of marriage when he composed his "Piano Concerto in A Minor". It is his best-known work described as being full of "a joy of life, amorous longing and youthful fire".

Major compositions

Incidental Music
Peer Gynt (1874-75)
Solveig's Cradle Song
Solveig's Sunshine Song

Orchestral
Piano Concerto in A Minor, Op. 16 (1868)
Peer Gynt Suites Nos. 1 & 2
  No. 1, Op. 46 (1888)
  (Highlights: Morning Mood, The Death
  of Aase, Anitra's Dance, In the Hall of the
  Mountain King)
  No. 2, Op. 55 (1891)
  (Highlights: Ingrid's Lament, Arabian
  Dance, Peer Gynt's Return, Solveig's Song)
4 Norwegian Dances, Op. 35 (1881)
  No. 1, D Minor,
  No. 2, A Minor,
  No. 4, D Major
4 Symphonic Dances, Op. 64 (1898)
Elegiac Melodies, Op. 34 (1880-81)
  Heart's Wounds, Spring
Holberg Suite (for strings), Op. 40 (1884)
2 Norwegian Melodies,
  Op. 53 – The First Meeting
Lyric Suite, Op. 54 (1891)
  Shepherd's Boy, Norwegian Peasants
  March, Nocturne, March of the Dwarfs

Chamber Music
String Quartet, G Minor, Op. 27 – Romance

Sonatas (Violin and Pianoforte)
No. 2, G Major, Op. 13 (1867)
No. 3, C Minor, Op. 45 (1887)
Sonata (cello and pianoforte),
  A Minor, Op. 36

Piano
Pictures of Folk Life, Op. 19 (1872)
  – Bridal Procession
Ballade, G Minor, Op. 24 (1875)

Songs (Over 150)
A Dream (Bodenstedt), Op. 48, No. 6 (1889)
Eros (Benzon), Op. 70, No. 7 (1900)
The Great White Host (Brorson),
  Op. 30, No. 10
I Love Thee (Hans Anderson),
  Op. 5, No. 3 (1863)
Spring (Vinje), Op. 35, No. 2 (1880)
(The) Swan (Ibsen), Op. 25, No. 2 (1876)
Two Brown Eyes (Hans Anderson),
  Op. 5, No. 1 (1863)
With a Waterlily (Ibsen), Op. 25, No. 4

Lyric Pieces (10 Books)
At the Cradle, Op. 68, No. 5 (1898)
Butterfly, Op. 43, No. 1 – "Papillon" (1886)
Erotik, Op. 43, No. 5 (1886)
Nocturne, Op. 54, No. 3 (1891)
To the Spring, Op. 43, No. 6 (1886)
Wedding Day at Troldhaugen,
  Op. 65, No. 6 (1896)

Grieg with his wife
**Grieg called his wife, who was a talented singer,
"the only true interpreter of my songs".
Their relationship was perfect and Nina's faith in
the genius of her husband was a great support to
him in his early years**

Another commentator found in the fiery concerto much to remind him of Liszt. In fact, when Grieg visited Liszt near Rome in 1870, the latter enjoyed playing the concerto, sight-reading it from the manuscript given him by Grieg. Liszt had fulsome praise for the concerto and advised Grieg to continue writing what came to him naturally and not be intimidated by criticism. The concerto really is a stunning piece which every virtuoso delights in performing.

Soon after the piano concerto, Grieg composed the incidental music for Ibsen's play *Peer Gynt*. Its two suites were very well received both within and beyond Norway, bringing Grieg many honours. It made him a national figure overnight and he received a pension from his Government in recognition of his contribution to Norway's culture. He also received several honours and Honorary Doctor of Music degrees from many countries, including England at Cambridge (1894) and Oxford (1906).

Grieg excelled in composing miniature pieces for piano and his Lyric Pieces were made up of short movements in contrasting moods.

In 1884, Grieg accepted a commission to write music commemorating the bicentennial of the birth of the Norwegian philosopher and playwright Ludvig Holberg. The resulting "Holberg Suite" is a five-movement piece for piano written in the manner of an 18th-century dance suite. Grieg later arranged it for string orchestra in which form the highly lyrical and graceful music soon became popular.

He spent the last years of his life in a charming villa among the hills and lived there happily with Nina. The English composer Delius and Australian, Percy Grainger, besides many other figures well known in the musical world, visited him there.

Grieg died, aged 67, dearly loved and deeply mourned, of exhaustion brought on by his several touring commitments. His ashes were placed in the hewed wall of a cliff that overhung a fjord close to his country home of Troldhaugen, near Bergen.

Grieg's place in music history

Like Schumann and Chopin, Grieg found himself most comfortable in compositions of modest dimensions which he could fill with an atmosphere of intimate feeling; he avoided large forms like the symphony and opera.

It was as a miniaturist that he excelled, and his music was highly individual, nationalist in flavour and universal in its appeal. Grieg also composed more than 150 songs, many of them so charming that they are part of the repertoire of famous singers to this day.

Piano Concerto in A Minor, Op. 16

This concerto is Grieg's best-known work. It was composed when he was 25 years old. The concerto is in the repertoire of every great pianist, not as a vehicle for display but as a beautiful utterance that explores the dramatic and tonal resources of the piano.

The first movement opens with "a long and ominous roll upon the kettle drums followed by a mighty chord in full orchestra. Then a furious descending passage for the piano and the first movement proper begins. The woodwind presents the most important theme of the movement... simple in rhythm and melody but which once heard is impossible to forget or dissociate from this great work. In a moment we hear it given voice to in the crystalline tones of the piano...

"The second section of the movement begins with more thematic material – an exquisitely flowing melody, lyric in character, yet containing within itself elements that are later developed into a furious outburst of passion.

"We hear this song first heard in the restrained voices of the orchestra; then it is given to the piano which makes of it a powerful and dramatic utterance. The formal working out section of the movement now takes form. Novelties of rhythm as well as unforeseen melodic development of the thematic material grow swiftly and surely out of the masses of tone that surge upward from both orchestra and solo instrument. Crashing chords from the piano and emphatic statement of the first theme in the full might of the orchestra's concerted voices brings us to the cadenza, or display passage for the piano. But it is more than a display passage; it is rather a sublimation of what has gone before, presented with the last iota of power and brilliance by the pianist... Underneath its glitter and its mighty chords lies the solid basis of the themes of the movement, and instead of distracting from the thought of the music, the cadenza merely glorifies and clarifies it in a burst of brilliant light.

"The second movement: The sombre feeling that is so often a characteristic of Northern genius is the underlying motive of this movement. But you will not confuse it with the abject melancholy of the Slav, for it is vital and moving; there is sadness, perhaps, but not deadly hopelessness. The melody is of simple lyric character, given to the piano after a somewhat lengthy introduction by the orchestra. There is a distinct feeling of climax, yet not departure from the sombre, almost elegiac character of the movement. With a very brief pause the third movement begins.

"The third movement begins after the dying away of the melodious conclusion of the second. In a moment the entire complexion of the music is altered. A bold passage on the piano ushers in a rhythm of almost violent force, and quaint dancing fingers which at times suggest the grostesquerie of 'The Hall of the Mountain King'. A climax of terrific intensity is reached, the piano ever revealing new influxes of power; new brilliancies, new and vivid colourings. And then once more come the pale Northern harmonies.

"Orchestra and solo instrument presently join again in a mad revel, the occasional dissonances – (Liszt loved them!) – adding spice and piquancy to the music. Mighty descending passages in octaves for the piano introduce a light and dance-like figure which presently involves, one by one, the various sections of the orchestra, and leads to the majestic finale, built not only of the themes of the present movement, but embodying, too, in heroic form, the once lyric song of the second section of the concerto. Mighty chords for piano and full orchestra bring the music to the close."

Grieg's grave
His ashes were buried in a cave hewn into the cliffside at his country home Troldhaugen

ANTONÍN **DVOŘÁK**

Born : Nelahozeves, Bohemia,
   September 8, 1841
Died : Prague, Bohemia, May 1, 1904

The village in which Antonín Dvořák was born and in which he passed his boyhood years, was a pleasant and happy place. His father, an innkeeper, was a jolly person who tinkled a zither to the music of which young village boys and girls danced. Young Dvořák learned to play folk songs on the violin before he started a serious study of music.

By the time he was 16, Dvořák had learned to play the piano, violin and organ so well that his parents permitted him to enter the Organ School in Prague.

Those were difficult times for the young musician and he sustained himself by occasional engagements with a band. For 12 years he had to support himself in whichever way he could. He played in a theatre orchestra for a while. In his humble lodgings, he studied borrowed scores and worked on compositions modelled on those of the great composers. Beethoven and Schubert were his gods.

In 1860 he graduated and that was the turning point in his life. His country, Bohemia (now part of the Czech Republic), had been freed from Austrian rule and along with the composer Bedřich Smetana, Dvořák was fired with the ambition of creating Bohemian national music for a free nation.

His first few compositions did not make an impression, but he persevered. His cantata "Hymnus" and a popular hymn "The Heirs of the White Mountain", both patriotic works, finally won him some recognition. He resigned his theatre job and became organist at St. Adalbert's Church in Prague: the changeover left him more time for composition.

Around this time he married Anna Čermáková, the younger sister of the girl he loved, and lived happily with her. When their little daughter Josefa died, he composed a Piano Trio (G Minor) and the religious cantata, "Stabat Mater", in mournful tribute.

A few months later, Dvořák submitted a set of sprightly and rhythmic dances, the Moravian duets for two voices and piano, for a State competition, and won the first prize (Brahms was one of the judges and became Dvořák's great friend and protector).

The Moravian duets became immensely popular and earned Dvořák a good income. The Slavonic Rhapsodies and Slavonic Dances that followed became equally popular. In these compositions Dvořák captured the spirit of Bohemian folk songs without employing actual folk song melodies; the melodies were his own.

Overnight, Dvořák became famous. Although he was bewildered by this sudden rise to fame and fortune, it did not go to his head. He was born a down-to-earth peasant and he behaved so to the end of his days.

Dvořák's growing fame led him to England and the United States of America. In London, in 1884, he conducted his "Stabat Mater" and other concerts, attracting large audiences. He returned to Prague with his pockets well lined with money.

Although by now he was the busy Director of the Prague Conservatoire, he found time to visit other countries. Everywhere he was honoured as composer, conductor and teacher. And always from his travels abroad he returned happily to Prague like a homing pigeon.

In the United States, which he moved to in 1892, he spent some of his happiest days in Spillville, Iowa, where some of his homesick countrymen had created a Bohemian village. Dvořák played national hymns on the church organ there and spoke in his own language at the village inn. Spillville was an oasis for him in America. Part of his famous "New World" Symphony, which he orchestrated there, was inspired by the Afro-American tunes that his students sang for him. At the first performance, in 1893, of the symphony at Carnegie Hall in New York, Dvořák received a tremendous ovation. From 1892 to 1895, Dvořák was the director of the National Conservatory of Music in New York City, at a then staggering annual salary of $15,000.

During the final years of his life Dvořák acquired a fine collection of honorary degrees and gold medals. In 1897 his great friend Brahms died and Dvořák grieved his loss. Death came to Dvořák as suddenly as had his fame. He was 63 when he died, having lived a full and simple life, of joys mixed with family tragedies.

Dvořák's place in music history

Dvořák is one of the greatest nationalist composers in the history of music. The American music critic Philip Hale has said: "Dvořák's music was best when it smacked of the soil, when he remembered his early days, the strains of vagabond musicians and the dances dear to his folk."

Paul Stefan, the Austrian music historian, called Dvořák "a true musician who seemed to draw directly from the extremely rich treasure of Czech folk music. Everything that he wrote was beautiful in sound and perfect in form."

Dvořák lived life simply despite all the honours that were heaped on him as a composer. This side of his character is to be seen in his music, where there is almost no deep passion or despair. His first aim was harmony and the emotion most notable in his music is joy. The nearest he comes to sorrow is the feeling of homesickness.

Major compositions

Operas
The Devil and Kate
The Jacobin
The Cunning Peasant, Op. 95
Rusalka

Symphonies (9)
No. 9, E Minor, Op. 95 "New World"

Orchestral
Carnival – Overture, Op. 92
Scherzo Capriccioso
Serenade for Strings, Op. 22

Concertos
Cello Concerto, B Minor, Op. 104
Piano Concerto, G Minor, Op. 33
Violin Concerto, A Minor, Op. 53

Songs
10 Biblical Songs, Op. 99
7 Gypsy Songs, Op. 55
  No. 1, My song tells of my love
  No. 4, Songs my mother taught me
The Girl Mowed Grass, Op. 73
The Maiden's Lament, Op. 73, No. 2
Slavonic Dances (16)
  Set I, Op. 46 – 8
  Set II, Op. 72 – 8

String Quartets (14)
Trio, No. 4, E Minor, Op. 90 "Dumky"
Quintet, A Major, Op. 81
  (piano and strings)
Humoresques (8), Op. 101
  (violin and piano)

Notes on select works

Symphony No. 9 in E Minor, Op. 95 – "New World"

This symphony is Dvořák's best-known work, taking its place among symphonies written by other great composers. It was composed in New York in 1893 and first performed on December 15 the same year. Anton Seidl conducted it and the composer was present at the performance.

"The first movement, *adagio, allegro molto,* in its introduction makes use of typical American syncopations in the *allegro* theme. The low strings give out the theme to which flutes and oboes reply, and after a climax of loud chords, in which horns and drums answer the strings, the *allegro molto* begins. The principal subject is stated by horns and woodwinds. The melodic second theme is stated by the flute and is derived from the Negro spiritual 'Swing Low, Sweet Chariot'.

"In the second movement, the *largo*'s principal theme is said to have been inspired by Longfellow's poem *Hiawatha*. The *largo* is one of the most appealing and best known pieces of music in all the literature of the orchestra. Its principal melody is considered one of the most beautiful solos for the cor anglais, or the alto oboe, in all music. The lovely melody is well known as the song 'Goin' Home'.

"The third movement, *scherzo, molto vivace,* contains an animated first subject by flutes and oboes, and then a placid cantabile theme. In the coda, allusion is made to the first subject of the opening movement.

"The fourth movement, *allegro con fuoco,* commences with horns and trumpets announcing a broad and fiery theme after an introduction. It is elaborated and then the clarinets introduce the second subject. Thereafter the first subject is again introduced, as are the main themes of the *largo* and *scherzo.* The coda combines the leading themes of the first and last movements."

Concerto in B Minor for Violincello, Op. 104

Good cello concertos are few in number. Dvořák's is among the best of them. This is an engaging concerto, unmistakably Slavonic, with episodes of dramatic fire.

"The first movement, *allegro,* opens with an orchestral introduction in which the main theme is heard at the start followed by a melodious folk tune. The entrance of the soloist is inscribed *quasi improvisando* and now the themes are taken up again with small scale motifs, which grow to a climax with the final repetition of the main theme.

"The second movement, *adagio ma non troppo,* is built on a three-tune song form. The simple quietly flowing main theme is taken from Dvořák's song, Op. 82, No. 1, and is especially noticeable in the dialogue between the cello and the orchestra at the close of the movement.

"The finale, *allegro moderato,* is a movement with a precise and effective

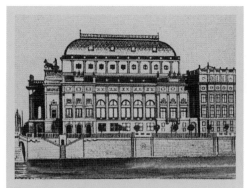

The National Theatre, Prague
The composer Smetana procured Dvořák a position here in his early days

main theme. This movement is like a rejoicing over a forthcoming journey home and brings with it lovely warm themes full of expectation."

Carnival Overture, Op. 92

In this merry composition Dvořák was very definitely Bohemian. In the overture he brought in the wild gypsy rhythms and passionately gay spirits of his native land.

The overture is the second of a suite of three: "Nature", "Life" and "Love".

"A carnival it is, glowing with vivid orchestral colours, and moving swiftly through wayward, wild and syncopated rhythm to a bacchanalian climax. In the very middle, a sober thought is intruded and we come upon one of the loveliest passages in all Dvořák's music. Here solo violin and English horn join in a passage of lyric sweetness, touched with melancholy. Flutes are attracted to this poignant strain... the impatient orchestra in agitation revives the colourful rout and brings presently a whirling, flashing climax of tremendous force."

Scherzo Capriccioso

"A delightful movement exhibiting Dvořák's distinctive and colourful orchestration, and some of the engaging rhythms of the Bohemian music of which he was so fond. The title indicates the light and free character of the music. The horns alone present a leaping figure as introduction; the orchestra puts forward the vigorous main theme.

"There is a particularly lovely passage in swaying waltz rhythm, and sung with intensity of feeling by the violins; and another section in which an English horn solo is conspicuous, reveals again a melody almost as beautiful as that of the slow movement in the 'New World' Symphony. The whole work is full of lovely melody."

EDWARD **ELGAR**

Born : Broadhurst, England, June 2, 1857
Died : Worcester, England,
February 23, 1934

Edward Elgar was born in the beautiful English countryside near Malvern in Worcestershire, which he dearly loved and spent countless hours exploring. He was one of seven siblings. His mother selected and read the best of English literature to the children. He received little formal education and left school at the age of 15.

His father owned a music business in the City of London. Young Elgar helped him in the shop selling musical instruments. His father was an organist at the local church and Elgar soon learned to play the organ from him. He showed an early aptitude for music. By spending hours in the family's music shop, Elgar taught himself how to play the violin, cello, double bass, bassoon, trombone and piano. He often participated in the musical activities of neighbouring Worcester.

When he was 23, Elgar composed "Salut d'Amour", which attracted much local attention. A series of cantatas and oratorios followed, but it was with the "Enigma Variations", one of his greatest works, that he really became well known.

The "Enigma Variations", dedicated to friends, is a brilliant orchestral composition in which 13 friends and the composer himself are characterised, one Variation to each person. Guessing which friend was whose Variation became an agreeable game at Victorian dinner parties.

By this time Elgar was 42 and had been married for 10 years to Caroline Roberts, daughter of a senior army officer. With his wife's encouragement, Elgar composed much music. Indeed, the story of Elgar's music is the story of his gradual building up of self-confidence. It was not until he married that he gathered the courage to unflinchingly face public criticism of his compositions. The understanding, encouragement and sure taste of his wife were valuable contributions to Elgar's maturity in holding his own.

Elgar at his home in Worcestershire where he composed his greatest works

Elgar's huge oratorio "The Dream of Gerontius", based on Cardinal Newman's long poem, did not make much of an impression in England and America but was very well received and appreciated in Germany where Elgar received special personal praise from Richard Strauss.

The oratorio was followed by six "Pomp and Circumstance Marches" (which included "Land of Hope and Glory" that rivalled the popularity of "God Save the King"), and "In the South" and "Cockaigne" overtures. These compositions were followed by "Introduction and Allegro" for string orchestra, the lovely violin concerto, the cello concerto and two symphonies.

With this spate of mature compositions came the honours. There were doctorates from Cambridge and Oxford as well as from Yale. Elgar was knighted at the coronation of Edward VII and a Chair of Music was created for him at Birmingham University. He became Master of the King's Musick in 1924, and was awarded the Order of Merit and given a Baronetcy in 1931.

After Lady Elgar's death, he stopped composing music. Gradually, he withdrew from public life. He died on February 23, 1934 in a nursing home after a long illness.

Elgar's place in music history

Elgar initiated a new epoch in British music. Not since the death of William Boyce (1720-79) had Britain produced a serious composer whose works were capable of standing comparison with even the minor compositions of the great composers of Germany, France and Italy. Elgar proved that England was after all a musical nation. He was a "nationalist" composer through and through by grace and not by adoption of folk song.

Hailed as the most British of all British composers, Elgar loved Brahms, Schumann and Wagner, whose slight influence was noticed in his earlier works. But he was a distinctive and original creator with his brilliant orchestration, exquisite harmony and typically English melodies. In many of his works we hear subdued echoes of the English landscape that he loved so much. Elgar believed in music education to create listeners, not merely performers. He therefore believed in radio and recordings, new to his generation, as aids to musical education.

Major compositions

Symphonies
No. 1, A-flat Major, Op. 55
No. 2, E-flat Major, Op. 63

Concertos
Violin Concerto, B Minor, Op. 61
Cello Concerto, E Minor, Op. 85

Orchestral
Bavarian Dances (3), Op. 27
Enigma Variations, Op. 36
Falstaff: Symphonic Study, Op. 68
Cockaigne Overture, Op. 40
Introduction and Allegro, Op. 47 (Strings)
Imperial March, Op. 32
Serenade in E Minor, Op. 20 (Strings)
Pomp and Circumstance, Op. 39 (Marches)
    No. 1, D Major "Land of Hope and Glory"
    No. 2, A Minor
    No. 3, C Minor
    No. 4, G Major "Song of Liberty"

Chamber Music
Salut d'Amour, Op. 12
  (in various arrangements)
Adieu (pianoforte, violin and pianoforte)
La Capricieuse, Op. 17
  (violin and pianoforte)
Serenade (pianoforte, violin and pianoforte)

Vocal
Dream of Gerontius: Oratorio, Op. 38,
  No. 6 "Land of Hope and Glory"
The Apostles: Oratorio, Op. 49
Caractacus, Op. 35,
Cantata: Coronation Ode, Op. 44

Notes on select works

Enigma Variations

This music has exercised a fascination more through its puzzling qualities than for any intrinsic value – which is not to say that it has none. On the contrary, the theme and variations are most engaging and worked out with a scholarly detail and finish characteristic of Elgar's best work. When, however, a composer poses a problem like this, it is but natural that his friends and admirers should try to guess the answers. But no one has completely solved Elgar's several indicated riddles.

"Enigma Variations" was performed for the first time in London under the direction of Hans Richter in 1899. It was the first contemporary English work and appealed greatly to the distinguished conductor. When he arrived in England from Germany to give a series of concerts, he was happy to be able to offer a native work of definitely outstanding musical value – a rare thing from the Continental point of view. Richter's brilliantly conducted performances of the Variations had much to do with establishing Elgar in English minds as a great musician.

"There is a basic theme called the 'Enigma' by Elgar himself and a set of 14 Variations. The composer desired that the work should be regarded as absolute music, without regard to the significance of the Variations – to which, nevertheless, he added the initials of certain friends, 'not necessarily musicians'. He wrote: 'The Enigma I will not explain – its dark saying must be left unguessed, and I warn you that the apparent connection between the Variations and the Theme is often of the slightest texture; further, through and over the whole set another and larger theme "goes", but it is not played.'

"This is something of a poser, but good guessers insist on exercising their peculiar gifts and several of the Variations have been identified with reasonable certainty. These are: the first, which is headed by the initials of Lady Elgar; the ninth, entitled 'Nimrod', suggests August Jaeger (German for hunter) who was a champion of Elgar's music; the eleventh, bears the initials of George Robertson Sinclair, organist of Hereford Cathedral and a friend of the composer.

"The main theme with which the music begins is of a sturdy and significant character, but in the Variations it is modified to fit the personality Elgar had in mind in each case. It is evident from the lighter and gentler mood of the music at times, that certain of the 14 friends are women."

> " *Elgar believed in music education to create listeners, not merely performers. He therefore believed in radio and recordings, new to his generation, as aids to musical education.* "

Symphony No. 1 in A-flat, Op. 55

Elgar spent several years planning and writing this symphony. It was finally completed in 1908 and played at Manchester, England, in December that year under the direction of Hans Richter, to whom it is dedicated. It created a furore and was performed over 100 times during the next 12 months.

The composer said of this symphony: "It is written out of a full life experience and is meant to include the innumerable phases of joy and sorrow, struggle and conquest, and especially between the ideal and actual life."

The first movement, *andante nobilmente e semplice,* has been called "the British Empire in music". A theme of noble simplicity appears in the introduction, gradually imposing itself on other contrasting, more exuberant and more agitated ideas. It reappears throughout the other movements, either fragmentarily or in more complete statements, and reaches a grandiose apotheosis in the finale. The mood of the symphony is sombre and introspective but powerful, and it reaches stirring emotional depths in the third movement *(andante)*.

Symphony No. 2 in E-flat, Op. 63

Elgar dedicated this symphony to the memory of King Edward VII and it was first performed in London in May 1911.

The symphony begins on a note of despair, the mood quickly lightens, breaking into sheer joyousness in the *rondo* of the third movement, and concluding on a serene note of triumph and optimism. The symphony as a whole is characterised by great clarity and directness of expression. The general impression of the symphony is purely one of spontaneous gaiety.

This atmosphere is common to each of the four movements. The second movement is a noble funeral march.

Violin Concerto in B Minor, Op. 61

The fly-leaf of the published score of this concerto bears the Spanish motto *"Aqui esta encerrada el alma de..."* (Here is enshrined the soul of...) indicating the wealth of personal feeling that Elgar expressed in the work. It is a reflection of his most intimate moods, ponderings and reveries. It is the only concerto by an English composer to have become an accepted item in the international repertory of violin music.

The concerto is dedicated to Fritz Kreisler and there was great excitement in the music world when it was played in London for the first time in November 1910, with Kreisler as soloist and the composer conducting. Later, Yehudi Menuhin made the concerto his own, as it were, and gave many performances of it. There is a historical recording of the concerto with a young Menuhin and the composer conducting at his advanced age.

"The first movement begins with passages for full orchestra in which several themes are announced and developed. Four distinct motives linked together, each having its particular sphere of activity, spring from the first subject. Then the broad singing melody, which, in its fuller development becomes the second theme, is softly hinted at by strings and wind choir in lower register. Gradually the phrase is brought forward in tender comment of woodwinds and strings. The orchestra then dwells principally upon the opening motives until a sustained tone for horn provides a background for the entrance of the solo instrument. It is a quiet entrance, but one of gripping beauty and warmth. As the music progresses, the theme becomes more

and more animated and colourful. The motives of the first subject are carefully developed, after which the lovely second subject is fully commented upon in passionate tenderness. The treatment of the material already stated holds the interest throughout the development and recapitulation. A vigorous reference to the opening motive terminates the movement.

"The second movement, *andante*, is in the key of B-flat Major, and is from beginning to end a poem of contemplation and tenderness. The orchestra states a prayerful theme. The solo instrument then repeats it, slightly altered, flowing along calmly and meditatively to a middle section which develops a second theme. Here the music acquires more warmth and intensity. Passages of deep tenderness for the solo instrument are matched against a sturdy orchestral background. Then, towards the close of the movement, the music re-establishes the mood of contemplation, dying away in serenity and peace.

"The third movement's animation is strongly contrasted to the quiet of the *andante*. Brilliant passage work for the solo instrument, punctuated by chords for the full orchestra, precede a surging of staccato scales of breathtaking rapidity. These recall the lovely theme of the preceding movement, stated first by the solo instrument and repeated by the orchestra; while the violin wreathes the whole with sparkling triplet figures. Material from the first movement now engrosses orchestra and solo instrument. A scintillating cadenza, which affords the soloist wonderful material for technical and interpretative display, follows. A rather mysterious effect is achieved in the orchestra by a *pizzicato tremolando* given to a portion of the strings. This is obtained by directing the players to drum softly on the strings with the fleshy part of their

fingers. A sustained trill for the soloist and a repetition of the opening motif for the orchestra, which is immediately silenced by the solo instrument, precede the end of the cadenza. Immediately, a vigorous passage in the solo instrument soars over a restatement of the material of the opening; then impressive chords for the violin lead to a short coda."

Fritz Kreisler
Dedicated to the violinist Kreisler, Elgar's is the only violin concerto by an English composer to enjoy acceptance in the international repertory of violin music

Yehudi Menuhin at the age of 12
The child prodigy created history performing Elgar's violin concerto, conducted by the composer himself at an advanced age

> " *Manuel de Falla is firmly established for his*
> *ebullient, rhythmic and lyrical music.*
> *He successfully shaped elements of traditional*
> *Andalusian music and created a colourful*
> *musical style distinctly his own.* "

MANUEL DE **FALLA**

Born : Cadiz, Spain, November 23, 1876
Died : Alta Gracia, Argentina,
November 14, 1946

Manuel de Falla's mother was a concert pianist and she gave him his early start in music. When he was in his teens he entered the Royal College of Music in Madrid, where Felipe Pedrell taught him composition. Pedrell, teacher and scholar, was a frustrated man as he had long laboured to interest people in his research into Spanish folk music with the idea of making it the basis for a national Spanish idiom. Pedrell was happy that Falla shared his enthusiasm for "root music".

Falla trained himself to be a concert pianist but found he was too shy for that career and so preferred to become a composer. His first lyric drama "La Vida Breve" (Life is Short) won him the top prize in 1905 in a competition for pianists at the Madrid Academy of Fine Arts. Shortly after that he won the first prize in a contest open to all pianists in Spain.

He thus found himself established in a dual career of composer and concert pianist. But the struggle to support himself was just beginning. He scrimped and saved for an excursion ticket to Paris. He fell in love with the city and remained there for seven years. Though poor, Falla considered himself rich in the friendship of such men as Claude Debussy, Paul Dukas, Gustave Charpentier and Maurice Ravel who shared his passion for Spanish rhythm and melodic forms.

In Paris, he began the composition of "Nights in the Gardens of Spain", symphonic impressions for piano and orchestra. This composition placed him as the foremost living Spanish composer. His next composition, the ballet-pantomime "El Amor Brujo" (Love the Magician) further enhanced his reputation.

He returned to Madrid after the outbreak of World War I and continued to gather folk songs which provided him a great deal of thematic material. He went to live in solitude and hermitic seclusion in

Granada in 1921. Mme Wanda Landowska was one of the very few friends he admitted to his monastic retreat and to whom he dedicated a beautiful three-movement concerto for harpsichord with chamber ensemble of flute, oboe, clarinet, violin and cello.

In Granada, among many other compositions, Falla wrote a score for a ballet, "El Sombrero de Tres Picos" (The Three-Cornered Hat). He played parts of it on the piano for Serge Diaghilev, the impresario, who commissioned him to make a ballet of it. Compounded of brisk action, uproarious comedy and typically Spanish humour, as well as song and dance, "The Three-Cornered Hat" has since become one of the most popular works in the ballet repertoire. The set design and costumes of its first performance were by Pablo Picasso.

After the outbreak of World War II, Falla left with a devoted sister to make his home in Argentina. Once there he worked on an oratorio, "Atlantida", on

> **" Though poor, Falla considered himself rich in the friendship of such men as Claude Debussy, Paul Dukas, Gustave Charpentier and Maurice Ravel who shared his passion for Spanish rhythm and melodic forms. "**

which he had already spent 10 years. His health was now poor, his means modest and he was homesick. He sank into a state of lassitude, weakness and depression, and died suddenly on November 14, 1946, leaving unfinished his scenic cantata "Atlantida", his most ambitious composition (it was later completed by his pupil Ernesto Halffter). Like his friend Maurice Ravel, Falla never married nor had children. He was known to have yearned for home, but never did return to his native Spain.

Falla's place in music history

*M*anuel de Falla is firmly established for his ebullient, rhythmical and lyrical music. He successfully shaped elements of traditional Andalusian music and created a colourful musical style distinctly his own. Later he re-created the polyphonic modes of the medieval Spanish masters.

Major compositions

El Amor Brujo (Love the Magician)

El Sombrero de Tres Picos (The Three-Cornered Hat)

El Retablo de Maese Pedro (Master Peter's Puppet Show)

La Vida Breve (Life is Short)

Nights in the Gardens of Spain

Harpsichord Concerto

Siete Canciones Populares Españolas (Seven Popular Spanish Songs)

CHARLES CAMILLE
SAINT-SAËNS

Born: Paris, France, October 9, 1835
Died: Algiers, Algeria, December 16, 1921

Charles Camille Saint-Saëns was born in Paris and brought up by his mother. He began music lessons early. By the age of 3 he had already composed his first piano piece. At 7, he began taking lessons in composition and soon gained a reputation in Paris as a child prodigy.

In 1846, at the age of 11, he gave a recital of the piano concertos of Mozart and Beethoven; for an encore he offered to play any one of Beethoven's piano sonatas from memory!

Saint-Saëns entered the Paris Conservatoire in 1848. Over the next five years, his dazzling gifts won both the friendship and patronage of the composers Rossini, Gounod, Liszt and Berlioz.

The 1860s were the peak years of his life. He acquired a formidable reputation as a composer and as a virtuoso pianist. In 1868 he wrote his Piano Concerto No. 2 in just 17 days, for which he received warm praise from Liszt.

Saint-Saëns taught at the École Niedermeyer between 1861 and 1865 and among his pupils was Gabriel Fauré. With like-minded musicians he founded the Société Nationale de Musique, to promote the works of French composers and to hold premières of important works such as those of Debussy and Ravel.

He was a brilliant intellectual whose reading interests were as wide as they were profound. He wrote not only on music and musicians but also on philosophy and literary matters. He was fond of travelling and on his return to Paris would write extensively about his experiences. Whoever met him was charmed by his personality and his conversational ability. He was highly respected and was the recipient of his country's Legion of Honour, among many other awards and degrees that were bestowed upon him in the course of years.

Major compositions

Opera
Samson and Delilah, 3 Acts

Symphonies (4)
No. 3, C Minor, Op. 78 (with organ)

Symphonic Poems
Dance Macabre, Op. 40
Le Rouet d'Omphale
 (Omphale's Spinning Wheel), Op. 31
Carnival of the Animals (orch./2 pianos)

Piano Concertos (5)
No. 2, G Minor, Op. 22 (1868)
No. 4, C Minor, Op. 44 (1875)
No. 5, F Major, Op. 103 "Egyptian" (1896)

Violin Concertos (3)
No. 1, A Major, Op. 20 (1858)
No. 3, B Minor, Op. 61 (1880)

Cello Concertos (2)
No. 1, A Minor, Op. 33 (1872)

Violin and Orch.
Introduction and Rondo Capriccioso,
 Op. 28
Havanaise, Op. 83

Saint-Saëns at the piano

Saint-Saëns's popularity among his colleagues, friends and with people in general, made so many demanding claims on his time that composing music in quiet surroundings, all by himself, was often difficult. He had to often leave Paris for distant places where he could be alone to pursue his work.

According to one account, he made one such trip to the Canary Islands. He went under an assumed name but word soon got around of a mysterious stranger who, under the alias "Sannois", spent the whole day in his room, seated at a table making suspicious marks on large sheets of paper. The police soon heard of this and tried to find out if he was a spy. Saint-Saëns changed his lodgings, but the police followed him and were determined to question him. As they confronted him, a Parisian tourist happened to pass by, looked closely at the composer, and raising his hat said: "Pardon me, you are Monsieur Camille Saint-Saëns, aren't you?" His cover blown and admirers following him on the streets, Saint-Saëns soon returned to Paris.

When he was on a visit to Algeria, the composer took ill and died there, far from home, on December 16, 1921.

Saint-Saëns's place in music history

Saint-Saëns composed prodigiously – piano and organ music; symphonies and symphonic poems; piano, violin and cello concertos; cantatas, oratorios, songs and choral works, and operas. It was a legacy of music that revealed a passion for order, clarity and precision as well as an always attractive and very French melodic charm. He composed with an easy facility, making it somehow seem that his art lacked seriousness and depth. He was and remained on the edge of genius, in a manner of speaking.

His best-known work was his opera "Samson and Delilah". Of his four symphonies, the "Organ" Symphony, No. 3 in C Minor, remains outstanding. His symphonic poems include "Dance Macabre" and "Omphale's Spinning Wheel". He composed three violin concertos, the best known being the third. His first cello concerto is the more prominent of the two that he wrote. Piano concertos No. 2 and 4 are impressive out of the five that he composed; the seductive and brilliant fifth, the "Egyptian", deserves the highest acclaim.

" Saint-Saëns was a brilliant intellectual whose reading interests were as wide as they were profound. He wrote not only on music and musicians but also on philosophy and literary matters. "

Among his orchestral works the "Suite Algérienne" is a very popular piece. His "Carnaval des Animaux" (Carnival of the Animals) was written as a private joke for a Parisian artists' club and Saint-Saëns strictly forbade its performance in public; however one of its sections, "The Swan", was a great hit even then and has remained so to this day.

Saint-Saëns was fond of the violin and wrote very felicitously for it, as evident from his "Introduction and Rondo Capriccioso" and "Havanaise", which are favourite pieces in the repertoires of all violinists.

Scene from "Samson and Delilah", Saint-Saëns's best-known opera

Notes on select works

Cello Concerto No. 1, A Minor, Op. 33

Its movements are:
i. *Allegro non troppo – Animato*
  Allegro molto – Tempo I
ii. *Allegretto con moto*
iii. *Tempo I – Un peu moins vite*
Più allegro comme le premier movement – Molto allegro
The concerto was composed in 1872 and first performed the following year at the Conservatoire by Auguste Tolbècque, a remarkable player. The cello at that time had little concerto repertoire of quality, a gap which Saint-Saëns nobly filled.

It has been said: "The concerto is small in scale and modest in virtuosity. It has great melodic vitality and undying charm. Like many concertos of the 19th century it contracted the standard three-movement form into a continuous single unit. Thus its energetic first movement is shortened only to recur in the final section after an otherworldly interlude suggesting a minuet of distant purity. The scoring here is most delicate and

Saint-Saëns's lifelong devotion to principles of restraint is not the least disturbed by the warmth that the cello can generate in such abundance. It is romantic without being passionate."

Violin Concerto No. 3, B Minor, Op. 61

Its movements are:
i. *Allegro non troppo*
ii. *Andantino quasi allegretto*
iii. *Molto moderato & maestoso –*
Allegra non troppo – Più allegro
Two of Saint-Saëns's three violin concertos were dedicated to the violinist Pablo de Sarasate, who was a close personal friend and did much to form the composer's ideal of the instrument. The concerto was written in 1880.

"In the brilliant opening *allegro* the soloist enters immediately with an impassioned theme of very decided gait; the short second subject (dolce espressivo) with its caressing triplets, has an almost Mendelssohnian sweetness. The *andantino* is a gentle barcarolle, the soloist always dominating, echoed or answered by the woodwind. The finale opens with a dramatic accompanied cadenza leading into the *allegro*. The staccato triplets and dotted rhythms of the first subject belong to the same world as the rondo capriccioso, and the secondary theme – which follows before the appearance of the true second subject – forms an appassionato contrast. In place of the normal development section Saint-Saëns inserts first a pianissimo cantabile chorale and then returns to the cadence, with which the movement opened, before embarking on the recapitulation."

Piano Concerto No. 2, G Minor, Op. 22

Composed in 1868, it was first performed at a concert in the Salle Pleyel, Paris. The Russian pianist-composer Anton Rubinstein conducted and Saint-Saëns himself was the pianist.

Earlier, Saint-Saëns had sent a copy of the concerto to Liszt. In acknowledging the composition, Liszt wrote: "The form of it is new and happy; the interest of the three portions goes on increasing, and you take into just account the effect of the pianist without sacrificing anything of the ideas of the composer, which is an essential rule in this class of work. At the very outset the prelude on the pedal G is striking and imposing; after a very happy inspiration you do wisely to reproduce it at the end of the first movement and to accompany it this time with some chords. The total of your work pleases me singularly."

In his book *Saint-Saëns*, Arthur Hervey writes: "In this work we have the composer in the plenitude of youth, teeming with spirits and with a wealth of musical ideas. In the first movement he sees the composer reminiscent of the organ -- lofty, romantic, tender, plaintive, and even passionate. The *scherzo* is the absolute musical realisation of the joy of living."

Symphonic Poems

Dance Macabre, Op. 40

This is the most popular of Saint-Saëns's works. It was inspired by Henri Cazalis's poem on the Dance of the Dead, on Halloween. Here is the free translation of the poem.

"Moonbeams break fitfully through ragged clouds. Twelve heavy strokes sound from the bell in the Church tower. As the last stroke dies away, strange sounds are heard from the graveyard, and the light of the moon falls on a ghastly figure: it is Death, sitting on a tombstone, tuning his fiddle. Shrieks are heard from the graves around and the wind howls through the bare tree tops.

"The sinister notes of Death's mistuned violin call the dead forth from their graves, and clad in white shrouds, they flutter round in a demoniacal dance. The quiet of the churchyard is rent by hollow cries and horrible laughter. Wilder and wilder race the rattling skeletons round the figure of Death.

"Suddenly, as if seized by a terrible suspicion, they stop. In the icy wind, Death's notes cannot be heard. A tremor runs through the ranks of the dead. The grinning skulls are turned, as if listening, towards the pale moon.

"But Death's goading notes once more shatter the silence, and once again the dead hurl themselves into the dance, wilder than before. The howling wind joins in the ghostly choir and moans in the bare linden trees... Suddenly Death stops his playing, and in the stillness that follows is heard the sound of a cock

crowing. The dead hurry back to their graves and the weird vision fades away in the light of dawn."

"Le Rouet d'Omphale", Op. 31

This is a brief and charming symphonic poem based on the story of Hercules, who once disguised himself as a woman to avoid becoming involved in certain unpleasant circumstances and who was put to work at spinning by Omphale, Queen of Lydia. It requires little imagination to discover in the strings' whirring figure the sound of the busy wheel; and in the lugubrious theme in the bass, the discomfiture of the mighty Hercules.

Watson Lyle, in the book *Camille Saint-Saëns: His Life and Art*, gives the following account of the inscription prefaced to the score:

"The subject of this symphonic poem is feminine seductiveness, the triumphant contest of weakness against strength. The spinning wheel is merely a pretext; it is chosen simply for the sake of its rhythmical suggestion and from the view-point of the general form of the piece.

"For sake of interpretation the poem may be divided into three sections: the power of feminine allurement – the triumphant struggle of weakness against strength – in fact, Omphale's fascination of Hercules; Hercules in bondage. Hercules groaning under the bonds which he cannot break; Omphale deriding the vain efforts of the hero.

"The opening figure of the composition is for purposes of rhythm alone and is indicative of the spinning wheel idea which persists throughout the entire poem. It is heard from the violins first and then on the flutes – a scoring which produces a peculiarly celestial impression. After some preludial material of the description, of gradually swelling

tone volume, the rhythm of the Omphale motive is announced by the wind. Thus, indeed, might Eve have beckoned to Adam when he first beheld her in the Garden. At any rate Omphale beckons to very considerable purpose. She becomes a little tearful, and then whirrs her spinning wheel and resumes her song, infusing into it greater intensity and a new significance. The Hercules motive is a theme of nobly expressive characters, and after a considerable struggle for supremacy, it triumphs. The Omphale theme mocks the fall of the hero – the desolation of a heart deceived and made light of – and, like a ghostly memory, is heard the whirring of the wheel and the thin, almost inaudible sound of a harmonic A on the first violins."

Fast to finish
Saint-Saëns loved speed and often composed in a hurry that, some say, made his works seem superficial

CLAUDE **DEBUSSY**

Born : St. Germain-en-Laye, France,
August 22, 1862
Died : Paris, France, March 25, 1918

*A*chille-Claude Debussy was the eldest of five children of very poor parents. His family could not afford to send young Claude (he had dropped the Achille early on) to school. But his mother taught him to read and write.

Despite the poverty of his surroundings, the young Debussy had markedly refined tastes. His father desired his son to have a career in the French navy. However, Mme Roustan, Debussy's musical godmother, intervened and he started piano lessons from the age of 7. He progressed so well that he entered the Paris Conservatoire when he was 11 years old.

Debussy remained at the Conservatoire for 10 years, studying improvisations with César Franck. He learnt to exploit the piano with technical devices as the "oblique" touch that produced an unearthly beauty of sound.

Like Berlioz, Debussy had ideas of his own which he expressed fearlessly. This cost him the coveted Prix de Rome prize for composition for two successive years; it was finally awarded to him for his cantata "L'Enfant Prodigue" (The Prodigal Son), which allowed him to study in the Italian capital.

He left for Italy in 1885 but he was miserable there and yearned for Paris. He remained in the Villa Medici, where he studied during his residency, for just two of the allotted three years. The only bright days of his stay in Rome, before he returned to Paris, were his meetings and friendships with Liszt, Verdi and Leoncavallo, among other composers.

When he was 25 years old, Debussy became acquainted with a group of poets led by the French Symbolist, Stéphane Mallarmé. Partly under their influence and partly because of a visit to Bayreuth, the stronghold of Richard Wagner, he became for a short while a Wagner enthusiast. But his Gallic delicacy had little in common with the thundering of the Teutonic

Titan. He responded positively, however, to the five-tone scale of Russian liturgical music, and he heard with delight the Javanese gamelan music when he visited the Paris World Exhibition in 1899.

For 10 years (1892-1902) Debussy had toiled on his exquisite opera "Pelléas et Mélisande" (after Maurice Maeterlinck's play). When the opera finally debuted in 1902, it was a great success and made him famous. It became part of the repertoire of every opera company of importance.

At this stage in his life, Debussy also wrote caustic music criticism which made him a lot of money, if not friends. He led a well-defined life, composing at night, sleeping in the mornings and going out for walks in the afternoons.

All his life Debussy crusaded for what he called French music – that is, music in the style of Rameau and Couperin, rather than Weber and Wagner. His plastic rhythmic patterns and his disregard of conventional structure proved to be the proper means to the end he had in view.

Debussy's private life was far from serene. His first love, Gabrielle (Gaby) Dupont, was a very loyal mistress. She was succeeded by Rosalie (Lily) Texier, whom he subsequently married. Both women shared his hopes and fears, his triumphs and failures for 10 years. Debussy's marriage to Lily was happy till he became acquainted with a well-to-do and cultured singer, Madame Emma Bardac, who made a deep impression on him. In 1904, Madame Bardac left her husband to live with Debussy. Lily attempted suicide and was taken to hospital with serious injuries. The scandal caused a tremendous sensation. From all quarters Debussy was accused of having sold himself to a rich woman and most of his friends renounced him.

> " *Debussy's objective was to liberate music from traditions, and as such Impressionist music represented the transition from Romanticism to 20th-century music.* "

Debussy, however, married Emma Bardac, and for the first time in his life he had a peaceful social and economic background for his art. He could live exclusively for his music and in comfortable surroundings. Moreover, he now had a daughter with Emma who they named Claude-Emma. Debussy loved the little girl dearly. She was affectionately called Chou-Chou and Debussy composed the "Children's Corner Suite" for her with its delightful "Golliwog's Cake-walk". Debussy loved Chou-Chou better than anyone in the world and she became his solace during the last nine years of his life.

In the years preceding World War I, Debussy undertook many concert tours and was highly successful as both conductor and pianist. After he developed cancer, his working capacity was considerably reduced. The War also affected him sadly. In 1915 he underwent a major operation and in the succeeding years he gradually became weaker.

On March 23, 1918 the Germans started bombarding his beloved Paris. Debussy died of his cancer two days later, in the late evening of March 25. He was 55 years old.

The Founder of Impressionist Music

Impressionism was the name of a movement initiated by 19th-century painters of France, which also affected its poets and musicians.

Debussy was more directly influenced by poets such as Paul Verlaine and Stéphane Mallarmé. Where Verlaine and Mallarmé used words to produce colour, and Edouard Manet used paints, Debussy used musical tones. In fact, among composers none have surpassed Debussy in tone-colour expertise.

Debussy's objective was to liberate music from traditions, and as such Impressionist music represented the transition from Romanticism to 20th-century music. Debussy's contribution to 20th-century piano music compares with Chopin's contribution to 19th-century piano composition. No one since Chopin so changed the character and technique of piano writing as did Debussy, who, it is said, "dealt in colours, shadows and mist". The new colours, nuances, effects and tonal atmosphere created by Debussy is largely through his harmonic writing and a new approach to resonance – all of which brought an expressiveness to the keyboard it did not convey even with Chopin and Liszt.

Debussy has been described as "a melodist, but of a different kind. His melodies were not phrase-long ones of Classical music. Instead, Debussy used shorter melodic fragments that fitted together like pieces of stained glass."

He effected a complete revolution in musical art, inventing new ways of associating chords hitherto regarded as "dischords" and using them to produce exquisite harmonies. He broke most conventional rules, making new ones designed to express fleeting sensations and delicate drifting emotions.

Debussy generally avoided composing heavily orchestrated music. He composed no symphonies, concertos or overtures. From first to last he was a master of the piano.

Major compositions

Opera
Pelléas et Mélisande, 5 Acts (1902)

Cantatas
L'Enfant Prodigue (1884)
La Damoiselle Élue (1887)
Le Martyre de Saint Sébastien (1911)

Songs
Beau Soir
Fêtes Galantes
3 Ballades de François Villon
3 Chansons de Bilitis

Orchestral
Danse sacrée et danse profane
  (harp and strings)
Images, Sets 1 & 2 (1905-07)
La Mer (1905)
Ibéria (Images, Set 3)
Nocturnes (1894-99)
  Nuages, Fêtes, Sirènes
  (with women's chorus)
Prélude à l'après-midi d'un faune (1894)
Printemps: Symphonic Suite (1886-87)
Rhapsody for clarinet and orchestra
Rhapsody for saxophone and orchestra

Chamber Music
String Quartet in G Minor (1893)
Petite Pièce
  (clarinet and pianoforte) (1910)

Sonatas
No.1, D Minor (cello and pianoforte) (1915)
No. 2 (flute, viola and harp) (1916)
No. 3, G Minor (violin and pianoforte) (1917)

Piano
Arabesques Nos. 1 & 2 (1888)
Suite Bergamasque (1890)
  Prélude, Menuet, Claire de lune, Passepied
Pour le piano – Suite
  Prélude, Sarabande, Toccata
Éstampes (1903): La Soirée dans Grenade,
  Jardins sous la pluie
L'Île Joyeuse
Reflets dans l'eau
Hommage à Rameau
Cloches à travers les feuille
Poissons d'or
Children's Corner – Suite (1908)
  i) Doctor Gradus ad Parnassum
  ii) Jimbo's Lullaby
  iii) Serenade of the Doll
  iv) The Snow is Dancing
  v) The Little Shepherd
  vi) Golliwog's Cake-walk
La plus que lente – Valse (1910)
Préludes (2 books of 12 each)
  Book I, No. 8, La fille aux cheveux de lin
  No. 10, La Cathédrale engloutie
Études, 12 (1915)

2 Pianos
Petite Suite (1889)
  En Bâteau
  Cortège
  Ballet

Notes on select works

La Mer

"La Mer" consists of three symphonic sketches: "From Dawn till Noon at Sea", "Play of the Waves" and "Dialogue of the Wind and the Sea".

"First we have an impression of the immense resting power of the ocean at dawn. Gradually the waters awaken. A lazy wisp of foam is cast aloft. A simple two-tone figure from 'Sirens' is the starting point of a development of astonishing imagination and mastery. Debussy is less concerned with conventional melody than with the play of minute fragments of rhythm and tonality, ever-changing reflections of sky, clouds and sunlight on his flashing, tossing orchestral sea. Towards the end, the depths themselves are set in motion with a brief but impressive chorale phrase which is to return at the climax of the last movement.

"In the 'Play of the Waves' the ocean lashes itself into a sportive fury. Rainbow colourings appear and vanish in the fountains of spray.

"A deep threatening voice, as of an approaching storm, opens the 'Dialogue of the Wind and the Sea'. A shiver of anticipation runs through the orchestra; there is a swift gathering of forces and the tempest seems about to break. Instead, there is a sudden lull, and from afar we hear a nostalgic call – the sirens of Debussy's imagination. The siren song is repeated and now it is answered by Triton's horns; the clamour grows and the creatures of the deep hold high carnival. The chorale of the first movement returns in an exultant climax till at last a curious, unresolved harmony ends the never-ending tale of the sea."

3 Nocturnes

"Nuages", "Fêtes" and "Sirènes"

In his nocturnes, Debussy takes nature – slow-moving clouds, dancing lights, the sea – as his subject. The title, as he himself explains, does not have the traditional significance of a nocturne. Here it has "a more general and above all a more decorative meaning".

The first nocturne, "Nuages" (Clouds), reflects, in Debussy's words, "the unchanging aspect of the sky, with slow and solemn passage of clouds dissolving into a vague greyness tinged with white". The high woodwinds weave soft, fluctuating patterns, which repeat and yet change as imperceptibly as the clouds. Underneath, the solitary voice of an English horn chants a melody of loneliness and contemplation.

The second nocturne, "Fêtes" (Festivals), reflects (again in Debussy's words) "the restless dancing rhythms of the atmosphere, interspersed with brusque bursts of light. There is also the episode of a procession – a wholly visionary pageant – passing through and blended with the argent revelry. But the background of uninterrupted festival persists – luminous dust participating in the rhythm of all things."

It opens with a dazzling burst of light and excited rhythm and vivacious little scraps of melody miraculously derived from the first nocturne. Debussy's orchestration is delicate and it achieves its greatest effect by its reticence. The most marvellous moment of the "Festivals" comes when, after a moment of silence, one hears the almost inaudible, throbbing rhythm of a march and over it the muted fanfare of distant trumpets. Debussy is the master of the half-spoken word. He can make a silence speak with more eloquence than the loudest roar of the orchestra.

For the third nocturne, "Sirènes", Debussy asks for a chorus of eight women's voices. It describes "the sea and its endless rhythm. Then, amid the billows silvered by the moon, the mysterious voice of the sirens is heard. It laughs and passes." The song of the sirens is without words for, as the American music critic Philip Hale said: "To each hearer on the ship of Ulysses, or to each hearer of Debussy's music, the sirens sang of what might well lure him."

L'après-midi d'un faune

This symphonic poem by Debussy was the first work to show the full and true characteristics of Impressionism.

The work was inspired by a poem by Stéphane Mallarmé, one of the Symbolist poets who sought to use rhyme and rhythm, and the sound of words, with something of a musical effect. Their object was to call to the reader's mind thoughts that are not directly expressed in the text, but that were present in the mind of the poet when he created his poem.

The story conveyed by the poet is along these lines. A faun wakes at dawn in the forest and tries to call the previous day to mind... Was he really visited by pure, gentle and beautiful nymphs, or was it only a dream? The picture of the white and gold bodies of the nymphs grows fainter, and becomes confused with swans swimming in a pool, or with a garden of lilies. The harder he tries to remember, the farther the delightful hour fades away from him. But the sun is warm and grass is soft; he drinks wine and then curls up for sleep, hoping to recapture his experience in a dream.

Debussy's music exactly reproduces this atmosphere of vague unreality. As we listen we feel the warmth of the sun, smell the fragrance of the wood and the flowers, and hear the faun muttering to himself as he struggles with his problem. "Since the whole work is sheer atmosphere, it is impossible to unravel it into 'themes'. There is no firm melody which one could hum or whistle, but at the end one blinks one's eyes as if one has experienced some strange dream."

Debussy's birthplace
Despite poverty marking his childhood, the young Debussy had refined tastes. Starting piano lessons from the age of 7, he progressed so well that he entered the Paris Conservatoire when he was 11 years old

> " *All his life Debussy crusaded for what he called French music – that is, music in the style of Rameau and Couperin, rather than Weber and Wagner. His plastic rhythmic patterns and his disregard of conventional structure proved to be the proper means to the end he had in view. Debussy is the master of the half-spoken word. He can make a silence speak with more eloquence than the loudest roar of the orchestra.* "

Children's Corner – Suite

This is a suite in six movements for piano. It was composed in 1908 when Debussy's only child, a little girl whose pet name was Chou-Chou, was 4 years old. The title page bears these words: "To my dear little Chou-Chou". The titles are in English as Chou-Chou's nurse was English.

Part I – Doctor Gradus ad Parnassum

Valued for his poetic insight into the Romantic period, the Franco-Swiss pianist and conductor Alfred Cortot writes that this piece "describes a child practising the piano, and pokes gentle fun at the unequal battle he is waging with Clementi's complicated monotony (Muzio Clementi wrote a collection of instructional piano compositions, *Gradus ad Parnassum*). What boredom, what immeasurable depression. What unconquerable desire to look out at a sunbeam or an opening rose! The child's feelings are shown in the sudden halting and slowing down of the music; then, towards the end, comes an irresistible spurt towards freedom and play."

Part II – Jimbo's Lullaby

Jimbo is Chou-Chou's toy elephant, and the music conveys an impression of its weight in the little girl's arms.

Part III – Serenade of the Doll

The title is due to Debussy's rather scanty knowledge of English. He meant "for the Doll".

Part IV – The Snow is Dancing

Part V – The Little Shepherd

Part VI – Golliwog's Cake-walk

Debussy heard the main theme played by the Grenadier Guards when he was on a visit to London and set it against a background, so he said, representing the atmosphere of the music halls at the turn of the century. In the middle section, "the love potion motif" from "Tristan and Isolde" is heard, followed by laughing sounds. Debussy is said to have had a bet with a friend that he could make him laugh at one of Richard Wagner's most beautiful tunes – and this is the result.

Small gems from Debussy

Debussy composed 75 "group" pieces for piano – Arabesques, Suite Bergamasque, Préludes, etc. – in which one part or parts of them have separately become better known than the rest. These include:
"Clair de Lune" – from Suite Bergamasque
"Jardins sous la pluie" from Estampes
"Golliwog's Cake-walk" from
    Children's Corner
"Fille aux Cheveux de lin" and "Cathédrale engloutie" from Préludes, Book 1
"Reflets dans l'eau" from Images, Set 1

Among his more memorable songs are:
 Il pleure dans mon coeur
 Balle des femmes de Paris
 Beau Soir
 La Flûte de Pan

MAURICE **RAVEL**

Born : Ciboure, France, March 7, 1875
Died : Paris, France, December 28, 1937

J osèphe-Maurice or just Maurice Ravel was
born in the Basque region of France in
the coastal town of Ciboure, close to the
Pyrenees. He remembered being lulled to sleep with
the rich regional folk songs. Some of them would
play a major role in his voice and instrumental
arrangements in the course of his musical life.

He was educated in Paris and later entered the
Conservatoire. He left the Conservatoire in 1895, but
returned to it two years later to study with Gabriel
Fauré who did much to develop Ravel's style.
Ravel would commemorate his revered teacher with
an exquisite tribute, his "Berceuse sur le Nom de
Gabriel Fauré" (for violin and piano).

While he was still in his twenties, Ravel
composed the glittering "Jeux d'Eaux" (Fountains)
and "Pavane pour une Infante Défunte" (Pavane for
a Dead Infant). He combined his delicate French
perfectionism with Spanish vigour and intensity in
such works as "Miroirs" and "Gaspard de la Nuit",
a three-part work for piano (1903), in which the
dazzling virtuoso writing serves to remind listeners of
his lifelong admiration for Liszt.

Ravel had, in fact, developed his own deeply
personal style that found musical expression in
diverse ways with some unconventional harmonies.
Some of these may be sensed, for example,
in the vital and brilliantly lyrical String Quartet
in F Major (1903).

Other works followed: "Histoires Naturelles" for
voice and orchestra, a comic one-act opera "L'Heure
Espagnole" and the heady "Rhapsodie Espagnole" for
orchestra. The most rewarding of his pre-War works
was the ballet "Daphnis et Chloé", composed for
Sergei Diaghilev's Ballets Russes. He later made it into
an orchestral suite, which is much favoured today.

Ravel was a master orchestrator and orchestral
arranger of the works of composers to which he
was strongly attracted. Memorable among these are

Mussorgsky's "Pictures at an Exhibition", Debussy's "Nocturnes" and "Prélude à l'après-midi d'un faune", and Schumann's "Carnaval".

Ravel was 39 when World War I rocked France. He was declared unfit for combat duty but patriotically volunteered to drive an ambulance. He was greatly shocked and saddened by the slaughter and mass suffering that he witnessed and his shattered nerves began to affect his health.

When after a long time he recovered, he composed "Le Tombeau de Couperin", a suite based on Baroque dance forms, which he dedicated to six of his comrades who had died on the battlefield. It first appeared as a piano piece and was later orchestrated by him.

In 1928, Ravel composed his unique "Boléro". It is not really great music and simply consists of a single theme repeated with increasing intensity and density of orchestration. He himself described it as "a piece for orchestra without music". But with its performance Ravel became famous, first in France and then in Europe, and not much later, all over the world. In 1929, even the great Italian conductor Arturo Toscanini introduced it to New York but at a pace that dismayed Ravel.

After the War, Ravel lived quietly in a villa near Montfort, near Paris. He never married, but an affectionately bullying housekeeper cared for him and kept open house for fellow musicians who came from Paris to talk and make music until the small hours. After the outstanding success of "Boléro", he was compelled to accept conducting engagements in Vienna, London and Paris.

Ravel's last works, in 1931, included his two piano concertos. The "Piano Concerto for Left Hand" was written specially for the pianist Paul Wittgenstein who had lost his right arm in the War.

An automobile accident in 1932 brought on a mental breakdown. Though he lived for another five years, his creative power was destroyed, his memory gone and he died on December 28, 1937 after a brain surgery.

Ravel's place in music history

There is no better way of beginning this section than by quoting Ravel's own expressed views on music: "I am not a 'modern composer' with a flair for writing radical harmonies and disjointed counterpoint because I have never been a slave to any one style of composition. Nor have I allied myself with any particular school of music. I have always felt that a composer should put on paper what he feels and how he feels it – irrespective of what the current style of composition may be. Great music, I have always felt, must always come from the heart. Any music created by technique and brains alone is not worth the paper it is written on."

Someone once protested that Ravel rehearsed orchestras driving them on as slaves. His curt response was "They *are* slaves!"

Ravel was a perfectionist. Though there are those who maintain that there is too much artifice in his art, that it is too well ordered, too formal, they also admit that within the pattern Ravel achieves original, graceful and intense beauty. Others have judged Ravel to be "more virile than Debussy. There are greater variations in colour, greater depth and more penetrating strength in his music."

" *In Ravel's orchestration of 'Pictures at an Exhibition' by the composer Modest Mussorgsky, he seems to have absorbed the totally different spirit of that craggy Russian as completely as he had done with the elegant and courtly Couperin.* "

Mussorgsky reinterpreted
Ravel orchestrally arranged the Russian composer's "Pictures at an Exhibition"

Author Karl Nef underlined the French nationalism of Ravel's work: "The picturesque has always been one of the main objects of French musical art, and in this respect Ravel is a master amongst the moderns. He is rich in new sound effects and even coaxes new sounds out of the piano. His compositions are truly French in their elegance and are thoroughly worked out to the last detail."

In his orchestration of "Pictures at an Exhibition" by the composer Modest Mussorgsky, he seems to have absorbed the totally different spirit of that craggy Russian as completely as he had done with the elegant and courtly Couperin. Ravel's highly charged orchestrated reworking of this originally pianistic composition established it in the repertoire of leading symphony orchestras.

With his death in 1937, French music lost one of its dazzling innovators in terms of both his development of pianistic technique and his unique, colourful orchestral writings.

Notes on select works

Ballets

Daphnis et Chloé (Second Suite)
Some of the paradox of classical Greek art comes to life in this ballet. For here is music that unites the traditional clarity and balance of form with the Dionysian frenzy of emotions that was typical of ancient Greece. Perhaps only a Frenchman could have achieved such a balanced paradox in beautifully scored music.

It was commissioned and first produced by Sergei Diaghilev's Ballets Russes, in Paris, in 1912. Nowadays it

Major compositions

Operas
L'Heure Espagnole (1907)
L'Enfant et les Sortilèges

Ballets
Daphnis et Chloé (1910)
Mother Goose (Ma Mère l'Oye) (1912)

Songs
Don Quichotte à Dulcinée (1932)
Histoires Naturelles (1906)
Shéhérazade (1903)

Orchestral
Boléro (1928)
Daphnis et Chloé – suites from the
 ballet (1911)
La Valse – Poème Chorégraphique (1920)
Le Tombeau de Couperin
 (after the piano suite, 1919)
Mother Goose suite (Ma Mère l'Oye) (1908)
Pavane for a Dead Infanta (1912)
Rhapsodie Espagnole (1907)

Piano Concertos
G Major (1931)
D Major (for left hand) 1931

Chamber Music
Quartet for strings, F Major (1903)
Introduction and Allegro in G-flat Major
 (for string quartet, harp, flute and clarinet)

Piano and Strings
Piano Trio, A Minor (1915)

Violin and Piano
Tzigane (Gypsy) (1924)
Pièce en forme de habañera

Piano
Gaspard de la Nuit Suite (1908)
Jeux d'eau (1901)
Le Tombeau de Couperin (1914-17)
Mother Goose (Ma Mère l'Oye)
 arr. for 4 hands (1908)
Miroirs (1905)
Pavane for a Dead Infanta
 (Pavane pour une Infante Défunte)
Prélude (1913)
Sonatine (1905)
Valses Nobles et Sentimentales (1912)
 (also for orchestra)

Costume design for "*L'Enfant et les Sortilèges*"

is seldom performed as a ballet, but the Second Suite, drawn from Ravel's score, has long been popular in the concert hall. Here is the background of this portion of the ballet, including "Daybreak", the "Pantomime" and "General Dance".

"There is no sound at break of day save the murmur of rivulets fed by the dew and the song of birds. Daphnis, asleep before the grotto of the nymphs is awakened and he looks about in anguish for Chloé. At last she appears and the couple rushes into each other's arms. She has been saved by the god Pan, in memory of the nymph Syrinx, whom he loved. Daphnis and Chloé mime the wooing of Syrinx by Pan. He fashions a flute of reeds and Chloé dances in imitation of the melancholy tune. The dance grows more and more animated until she falls into his arms. They are joined by girls dressed as bacchantes and a group of young men, and the suite ends with the joyous tumult of the danse generale.

"With all its melodic imagination, brilliant orchestration, intoxicating colour, sensuous harmonies and orgiastic rhythm, 'Daphnis et Chloé' remains an essentially patrician score. Ravel was a spiritual aristocrat. Yet he knew the elemental drives and could express them in music. His is the supreme artistic achievement of appearing to give full rein without once relaxing his potent instinct for form."

" 'Great music, I have always felt, must always come from the heart. Any music created by technique and brains alone is not worth the paper it is written on,' Ravel said. "

Mother Goose (Ma Mère l'Oye)
This suite was first performed in London, with Ravel conducting the orchestra. The programme notes listed five sections: Pavane of the Sleeping Beauty,

Tom Thumb, Little Ugly Girl (Empress of the Pagodas), The Conversations between Beauty and the Beast, and The Fairy Garden. In French, as in English nurseries, the collection of fairytales under the title of "Mother Goose" was in high favour with children. Ravel's delicate, fanciful and whimsical genius is well suited to the illustration of these stories of "once upon a time". The scenario of the ballet from which the suite is taken, was written by Ravel himself.

Pavane of the Sleeping Beauty
The pavane is a slow solemn dance much in vogue during the 16th-17th centuries and is said to have originated in Padua, Italy. Pavanes were frequently introduced into weddings and other solemn ceremonies. The pavane leaves an impression of something wan and remote, a strain of music heard through the veil of sleep.

Tom Thumb
This section is preceded by the following quotation from the tale: "He thought he would easily find his way back by means of his bread, which he scattered as he passed along; but to his surprise he could not find a single crumb, for the birds had eaten all the crumbs." A continuous quaver figure in the music seems to suggest the long, winding path through the woods, while the solo oboe sings a little wanderer's song above the moving accompaniment. There is a short middle section containing some realistic bird music, the solo being transferred to the bassoon. Then the wandering figure is resumed and the air passes to solo piccolo. A few bars, in which the violas have a more agitated figure and the cello's sustained harmonies, are perhaps intended to depict Tom Thumb's fear and dismay.

Little Ugly Girl (Empress of the Pagodas)
"She undressed and entered the bath, and immediately the Pagodas, male and female, started singing and playing on various instruments; some had lutes, made of nutshells: others, viols made of almond husks; for they had to make their instruments in proportion to their own size."

This quotation explains the many quaint and miniature orchestral effects crowded into this movement – the muted strings and the delicate harmonies. Harp, celesta, keyed glockenspiel, xylophone, gong and cymbals are all employed in the scoring.

The Conversations between Beauty and the Beast
The programme note to this composition gives an outline of the conversation between the Beauty and the Beast, which

Ravel then tries to capture and depict in the music. Thus, when the Beast meets Beauty he tells her how much he adores her, but at the same time confesses that the chances of Beauty reciprocating his love are virtually a dream for he is after all an ugly Beast. Beauty, however, consoles the Beast by saying that she is aware that he has a kind heart which is far more important than physical ugliness. The Beast thanks Beauty for her understanding nature and declares that now having heard her, he would be happy to end his life. Greatly perturbed by the Beast's intention, Beauty impulsively tells the Beast that he should rather live to be her husband.

"At these words the Beast disappears, as the evil spell under which he was held is broken and Beauty finds at her feet a Prince as handsome as the god of love himself.

"The music, as it opens, is in valse rhythm. Over an accompaniment for muted strings, harps and flutes, the amiable speeches of Beauty are heard from solo clarinet. Presently, the Beast speaks: his accents are interpreted by a double bassoon. He ends with a prolonged sigh, during which there is a roll on the bass drum and the cymbals vibrate, while all the strings tremble mysteriously.

"A dialogue follows, the Beast being always represented by double-bassoon, while Beauty's phrases are now assigned to flute and now to oboe. The music grows more animated. Beauty's expressive theme appears to indicate her understanding and pity.

"A clash of cymbals suddenly indicates that the evil spell over the Beast is shattered. Beauty finally speaks in a violin solo, and the Beast, now humanised, answers in a new voice from a cello solo, and so the tale comes to a gentle and tender conclusion."

The Fairy Garden

"This is the final apotheosis: the awakening of the Sleeping Beauty. Prince Charming enters and finds the Princess asleep. At a passage marked by the ethereal sound of the celesta, she awakens, the sun rising at the same moment. All the fairytale characters of the ballet reappear and group themselves round the united lovers, while to the sound of triumphant fanfares a fairy arises and blesses the happy couple."

Boléro

Ravel's most famous work has been thus described: "It is more of an exercise in orchestration. The use of an unvarying rhythm beyond the point of boredom, to the verge of madness, is not a new idea in music – but its execution in Boléro is original and superbly effective. It is impossible to convey, except through the orchestra itself, the power and the fascination of the cumulative effect. The tune never becomes monotonous;

the rhythm established and maintained in the accompaniment is monotonous to an amazing degree – which is precisely the effect the composer wanted to create. It is hardly great music, as music per se. It is, nevertheless, a gigantic masterpiece of orchestration and reveals the enormous dynamic powers of the orchestra, and the almost infinite variety of tonal colour of which the symphony organisation is capable.

"The music itself is not truly a boléro. The characteristic dance of this name is one of dignity and modesty, not unrelated to the minuet; also, it is usually in double time, whereas the Boléro is in triple rhythm. At any rate Boléro is highly flavoured with Spanish essence, and the theme itself, if not Spanish in origin, is sufficiently typical to have originated south of the Pyrenees.

"The work is dedicated to the great dancer Ida Rubinstein and was first presented by her in Paris in November 1928. It was staged as a ballet divertissement, the setting suggesting a Spanish inn, the dance performed on a large table. The Rubinstein performance almost resulted in a riot. The mounting excitement of the music, the hypnotic power of the persistent rhythm and the magically suggestive performance of Rubinstein herself brought about a disordered scene in which the dancer barely escaped injury, and both audience and the actors became involved in a violent and dangerous melee.

"Ravel himself called his composition a danse lascive (lewd dance) and marked it in comparatively slow tempo (to last 17 minutes) and was annoyed when the great Toscanini played it considerably faster in introducing it to New York in 1929.

"The music of Boléro opens with a theme in two distinct parts. The first part

of the basic subject, after a few bars of an insinuating rhythmic figure established by the drums, is projected in the solo voice of the flute. The second section of the theme comes a little later, played solo by the clarinet. The wind instruments in turn, beginning with a solo bassoon, present the curious wayward melody or some closely similar derivation of it. It is heard solo in the oboe d'amore and in the flute again. It comes successively in muted trumpet, in tenor and in soprano saxophone. Finally as the crescendo which begins almost with the opening note exceeds the possibilities of solo instruments, the theme is transferred to groups of instruments. Almost without exception, these groups bring into being weird and brilliant and novel qualities of tone. The first group creates a strange effect – celesta in octaves, piccolo and the melody in the solo horn. Another bizarre presentation occurs when the theme

Costume design for "Boléro"

comes in a combination of oboe, oboe d'amore, English horn, clarinet and bass clarinet. Still later, with a slight recession of dynamics, the theme is revealed as a trombone solo.

"With every representation of the theme, the orchestra's powers are more heavily drawn upon, and the endlessly varied and brilliant colour of which it is capable more wonderfully revealed. Ravel commences using the instruments in pairs, contrasting yet blending with one another in the most fantastic combinations. Underneath moves the maddeningly persistent rhythm, enforced now not only by drum, but by dissonant chords of the harp and pizzicato strings. The theme is transferred to bowed strings, and again to the first and second violins divided in weird harmonies against similarly divided and harmonised woodwinds. Not content with matching all the orchestral voices against each other, Ravel is by no means at the limit of his resources, but changes the character of the total effect by still further reinforcing the harmonies of one instrument with the fundamental of another.

"Ultimately the whole orchestra sways in the wicked rhythm, and with a potency of utterance that seems to exact its ultimate powers. But the end is not yet! At the very peak of this mountain of vibrant sound, Ravel introduces a slight change in the melodic line and in tonality – most noticeable in violins and woodwind – which somehow seems to add still more power, though actually it does not. There are short syncopated phrases which have not been noticed before; new accretions of power in the brass, and finally, after poisonously dissonant glissandos in which the trombone's coarse bray is most conspicuous, the piece ends in a single crushing mass of tone."

Rhapsodie Espagnole

"The mystery of a Spanish twilight, charged with secret yearnings, sweet scents, and sensuous suggestions; the provocative rhythms, the ecstasies of Spanish dances, the flaming colour and vivid life of a Spanish festival – these are the textures of this rapturous and incandescent music. It is not strange that Ravel exhibits Spanish influence, for he is from the Basque country, the high country of those strange people who are neither Spanish nor French, but reveal certain sympathies with both.

"The Spanish Rhapsody was first performed in 1908 and is divided into four sections – Prélude à la nuit, Malagueña, Habañera and Féria – played continuously."

Prélude à la Nuit

"There is something acrid, yet sweet in the complaining phrase of muted strings in the beginning; and paradoxically, as the hard light of day fades, and the loveliness and loneliness of darkness penetrate the music, there is growing warmth, there are anticipations of promised ecstasy in fierce little bursts of harp and woodwind. Two clarinets course over a rapturous cadenza, and a little later, the shadowy tones of the bassoons imitate it, with a quartet of violins abandoned to trills and moving harmonies. There are languorous chimings, and at the end, the lingering liquid sweetness of the celesta."

Malagueña

"A fascinating rhythm moves through basses and, presently, bass clarinet, to ensure a typically Spanish dance melody. Suggestions of it appear in plucked strings, and in woodwinds almost glissando in the rapid smoothness of their scales; a distant and muted trumpet adds its penetrating phrase, and a fierce brief climax brings a suggestive pause. Then the cor anglais, against trembling strings and celesta, intones a languid melody; the plaint of the strings from the opening passages return briefly, as does the rhythmic introduction to this section. A delicately flirtatious flick of string tone dismisses the yearning sentiment, and ends the dance."

Habañera

"The Habañera derives its name from Havana and it originated in Cuba. Ravel's version is a seductive and languorous dance, artfully syncopated and slow; the clarinet first establishing the rhythm, and woodwinds later introducing a melody typically Spanish in outline. Little climaxes and restless hastening of the rhythm occur; then, wearied with ecstasy, the dance ends in faint sweet tones of celesta above the clarinet's insistent figure."

Féria

"Here is a glowing picture of the colours and movement and variety of a country fair in Spain. Here, too, for the first time in music, the orchestra speaks with its fullest power; now in swift climax, in fragmentary dance tunes, ultimately in a wild mélange of all the burning colour and febrile activity of the scene. But there is a section wherein all the blinding brightness and distractions of the fair are forgotten, and the cor anglais sings of romance and of passion with little ecstatic rushings of the strings – all against the very Spanish melody boldly sung forth in strings. Presently dances and wild songs come once more, and the persistence of the rhythm, emphasised in mighty chords of full orchestra is almost maddening in its excitement and power. The end comes abruptly on a swift climax."

Capturing ethnic colour and movement came naturally to Ravel

Tzigane

This violin rhapsody with piano or orchestral accompaniment was composed in 1924. The work was dedicated to the soloist who gave it its first performance in London, Jelly d'Aranyi, grand-niece of the Hungarian violinist Joseph Joachim. It is said that she had only two or three days in which to study the piece but mastered it so brilliantly that Ravel apologised for not making it more difficult. "Tzigane" is, in fact, one of the most difficult of all violin pieces. Ravel added new virtuoso tricks to all the old ones. It has been said that to play this work one must indeed be a musical magician.

" Rimsky-Korsakov was the creator of the Russian symphony and the Russian tone poem. His expert knowledge of the tonal colour and range of each instrument was the unique feature of his works, which were often built on Russian folk songs and dances. "

NIKOLAI
RIMSKY-KORSAKOV

Born : St. Petersburg, Russia, March 18, 1844

Died : St. Petersburg, Russia, June 21, 1908

As the son of aristocratic parents, Nikolai Rimsky-Korsakov received an education befitting his status, which included music. Since one of the very few professions regarded as suitable for a young man of his birth was the Navy, Rimsky-Korsakov joined the Corps of Naval Cadets in 1856 at the age of 12. He served until he was almost 30 years old.

He was popular among his colleagues, and often regaled them with performances on the violin and cello. It was during the long sea voyages that he composed his First Symphony.

After leaving the Navy, Rimsky-Korsakov became part of the important group of Russian composers who formed the "Neo-Russian school". He accepted the importance of Russian music for Russians as propounded by Balakirev, the guiding spirit of the group of composers, who became his special friend. Known also as "The Five", "The Mighty Handful" and "Les Cinq" in French musical circles, their "Orientalist" style depended on Eastern themes and harmonies. (The Five were Balakirev, Borodin, Cui, Mussorgsky and Rimsky-Korsakov.) The association didn't last long: Rimsky-Korsakov parted from them as they distrusted formal musical education.

Rimsky-Korsakov's more active interest in music was kindled by attending Glinka's operas, "Life of the Tsar" and "Russlan and Ludmilla", which enchanted him. Following his first symphony came two compositions that brought him to the attention of the Russian musical school: the symphonic poem "Sadko" from his opera of that name, and the opera "The Maid of Pskov".

After his retirement from the Navy, Rimsky-Korsakov accepted the position of Professor in the St. Petersburg Conservatory. He thereafter held a series of musical posts and as a teacher was conspicuously successful. Among his pupils were such noted musicians as Lyadov, Sacchetti, Stravinsky, Gretchaninov and Glazunov. A publishing house was founded to promote their works and a symphony orchestra, directed by him, to perform them.

Rimsky-Korsakov's capacity to learn while he earned is evidenced in his *Practical Manual of Harmony and Principles of Orchestration*. He also edited works by his colleagues Borodin, Mussorgsky and others.

He married Nadezhda Purgold, a concert pianist, and this brought still more music into his life and spurred him to compose in a variety of musical forms.

In 1888, Rimsky-Korsakov heard the first performances of Wagner's "Ring Cycle" and was so overwhelmed that he decided in future to write only operas. This resolve resulted in the fairy opera ballet "Mlada", the epic opera "Sadko" and his only non-Russian opera, "Mozart and Salieri" (1898), among others. The "Tale of Tsar Saltan" is perhaps best remembered outside Russia for its famous "Flight of the Bumble-bee", an orchestral interlude since arranged for all manner of virtuoso instrumentalists.

His last opera but one, and possibly his greatest success in Russia, was "The Legend of the Invisible City of Kitezh" (1906), which has been referred to as the "Russian Parsifal". His last, in 1907, was "Le Coq d'Or" (The Golden Cockerel), a bitter satire on autocratic and bureaucratic stupidity, banned by the government which permitted its staging only posthumously.

During the political protests of 1905, Rimsky-Korsakov bravely showed that his sympathies lay with the revolutionary students at the St. Petersburg Conservatory. He composed "Dubinushka" (The Little Hammer) whose programme of growing student unrest further inflamed the authorities: it musically depicted a hammer which with orchestral crescendo turned into a mighty revolutionary mallet! For taking this stand he was dismissed from his post. This made him a hero to the students and to a large section of the public. He was soon given back his post, but his political allegiances remained unaltered. He was honoured not only as a leading Russian composer and teacher, but also as a revolutionary for his political beliefs and musical idiom.

It was on June 21, 1908 that Rimsky-Korsakov died suddenly at his country estate, of a heart attack.

Major compositions

Operas
May Night (1878-79), 3 Acts, 4 Scenes
The Snow Maiden (1880)
  Prologue and 4 Acts
Sadko (1895), 7 Scenes
The Tale of Tsar Saltan
  Prologue, 4 Acts, 7 Scenes, Op. 34 (1899)
The Golden Cockerel (Coq d'Or)
  3 Acts (1907)

Orchestral
Symphony No. 2 (Antar)
Capriccio Espagnol, Op. 34 (1887)
Scheherazade, Op. 35 (1888)
Russian Easter Festival Overture (1888)
Dubinushka (1905)

Songs
It is not the Wind, Op. 43, No. 2 (Tolstoy)
The Rose and the Nightingale,
  Op. 2, No. 2 (Kostov)

Rimsky-Korsakov's place in music history

Rimsky-Korsakov's great talent lay in orchestration – it was brilliant, evocative, colourful and had earned great praise from none other than Tchaikovsky himself. The picturesque and especially the Oriental side of Russian life made his music very interesting, though his forms were always West European.

He was the creator of the Russian symphony and the Russian tone poem. His expert knowledge of the tonal colour and range of each instrument was the unique feature of his works, which were often built on Russian folk songs and dances.

Rimsky-Korsakov revised, orchestrated or completed a number of his colleagues' works such as Dargomyzhsky's "The Stone Guest", Glinka's operas, Mussorgsky's "Khovantschina" and "Boris Godunov", and Borodin's "Prince Igor".

Notes on select works

Scheherazade, Op. 35

"It would be difficult to conceive a more fitting subject for exploitation by a composer of Rimsky-Korsakov's particular gifts than the *Arabian Nights*, or more properly, *The Thousand and One Night Stories*. The Orient is but next door to Russia, and few are the Russian composers who did not feel its subtle influence. Rimsky-Korsakov was almost unique in his ability to write music pervaded with the perfumes, the glowing colours, the brilliant and exotic life of the oldest part of the Old World...

"Rimsky-Korsakov himself declared explicitly that in the Suite he had no intention of depicting, in detail, any of the *Arabian Nights* stories. All he desired was that the hearer should carry away the impression that it is beyond doubt an Oriental narrative of some numerous and varied fairytale wonders."

The story that inspired Scheherazade

"The Sultan Schahriar, holding the conviction that all women are false and faithless, vowed to put to death each of his wives after the first nuptial night. But the Sultana Scheherazade saved her life by entertaining her lord with fascinating tales which she continued telling him for a thousand and one nights. The Sultan, consumed with curiosity, postponed from day to day the execution of his wife and finally repudiated his bloody vow entirely.

The Sea and the Vessel of Sinbad

"As the music begins we perceive the menacing figure of the stern Sultan. The bold phrase, given in unison by trombone, tuba, horns and the woodwind and strings in their lower range at the very beginning of the suite, might represent the severe monarch. There is a little interlude, rather tentative in character, and then the violin, trembling and diffident, yet shining clear against rich chords from the harp, utters the lovely little song that typifies Scheherazade, the Narrator.

"Now we feel the long swell of the sea, the heaving restless sea; we hear the strange mysterious sounds of water lapping at the smooth sides of the vessel; we see the billowing sail and the bending mast, the white-capped blue of deep water, and the brazen sun hanging in a brazen sky. Sinbad the Sailor looks along the rail and thrills to the unceasing motion, the ceaseless susurrus of the ocean. The music has the long rolling motion of the deep sea. But not for long. A short fierce storm rages invisibly in the infinite blue depths and the sea heaves up as a weary giant. Suddenly the stern voice of the Sultan is heard (the same theme as at the opening of the movement) and the tremulous accents of Scheherazade go bravely on. In the calm that closes the movement we have assurance that for one day, at least, she has postponed her terrible fate."

The Tale of the Prince Kalender

"The motif of Scheherazade, a little more confident, a little more certain, opens the second movement of the Suite. A tenuous shining thread of tone, changing in expressiveness as the dainty Sultana's face must have altered to meet the smile or frown of her lord. Ending in a cadenza of extreme brilliance and difficulty, it leads us into the main theme of the movement, assigned to the bassoon. Here it is a golden opportunity for 'the clown of the orchestra' (the bassoon). After a space the tearful voice of the oboe takes up a little song derived from that of the bassoon and a brightness comes over the

Rimsky-Korsakov
The most representative of the Russian nationalists

music. The violins join in a livelier rhythm and toward the close of the first section of the music we hear what might be the accompaniment to a wild exotic dance.

"The placid opening of the second section is deceptive, for suddenly we are in the midst of a scene of wild barbaric splendour. Fanfares of the brass, flying phrases of string and woodwind are combined in a whirling, glowing flux of tone; incandescent masses of colour are thrown out like bright jewels from the garments of some dancer of the Orient. Commanding phrases are uttered boldly by the trombones, and echoed in the mysterious distance by a muted trumpet; secretive sentences come from plucked and muted strings; that tragic comedian, the bassoon, mutters strangely to itself.

"Here, as in nowhere else, Rimsky-Korsakov develops the themes in conventional symphonic style. This is particularly noticeable in the third part of the 'Kalender Prince' yet not the slightest degree of novelty, or of vitality, or of sustained interest is lost in the process."

The Young Prince and the Young Princess

"What a delightful contrast in these naïve melodies! Here the significance of the music is not Oriental, but simply human. It sings of love, love of the idyllic kind; not without passion, but without the fierce selfish hunger of passion; not without ecstasy, but with the ecstasy of love fulfilled and not satiated.

"The Prince speaks first, and to him is assigned the tender melody of the violins at the very beginning of the movement. We might picture him singing to his love

> " Rimsky-Korsakov was honoured not only as a leading Russian composer and teacher, but also as a revolutionary for his political beliefs and musical idiom. "

'on a terrace above a dark pool, while behind them a carven moon, without faintest aureole, a voluptuous moon, mysteriously marked, holds her hand upon the circle of her breast'. Presently the young Princess speaks, in the reedy sweetness of the clarinet – a tender little song, with rapturous flights of tone and arch phrases. Later we hear her accompanied in her song by snare drum, tambourine, cymbals and the tinkling triangle. The Young Prince sings again his amorous lay, and then, near the end, we remember once more that it is a story, as the shy Scheherazade appears."

Festival at Baghdad
The Sea Vessel is Wrecked

"Once again the stern-voiced Sultan is heard in his dreadful resolution, but Scheherazade hastens on with her stories, diverting him with a glowing description of a Baghdad festival. A brief but brilliant violin cadenza leads us to this lively and colourful scene. Wild dancers weave sinuously in strange arabesque figures, gaily coloured draperies stiffen in the breeze, the hubbub of the market place runs like a powerful undercurrent beneath the more assertive sounds of the festival. Snake charmers pipe magic tunes to their hooded charges, fakirs cry their wares and perform strange feats before a thousand curious eyes. Ivory-skinned girls peer seductively from shadowy shelters of richest rugs and rare fabrics. Imperious camels carry some lordly satrap and his train through the chattering crowds. Rare perfumes, mingled with the penetrating odours of spices and the unforgettable scent of the streets and crowds. It is the Orient with all its brilliantly glowing life and sound and colour.

"Once again the ominous accents of the Sultan are heard, but briefly now and with less determination, while Scheherazade bravely continues with her tale, desperately achieving new climaxes, more bewildering pictures of beauty. Suddenly we are once more on the sea, on the broad decks of Sinbad's ship.

"But it is not the quiet ocean we have known. Rather its gigantic surges heave themselves up to terrifying heights, the vessel trembles to its very keel; the sails crack like giant pistols under the impact of sudden fierce gusts from the empty skies. Masts bend and strain.

"The sailors turn ashen faces towards a great rock, surmounted by a warrior of bronze. And towards the rock the ship turns too, drawn irresistibly by some occult force.

"A heaven-splitting crash, and the ship is gone, her proud hull splintering and grinding against the refractory rock and only the wandering winds to mourn her. Now Scheherazade rehearses the little, almost articulate, phrase (woodwind) with which she prefaced her stories, and presently we hear her own lovely motive, as before in the voice of the violin.

"The Sultan finally speaks – but now gently, amorously, and the violin rises to an incredible triumphant height against the glowing harmonies that end the movement."

Capriccio Espagnol, Op. 34

It is a curious fact that before Ravel and certain contemporary Spanish composers, the musical spirit of Spain was more vividly expressed by Slavic composers than by Spaniards. The many dance and song forms, the captivating and sensuous rhythms, the folk and gypsy melodies of Spain fascinated all great musicians who heard them at first hand and, as a result many adapted them to their own musical purposes.

Rimsky-Korsakov had originally planned this work as a fantasy for violin upon Spanish themes, but changed his mind as the glamour and glitter that he wished this music to express could be conveyed far more effectively through the orchestra. He was singularly proud of this music. There is little to compare with it in dazzling brilliance of orchestration, its fantastic and glowing sound pictures.

The first performance of the work was at St. Petersburg, on October 31, 1887, with Rimsky-Korsakov conducting. At rehearsal, the musicians were so impressed with the work that they stopped and applauded. Warmed by their enthusiasm, the composer dedicated the Caprice to the men of the orchestra, and the name of each one appears on the fly-leaf of the score. The music is in five sections, played without pause.

Alborada
"A morning song, and one to which the deepest sleeper should awaken, for it bursts into vigorous life with a theme powerfully projected in full orchestra. Later, plucked strings, with woodwind and horn in accompaniment, supply a background against which the solo clarinet repeats the opening theme. A violin cadenza, technically exacting and musically beautiful, ends this section of the music."

Variations
"The basis of the Variations is a subject issued by the horns at the beginning. Upon it the composer constructs five

Rimsky-Korsakov was almost unique in his ability to write music pervaded with the perfumes, the glowing colours, the brilliant and exotic life of the oldest part of the Old World.

ingenious elaborations, each presented in different tone colours. The first begins in the strings, gracefully rising directly out of the subject matter. The second combines the round full tone of the horn with the melancholy reediness of the cor anglais. The third is boldly put forth by practically the entire orchestra. The fourth is sounded in a delicious combination of paired horns and cellos, against accompaniment by clarinet and violins. The last again calls forth the full colour range of the orchestra, and is succeeded by one of the brilliant display passages originally written for the violin, now played by flute."

Alborada
"This section, in its musical material, is practically the same as the opening part of the work, but its orchestration is ingeniously arranged so that it almost sounds new. The most noticeable feature is the exchange of parts between violin and clarinet. The solo previously given to clarinet is now played by violin, and vice versa."

Scene and Gypsy Song
"It is difficult to connect this music with 'Scene' – if we are looking for details; for the first part is no more than a series of display passages, dramatic enough, to be sure, but certainly not translatable from the language of music into any other. There is a long roll on the snare drum, and a brilliant, syncopated passage for a sharp-edged combination of horn and trumpet. The rattling of the drum fades, and the solo violin traces a delicate figure, imitated by the clarinet and the flute.

The bright tones of flute dance over a heavy sounding of the timpani; the rapidly beaten cymbal makes a brilliant foil for the full richness of the solo clarinet. The 'Scene' is ended by the iridescent glitter of harp and triangle.

"An ecstatic glissando on the harp ushers in the passionate gypsy song, sung with fierce emphasis by the violins with a brassy accompaniment from trombone, tuba and cymbals. The orchestra remembers the violin solo from the preceding section and puts it forward with vehemence. The music grows more complicated, warmer, and more lustrous and gypsy song, the previous theme of the violin, a solo for cello, and certain imitations of the finale that is still to come, are all woven together with incredible richness and brilliance of orchestration. The resources of the orchestra seem endless as they are summoned forth, one by one; the tempo increases to furious speed and rushes the orchestra into the fandango."

Fandango of the Asturias
"The fandango is a gracefully seductive dance, probably of Moorish origin, certainly very ancient. It is subtle, full of delicate and tempting manoeuvres, its flaming passion concealed – for the most part – beneath a mask of suavity.

"But here the dance rises to a fury, to an overpowering degree of madness and abandon. Occasionally a single instrument speaks, but for the most part the orchestra is enslaved to the intoxicating rhythm.

"At the peak of intensity, the trombones speak as they spoke at the beginning of the movement; the dance suddenly changes to the music of the first movement, and in concluding passages of incandescent warmth and terrific power, the Capriccio is ended."

PETER ILYICH
TCHAIKOVSKY

Born : Votkinsk, Russia, May 7, 1840
Died : Moscow, Russia, November 6, 1893

Peter (Pyotr) Ilyich Tchaikovsky grew up in an upper class family that unfortunately had no interest in music. Nevertheless, he learned to play the piano at an early age and developed a love of music by improvising for hours. When he was 10 years old, the family moved to St. Petersburg and Tchaikovsky was sent to boarding school. He displayed no exceptional ability in any subject. But while a schoolboy he heard a symphony orchestra for the first time and the experience made such an impression on him that he raved about it all night in his sleep.

His father decided that the boy should study law, but allowed him to have music lessons at the same time. At 19, Tchaikovsky took up a clerical post at the Ministry of Justice, yet showed very little interest in his work. On the other hand, his involvement with music grew steadily stronger, and he became a frequent visitor to the concert hall and the opera.

After four years he gave up his clerical post and entered the St. Petersburg Conservatoire where he showed an industry and eagerness that impressed his teachers. (One of the things he did in a single night was to compose 200 variations on a given theme.)

His first printed work was a Scherzo and Impromptu for piano, and his first orchestral composition to be performed was a waltz, "Haymaker's Dance", directed by Johann Strauss at Pavlovsk in 1865. Tchaikovsky retained his love of the waltz form and often made use of it.

In 1866, Tchaikovsky took up a post as teacher of theory at the Moscow Conservatoire and set about composing his First Symphony, working with such concentration that it began to affect his health. Back in St. Petersburg, only two of the movements of that First Symphony, "Winter Daydreams", were performed and Tchaikovsky never forgave the director of the St. Petersburg Conservatoire, Anton Rubinstein, for thus mutilating the work. Tchaikovsky's bitterness developed into a hatred of everything to do with the city of St. Petersburg, its musical authorities, press and public. Nor did he have any great success with his works in Moscow. His financial situation became critical and to earn a little extra money he took up, much against his will, a post as music critic.

One day Tchaikovsky received the first of several letters from a young woman pupil, Antonia Milyukova, declaring her love for him. Finally he visited her and tried to explain that he did not love her and could never make her happy. When she threatened to kill herself, he consented to marry her despite his homosexuality. The marriage was tragic in every respect. After nine days of it with this apparently psychopathic woman whose very sight disturbed him, Tchaikovsky in desperation tried to commit suicide by standing up to his neck in the ice-cold water of the river Neva.

At this time, in 1877, there occurred a turning point in Tchaikovsky's life. A wealthy music lover, Mme Nadezhda von Meck, who was the widow of a railway magnate, had conceived a great interest in his works. When she heard of his difficult financial situation, she decided to help him. She began by commissioning compositions from him, paying for them in princely fashion. A correspondence developed between them and soon Nadezhda von Meck paid off all Tchaikovsky's debts, then offered him an annual "salary" of 6,000 roubles. She made only one condition: that they should never meet. After 14 years she abruptly withdrew her support, but by then Tchaikovsky was well off. Tchaikovsky travelled extensively, living in both Italy and France. He was particularly fond of

Italy, its music and its people. He also travelled and performed in the United States of America and was specially invited there for the gala opening of Carnegie Hall. In England he was much feted as well and received the Doctorate in Music from Cambridge University.

Tchaikovsky's last great work was his Sixth Symphony, the "Pathétique". Five days after the date of its first performance he took ill. He had slept badly and did not come down for breakfast as usual. When he did and sat at table with his brother and nephew, he ate nothing. Then he took up a glass of unboiled water and drank a deep draught. As there was a cholera epidemic in the city, those present were appalled at his carelessness. His condition rapidly worsened and was diagnosed as cholera. He died a week later on November 6, 1893.

Tchaikovsky's place in music history

Tchaikovsky is unquestionably the most loved and the most expressive of Romantic composers that Russia has given to the world. His great genius was in creating melody. His temperament was basically emotional with pessimistic overtones. Strangely, many of his major compositions were not received well in their first performances – and sometimes even in subsequent ones – causing him much mental distress and morbid introspection in which he doubted his own talents as a composer. The list of such compositions, which later became universally famous, included his Violin Concerto, the B-flat Minor Piano Concerto, the Fifth Symphony, the operas "The Queen of Spades" and "Eugene Onegin", the music of the ballets

"Swan Lake", "Sleeping Beauty" and "Casse Noisette" (the "Nutcracker") and even his Sixth Symphony – the "Pathétique" – arguably his greatest composition.

Tchaikovsky is held in high regard for his orchestral works in many forms. He drew freely on Russian folk music – the *andante cantabile* from his Quartet Op. 11 is based, we are told, on a street singer's song. He also wrote over 100 songs, the best known being the setting for Goethe's poem *None but the Lonely Heart*.

Music scholars have pointed out though, that an overall visualisation was the weakest aspect of his art. "He worked prodigiously, quickly and easily, but the planning of a great work, the cool reflection on all its possibilities, the logical development and clear embodiment of ideas, were not his forte. He wrote essentially from the heart, and an intuitive sense of the completeness and unity shaped his work. Tchaikovsky had a rich vein of melody, and when he openly and fully gave himself up to it he could swing his melody into unique breadth and power. With his great lyrical ability, he had a pronounced instrumental imagination that gave flow and passion to his orchestral works."

Notes on select works
Violin Concerto in D, Op. 35

If a list was drawn up of the top violin concertos of the world, this concerto would certainly be included among the first five. And yet, it had an unhappy start. Its original dedicatee, Leopold Auer, then the foremost violin teacher of his time, returned it to Tchaikovsky saying it was "unplayable". However, another violinist, Adolf Brodsky, first became interested in it and the concerto, now re-dedicated to him, was performed by him several times with increasing success.

The first movement, *allegro*, begins with an orchestral prelude, which gives a hint of the main theme, but it is only after the soloist has entered with an improvisation that the theme, which has the character of a gracious dance, really breaks through. This grows into a richly developed solo passage which quietens down into an evocative song theme. Throughout, the soloist has very difficult passages, which reach their climax in a cadenza. The effect is further enhanced in the brisk and brilliant coda.

The second movement, *canzonetta* (*andante*), opens with a short introduction from the wind instruments. The soloist takes up a sad, typically Slavonic melody. The introduction is heard once more and then gradually dies away, until suddenly, without break, we pass straight into the third movement.

The *finale, allegro vivacissimo*, after an orchestral introduction, prepares the main theme. A short violin cadenza follows, lively dance rhythms appear. The theme is developed wittily and elegantly, the soloist having the upper hand throughout. The movement ends in a searing spurt.

Piano Concerto No. 1, B-flat Minor, Op. 23

This concerto takes its place as the second most popular of all piano concertos (after Beethoven's Fifth Concerto, the "Emperor").

As with the violin concerto, this work also had an unpromising start. Its first performance was played on Christmas Eve 1874 before Nicholas Rubinstein, head of the Moscow Conservatoire. After it ended, Rubinstein declared it unplayable and trivial. Tchaikovsky was disappointed and

Major compositions

Operas and Orchestral
Eugene Onegin
Joan of Arc
Queen of Spades
Mazeppa

Symphonies (6)
No. 4, F Minor, Op. 36
No. 5, E Minor, Op. 64
No. 6, B Minor, Op. 74 "Pathétique"

Ballets
Swan Lake, Op. 20
Sleeping Beauty, Op. 66
The Nutcracker (Casse Noisette), Op. 71

Symphonic Poems and Overtures
Coronation Cantata (for Alexander III)
Two Masses
Manfred
Romeo and Juliet – Overture Fantasia
Hamlet – Overture Fantasia, Op. 67
Tempest – Symphonic Fantasy
Francesca da Rimini
  – Symphonic Fantasia, Op. 32
Capriccio Italien, Op. 45
Marche Slave (Slavonic March), Op. 31
Ouverture Solennelle, Op. 49
Serenade, C Major, Op. 48
  (String Orchestra)
Suite No. 3, G Major, Op. 55
  – Theme and Variations
Suite No. 4, Op. 61 "Mozartiana"

Piano and Violin
Piano Concerto No. 1, B-flat Minor, Op. 23
Piano Concerto No. 2, C Major, Op. 44
Violin Concerto, D Major, Op. 35
Sérénade Mélancolique for violin and
  orchestra, Op. 26
Variations on a Rococo Theme for
  cello and orchestra, Op. 33

Chamber Music
String Quartets (3)
No. 1, D Major, Op. 11 (Andante cantabile)
  Piano Trio, A Minor, Op. 50
  Souvenir d'un lieu cher, Op. 42
    for violin and piano
No. 2, Scherzo
No. 3, Melody (E-flat Major)

Piano
Dumka, Op. 59, No. 1
Humoresque, Op. 10, No. 2

Songs (over 100)
A Ballroom Meeting, Op. 38, No. 3 (Tolstoy)
Don Juan's Serenade, Op. 38, No.1 (Tolstoy)
None but the Lonely Heart,
  Op. 6, No. 6 (Goethe)
Lullaby, Op. 54, No. 16 (Aksakov)

Inspired notations
The score of a page from the Pathétique symphony

re-dedicated it to the conductor, virtuoso pianist and composer Baron Hans von Bülow, who was enthusiastic about it and made it popular.

The first movement, *allegro non troppo* and *molto maestoso, allegro con spirito,* opens with a broad orchestral melody in unison. But strangely, this fine theme never re-appears. The main theme of the first movement, *allegro con spirito*, follows, with the piano's quick passages in double octaves. Tchaikovsky utilised the tune which he recalled having heard sung by beggars on the streets.

The second movement, *andantino semplice, allegro vivace assai,* makes use of the refrain of an old French song among its motifs which Tchaikovsky used to sing and whistle in his young days.

The third movement, *allegro con fuoco,* is a pyrotechnic display of sound in which a singular folk tune, a kind of Cossack dance, plays the leading part.

String Quartet No. 1 in D, Op. 11
The second movement of this quartet, *andante cantabile,* based on a Russian folk tune, is of great beauty and is often performed separately. The entire quartet, including its well-constructed first movement, the Grieg-like *scherzo* and the gay finale, is sometimes now played.

Symphony No. 4, in F Minor, Op. 36
Dedicated to Mme Nadezhda von Meck, Tchaikovsky's "best friend" and benefactor, its first movement, *andante sostenuto, moderato con anima,* in its introduction projects the key to the symphony's principal idea which is that it is Fate that hinders one from reaching the goal in the quest for happiness. Fate watches

> *"Tchaikovsky is unquestionably the most loved and the most expressive of Romantic composers that Russia has given to the world. His great genius was in creating melody."*

jealously to see that calm does not last long and the sky is not free from clouds. The second movement, *andantino in modo di canzone,* shows another phase of suffering. This is the melancholy feeling that besets one when sitting alone at home of an evening, tired after the day's work. You are lost in memories of youth, happy and sad. The third movement, *scherzo, pizzicato ostinato,* does not give expression to any definite feelings. The mood is neither joyful nor sad – one is simply not thinking of anything.

The fourth movement, *finale, allegro con fuoco,* makes you want to find happiness in yourself by going amongst people, seeing how they enjoy themselves. There is still some joy left to find, simple and sincere pleasure. Rejoice in others' joy and life goes on.

Symphony No. 5 in E Minor, Op. 64
The symphony opens with a theme on the clarinet and low strings. The so-called "Fate theme" recurs in all the movements, appearing finally in the last movement in the major key.

After the *andante* introduction there appears, in *allegro con anima*, the peculiarly syncopated main theme. A couple of very expressive waltz themes occur, strongly syncopated in places, but the movement ends with the restless main theme.

The second movement, *andante cantabile,* has all of Tchaikovsky's melodious charm, but the happy mood is interrupted by the "Fate theme".

The third movement is a gracious waltz, *allegro moderato,* partly based on a street song. The "Fate theme" is heard

this time only as a distant memory and without its usual menacing accent.

The fourth movement, *andante maestoso,* introduces the "Fate theme" in the major. This is modified into a kind of Russian hymn. There then follows *allegro vivace,* an energetic and characteristically Russian theme, which has almost the stamp of a folk dance. The "Fate theme", now in its new shape, carries the movement and brings it to a triumphant conclusion.

Symphony No. 6 in B Minor, Op. 74 – "Pathétique"
This is Tchaikovsky's last symphony and also reckoned among his greatest works. He gave the symphony its name.

The first movement, *adagio, allegro non troppo,* opens with a slow introduction, which contains the thematic material and gives the basic mood of the work. The main theme is based on motifs from the introduction.

The second movement, *allegro con grazia,* is a kind of waltz, with an elegy as trio.

The third movement, *allegro molto vivace,* features a cheerless march. This dazzlingly orchestrated movement is restless.

The fourth movement, *adagio lamentoso,* in its introduction theme appears as an expression of the deepest despair and is succeeded by a theme filled with bitter lamentation. Then follows what is the chief motif of the movement, a mood of peaceful resignation. The work dies away in the quietest pianissimo.

Ballet Music
Tchaikovsky enjoys worldwide acclaim for his ballet music. He wrote the music for three ballets – "Swan Lake", Op. 20; "Sleeping Beauty", Op. 66 and "The Nutcracker" (Casse Noisette), Op. 71.

Swan Lake

Tchaikovsky was spending the summer of 1871 with relatives in the countryside, and to entertain his sister's children, wrote a little ballet that was given the name "The Swan Lake". Four years later, he made use of this music he had written for the children in a major composition.

"At the magnificent court of Prince Siegfried his coming of age is being celebrated in high style. His mother upbraids him for not settling down and decides that he must choose a wife at the next ball. Siegfried sets out on a hunt with his friends at a nearby lake.

"The Second Act is by the Lake. Gliding over it are some swans, which on touching the shore change into beautiful girls. Rotbart, a magician, watches with interest. Siegfried and his friends are about to release their arrows when Odette, the leader of the swans, begs them to refrain, explaining that Rotbart's spell permits them human form for only a few hours after each midnight. Siegfried falls in love with Odette. Invited to the forthcoming ball, to be chosen as Siegfried's wife, Odette declares her presence impossible unless the magician's spell is broken. She reminds Siegfried that if he breaks his promise she and all her friends will die.

"The Third Act is a resplendent ballroom, which is soon filled with guests. Six girls of blue blood dance before Siegfried, but he shows no interest in them. After a feast of dancing a fanfare heralds Rotbart, disguised as a black swan, with his daughter Odile, dressed to resemble Odette. Deceived by the likeness, Siegfried woos her and announces that she is to be his wife. Rotbart is delighted – the Prince has broken his vow. He and his daughter disappear suddenly and it is then that Siegfried realises his mistake.

"Act Four is by the Swan Lake. Odette is in despair at Siegfried's betrayal, and it is not until he discloses the trickery that she forgives him. The reconciliation is however marred by a storm that Rotbart engineers. The girls are terrified that they will perish in the rapidly rising waters, and Siegfried, seeking a nearby slope with Odette in his arms, declares his willingness to die at her side. This devotion breaks the evil spell and at last all the swans become human beings."

The Sleeping Princess/Beauty, Op. 66

Since 1946, the composition has been called "The Sleeping Beauty".

Based on *La Belle au Bois dormant* by the French fairytale writer, Charles Perrault, the composition comprises a prologue and three acts. The story is the well-known tale of the Princess placed under a spell by a wicked fairy to sleep until awakened by the kiss of a Prince.

The composition is very popular, and continues as one of the mainstays of the former Soviet Ballet. Its music, however, has been held by purists to be too symphonic.

The last act of the ballet – the celebration scene – is often performed by itself under the title "Aurora's Wedding".

The Nutcracker Suite (Casse Noisette), Op. 71

In this ballet toys come to life and children play and dream about them on Christmas Eve and Christmas Night. The Nutcracker, trying to split a nut that is too big for it, breaks into pieces. There is a battle between the toys and the mice, with the Nutcracker as commander. He is transformed into a Prince, and all the toys rejoice and display themselves, each in its own dance, viz. Dance of the Sugar-plum Fairy, Russian Dance, Arab Dance and Chinese Dance, and, of course, the Waltz of the Flowers.

Serenade in C Major, Op. 48

This is a suite in four movements, none of them very long and all quite attractive. Tchaikovsky was a great melodist, never happier than when writing for the string family of instruments. First, there is a "Piece in the form of a Sonatina", formal but very pleasant. Then follows a waltz so lovely, it is a sheer delight to hear. Even Johann Strauss at his best did not surpass Tchaikovsky when in a waltz-writing mood. After this, a quiet reflective movement, Élégie, and to finish, a spiritual Finale based on two Russian folk tunes, the one a boat-hauling song and the other a lively street song. Here the music works itself up to a climax, with an infectious rhythm.

Capriccio Italien, Op. 45

This composition is a bundle partly of Italian folk tunes, as Tchaikovsky himself admitted, taken from published collections and partly a record of popular airs that he heard in Florence.

The music relies entirely on its brilliant orchestration. The musical value of the work is little, but the colouring is vivid and fascinating, and the movements animated.

RICHARD **STRAUSS**

Born : Munich, Germany, June 11, 1864

Died : Garmisch-Partenkirchen, Germany, September 8, 1949

Richard Strauss's father Franz was a famous principal French horn player of the Munich Court Orchestra. Indeed, he was known as "the Joachim of the French horn", who saw to it that in addition to thorough musical coaching his son received a thorough German education, which was the envy of other countries.

Franz Strauss disliked Wagner's music and tried to keep his son clear of its contaminating influence, exposing him instead to the Classical composers. But when Richard was 20, to his father's disgust, he openly became an admirer of the musical Romantics – Wagner, Liszt and Berlioz.

Strauss's first great composition was a symphonic fantasy, "Aus Italien", in which he translated the impressions of his rambles through Italy into music of Wagnerian proportions, foreshadowing the massive tone poems that were to follow: "Don Juan", "Macbeth" and "Death and Transfiguration", that appeared in quick succession.

By the age of 30, Strauss was comfortably settled, successful and married to the soprano Pauline de Ahna in September 1894. He embarked upon a pleasant career of composing pieces that he often guest-conducted. Deaf to what the critics said – and they fulminated – Strauss turned out more tone poems between 1895 and 1899 such as "Till Eulenspiegel", "Also sprach Zarathustra", "Don Quixote", "Ein Heldenleben" (A Hero's life) and "Sinfonia Domestica".

Strauss visited Bayreuth in 1891 where, with one principle in mind – "Anything Wagner can do, I can do better" – he started composing operas like "Salome", "Elektra" and "Der Rosenkavalier". Fifteen operas were to emerge from his pen. In all these tone poems Strauss followed the form of the symphonic poem set by Franz Liszt. But he enlarged it, working at the same time towards a descriptive musical language that everyone could appreciate. He supplied programmes which explained in words the humour, satire or irony, the rage, hysteria or perversity that the music depicted. His symphonic poems were, therefore, rightly called "programme" pieces.

In 1889, Strauss became director of the Weimar Court Orchestra. Here he gained recognition with his symphonic poem "Don Juan" and established a reputation as the most significant German composer since Wagner.

The period from 1894 to 1902 was one of intense activity during which Strauss continued composing a series of tone poems and used instruments to tell a story or illustrate a theme. Among these, "Also sprach Zarathustra" was one of the grandest, based on the text by the German philosopher Friedrich Nietzsche, making use of huge orchestral forces to depict the evolution of the human race.

Strauss's "Don Quixote" portrays scenes from the classic novel of the same name by the Spanish writer Cervantes in which the cello represents the Knight and the viola, his servant Sancho Panza. The "Sinfonia Domestica" describes in music a day in the life of Strauss's own household.

His third opera, "Salome", based on the play by Oscar Wilde, received a passionate response when it was performed in 1905. This sensual and erotic work was received with such enthusiasm at the first performance that Strauss had to make 38 curtain calls. It dealt with a biblical subject, but the music was dramatic and sensual in a manner that had never before been heard and the scandal it provoked led to huge attendances across Germany.

In 1909, Strauss produced "Elektra", his first opera to a libretto by the German poet Hugo von Hofmannsthal. The emotionally charged music and the story of vengeance again attracted media attention; the opera house was packed with audiences wanting to hear "the decadent and immoral music".

Strauss's next opera "Der Rosenkavalier" was Mozartian, full of tunes and Viennese waltzes. It is a warm, human work with universal appeal.

A remarkably well-read man, Strauss in his earlier years at the University of Munich had studied philosophy, aesthetics and the history of art. He collected paintings by Renoir, Tintoretto and Utrillo. Throughout his life he earned well by conducting and used his free time to compose.

Easy success and comfortable living had not prepared Strauss to defy the Nazis when they came to power and invited him to head their Reichsmusikkammer (Chamber of State Music), in 1933. His acceptance discredited him with the anti-Nazi world. After a brief tenure in office, he found he could not stomach the Nazi doctrine and resigned.

Fortunately, after the War, in 1948, he was cleared by a de-Nazification Board of all taint of collaboration and died the following year, with his reputation restored.

Among Strauss's last works is the conversation piece "Capriccio" which discusses the relative importance in opera of words and music.

Strauss had continued to compose throughout World War II and was moved by its horrors to a final outpouring of compositions. His "Metamorphosen" (1945) for 23 strings is an elegy for pre-War German musical life shattered beyond recognition by the conflict.

Strauss died in 1949, at the age of 85, a year after completing the serenely beautiful "Four Last Songs", settings of poems by Hesse and Eichendorff for sopranos and orchestra.

Major compositions

Operas
Salome, 1 Act (1905)
  Salome's Tanz
    (Dance of the Seven Veils) – Orch.
  Finale: Du wolltest mich
Elektra, 1 Act (1909)
Der Rosenkavalier, 3 Acts (1911)
  Orchestral Suites
  Waltzes, Act 2 (violin and pianoforte)
  Waltzes, Act 3 (Walzerfolge)
  Act 1: Di rigori armato (T)
  Kann mich auch an ein Mädel erinnern
  Act 2: Herr in Himmel
  (Presentation of Rose)
  (Letter & Waltz Scene) Da lieg ich
  Act 3: Hab' mir's gelobt (Trio)
  Ist ein Traum (25) (arr. orch. and pf)
Ariadne auf Naxos, 1 Act (1912)

Orchestral
Alpine Symphony, Op. 64 (1915)
Also sprach Zarathustra
  (Thus spake Zarathustra), Op. 30 (1896)
Burleske (pianoforte and orch.) (1883)
Don Quixote, Op. 35
  (violincello and orch.) (1897)
Ein Heldenleben, Op. 40 (1898)
Sinfonia Domestica, Op. 53 (1903)
Till Eulenspiegels Lustige Streiche,
  Op. 28 (1895)
Death and Transfiguration
  (Tod und Verklärung, Op. 24 (1888-89)
Metamorphosen, 23 strings (1945)
Four last songs (voices and orch.) (1950)

Strauss's place in music history

The last of the great Romantics, Richard Strauss left an extraordinary catalogue of works whose power and warmth have earned him a unique position in music's hall of fame. His music is alive with vigour and vitality. It is music of glowing colour, for Strauss was a master among masters of the art of orchestration. His reputation rests on his operas, art songs and the ear-filling vital, realistic tone poems.

Strauss developed and perfected the tone poem. He elaborated the leitmotif, or musical phrase attached to a definite person, place, thing or situation. He projected a new conception of counterpoint in which simultaneous melodies are considered separately as melodies without regard to their mutual harmony or dissonance.

In the treatment of programme music he was a pioneer of musical realism. Whereas Wagner claimed that the symphonic poem as programme music could not be understood without the aid of the stage, Strauss made no attempt to conceal his intention to establish a direct association between music and the daily round, and so developed its descriptive possibilities that it becomes possible to portray a teaspoon in tone.

"To call Strauss's music merely 'programmatic' is to slander it. For he seldom descends to mere imitation of familiar sounds or stereotyped musical idioms, for the suggestion of 'falling waters' or 'galloping horses' or similar picturesque incidents of ordinary 'programme music'. With Strauss a fanfare of brass may mean not merely a call to arms but the cause of an empire's downfall; a fluttering of strings may signify not a springtime zephyr but a storm within the soul. Though it may revolve about material beings and objects, the music of Strauss is nevertheless powerfully subjective and symbolic.

"Strauss's complete mastery of musical media is apparent everywhere in his works. He could do anything he wished with the notes, and constructed his works with clear and calculating intelligence. He selected his self-imposed tasks with boldness, imagination and wisdom."

Notes on select works
"Ein Heldenleben" (A Hero's Life)

"A Hero's Life" is not a musical biography of some actual or mythical human being. It is rather the depiction of the life of an ideal man – a hero only in the sense that he meets his problems, victories and defects, the force of evil and of destruction, the supreme experience of love, the demands upon his physical and spiritual powers, and the autumnal peace of his closing years, with all the nobility and vitality of his manhood.

❝ With Strauss a fanfare of brass may mean not merely a call to arms but the cause of an empire's downfall; a fluttering of strings may signify not a springtime zephyr but a storm within the soul. ❞

"The Hero is, then, an ideal, a subjective personage. We must not therefore look to the music for two well-defined incidents. The underlying idea is treated broadly, subjectively and with symbolism. Yet the Hero is human; he lives and loves; knows victory and defeat, tears and laughter. He wields a sword, and achieves even more powerfully in fields of peace and at length, himself knows the great peace of fulfillment.

"Whether or not he wishes to be so considered, Richard Strauss is generally regarded as being the hero of 'Ein Heldenleben', not, as has been implied above, as a singular and well defined personality, but as experiencing, in his own career, much of the antagonism and much of the superb defiance of his adversaries that distinguishes the Hero of the tone poem. He created this musical epic, certainly not in any mood of self-glorification, but perhaps with much the attitude which begot Wagner's 'Meistersinger'.

"While Strauss, in the score of 'A Hero's Life' sets forth no arguments, no programme, no clue to the story which lies implicit in the music, the following may be accepted as a broad outline of the Hero's life.

"At the opening of the music, the Hero is in full powers of young manhood. His personal, spiritual characteristics are distinguished and noble. He is proud, sensitive, imaginative, sympathetic and powerful of will. When such a personality comes in contact with meanness, there is conflict. The conflict of the Hero with his adversaries, who are pictured as stupid, envious, malicious, together with the Hero's disquietude, make up the second section of the work.

"The third section introduces the Hero's Beloved, in her various engaging moods. She is playful, seductive, angry, scornful and demure by turns. He woos her with a quiet passion that one feels must eventuate in his triumph in the lists of love, as indeed it does.

"The fourth section sees the Hero torn from his Beloved to face the heat and strife of battle. The military note is unmistakable. The Hero departs for the battle front, and there are marvellous pictures of flashing swords, of uproar and of slaughter; and we hear the conflict of the Hero's theme with that of his adversaries. Occasionally there are recollections of the theme of his Beloved that urge him on, supporting him until at last the victory is won.

"The fifth section depicts the Hero's victories in the fields of peaceful endeavour. These are victories of the mind and spirit, and it is this section of the work that implies most strongly that Strauss himself is the Hero. Now we hear musical allusions and quotations from his previous works... works which achieved success only after the most vitriolic criticism and unrelenting attacks.

"The final section of the tone poem is perhaps the most subtle. Here we discover that, though the Hero has triumphed, his achievements are belittled by his stupid adversaries, and his reward is envy and contempt. At first he rebels; then gradually he realises that his true triumph lies in the inward satisfaction of his own spirit and conscience, and though there are occasional distressing memories of scenes of strife and bitterness, peace finally broods gently over the Hero's soul. It is the peace of fulfilment and of contentment.

"His work is achieved – and nobly. He knows that in the depths of his soul. Thereafter, nothing can disturb his tranquillity."

Salome's Dance
(The Dance of the Seven Veils)

"This highly dramatic and frantically voluptuous music is extracted from Strauss's musical setting of the one-act drama *Salome*, written by Oscar Wilde. It does not necessarily depict the tense situation in which the dramatic action is suspended at the moment when Salome begins her choreographic undoing of Herod, but it does very powerfully suggest the succeeding waves of voluptuous excitement and exhaustion which marked the dancing of the vengeful and sadistic Salome.

"The cries of John, imprisoned, fill the dancer with sweet torment. She burns with the fury of a woman scorned; she pants for revenge, yet at the same agonising moment she is tortured with love for her intended victim. Upon the bloated Herod she casts a mysterious glance, languishing and submissive, yet determined; promising, yet remote. From the forbidding countenance of her mother, the governor's wife, she turns her face away.

"The music begins, and Salome, as if waiting for a significant phrase, stands motionless, beautiful and deadly. The

Richard Strauss at the age of 10

mad excitement of the music is restrained as she begins the sinuous weaving and posturing, the fluid rhythms that beguile and seduce the sensual Herod, the half-revealing, half-concealing veils floating like a rosy mist about her. In the orchestra the viola and flute put forth a wickedly innocent phrase, and again, a lovely line of melody is traced by horn and strings and woodwind, with the Oriental accent of the cor anglais lending warm and dark colour. The fainting ecstasies of the dancer, and hard upon them new influxes of power and passion, are reflected in the changing rhythms and intensities of the music, until in a wild and abandoned climax, the orchestra indicates the last convulsive leaps and whirlings of the dancer's white body – and afterward, her quivering prostration at the feet of Herod."

Till Eulenspiegels Lustige Streiche (Till Eulenspiegel's Merry Pranks)

"It is not important whether or not Till Eulenspiegel ever existed in the flesh; certainly he lives now, in this merry, naughty, diabolically ingenious music. In providing this delicious musical entertainment, Strauss indulges, as he has done nowhere else in his scores, a sardonic, a wry, and sometimes macabre humour, none the less apparent because of the extraordinary complicated orchestration. It is possible, though not at all necessary, to fit this music into a rough form; the thematic treatment lends itself to such a humourless diversion. It is much more pleasant, however, to sit back and listen and laugh, and perhaps sometimes not to laugh – noting, meanwhile, such details as seem to be of indubitable significance.

"Here again Strauss indicates, by the title, a theme that is certainly programmatic; yet he has never

authorised, though he has tolerated, the publication of a 'story' or programme for this music. To search painfully through the score, and to detach therefrom every phrase that can be detached without dislocating the whole structure; and to identify every such phrase with some particular activity or characteristic of Till is a distasteful task that may well be left to more pedantic scholars. There is no authentic story. But we should know this:

"Till Eulenspiegel (Till Owlglass) is a wickedly mischievous fellow much given to practical jokes. He rides his horse through a crowded market place, scattering housewives, merchants and goods in every direction; he disguises himself as a member of the clergy, or a dandy, or an ordinary respectable citizen, and while so disguised perpetrates his most annoying mischiefs – some of them too nasty for description; he makes love to village maidens, playing, so to speak, 'touch and go' with them. But eventually

he is caught, tried and (in the musical version) hanged. The last joke is on Till.

"The atmosphere of the introduction clearly suggests the folk-tale inspiration of the music. Considerable thematic material is introduced here, and a climax in which most of the orchestra joins brings us to the point at which Till first walks, hops, skips or jumps upon the scene. He appears in a sly phrase of the clarinet one to mark well, for in various guises and mutations this motif will appear often and meaningfully. There is some sport with the theme, developing into a climax of considerable power. Then we hear Till again. He is putting on his Sunday best, and presently appears in silken string tone, in viola and basses; even in the polished tones of the flute.

"The first of his naughty pranks is the insolent trampling down of the stalls in the market place, as he spurs his horse through chattering crowds (woodwind). Crashing of household utensils as they are scattered about, and Till's precipitate flight, are clearly indicated in the music.

"Now our hero has an inspiration. He adopts the protection of 'the cloth', masquerading as a priest of exceptionally unctuous appearance and manner. He doesn't quite know how to handle a cassock, however, and through the quasi-religious atmosphere we can see the rascal (clarinet: Till's theme) beneath the priestly robes.

"Again the theme of Till comes, now bold and somewhat military in suggestion. Till is a plumed knight, a very devil of a fellow, a gay Lothario. How the ladies love him – or do they?

"Episode after episode, each delineated in the most ingenious orchestration, keeps us wondering 'what next'; wondering too, at the really marvellous mastery of the orchestra's resources the composer displays here.

Till gets into and out of trouble time after time, but eventually he is caught. He is arrested; he is brought into court. And terribly the court thunders its accusations. Till answers with customary insouciance (Till's theme). The court recalls another of his crimes; Till denies it.

"He is found guilty anyway, perhaps on the theory that even if he had not done what he was presently charged with, he should be punished anyway for other crimes, unknown to the court. So they hang him, and there is a grisly humour in the squeakings of the orchestra as poor Till does his airy dance.

"It is characteristic of Strauss that he is not through with Till until he has forgiven the rascal. The concluding measures at least suggest such an attitude to some listeners. The original themes reappear; Till is seen in the light of distance and legend. The laughs that he caused are remembered; the cruelty and coarseness are forgotten. Yet the concluding bars, presented fortissimo, leave the problem unsolved."

Don Quixote

This presents fantastic variations on a knightly theme for full orchestra. Each variation illustrates an episode from Cervantes's famous novel.

Cervantes created two immortal characters: the romantic, idealistic Don Quixote, who, dressed in an old suit of armour, rides out on his broken-down old horse Rozinante into a world packed with imaginary dangerous adventures; and his esquire, the shrewd and materialistic farm lad Sancho Panza.

The composer himself set out the following programme –
Theme: Don Quixote, Knight of the Rueful Countenance (solo cello).
Sancho Panza, his esquire (bass clarinet, tenor tuba and solo viola).

"1st Variation: The strangely assorted pair ride away, bidden farewell by Dulcinea del Toboso. Incident with windmill.

"2nd Variation: Vigorous fight with the army of mighty Emperor Alifanfaron (actually a flock of sheep).

"3rd Variation: Conversations between knight and esquire. Sancho pours out questions, sayings and proverbs. Don Quixote teaches him and sets his mind at rest, promising him a great reward (viz. the princess's handmaiden).

"4th Variation: Unfortunate encounter with a procession of pilgrims carrying in prayer and penance the image of a saint, arrayed in woman's clothes. Don Quixote scents an abduction and tackles the pilgrims, only to be driven off himself.

"5th Variation: Don Quixote's vigil. He thinks lovingly of his far away Dulcinea.

"6th Variation: Meeting with a peasant girl, whom Sancho presents to his master as the bewitched Dulcinea.

"7th Variation: Journey through the air. Some noble ladies blindfold the knight and delude him into believing that he is flying through the air.

"8th Variation: Disastrous voyage in the bewitched boat (Barcarolle). The boat capsizes under some mill wheels, which Don Quixote thinks are a fortress.

"9th Variation: Fight against supposed wizards (two priests on their mules).

"10th Variation: Duel with the Knight of the Shining Moon. Don Quixote is defeated, renounces the profession of arms and returns home to be a herdsman.

"Finale: Having returned to his senses, he spends his last days in realisation of his foolishness. Death of Don Quixote."

Also sprach Zarathustra (Thus spake Zarathustra)

Of this tone poem for orchestra Strauss himself wrote in a letter: "I did not intend to write philosophical music or to portray in music Nietzsche's great work. I meant to convey by means of music an idea of the development of the human race from its origin, through the various phases of its development, religious and scientific, upto Nietzsche's idea of the Ubermensch.

"The whole symphonic poem is intended as my homage to Nietzsche's genius, which found its greatest exemplification in his book *Thus Spake Zarathustra.*"

Perhaps the last sentence of the quotation comes nearest to the mark. The music pays tribute to the great German philosopher by adopting, as the basis, for certain more or less illustrative musical developments, passages from the philosophical poem of the same name. Music cannot convey an idea of the development of the human race, except in a historical and evolutionary sense. The test of that statement is this: how much of the history of the race, or its religious and scientific development, would be deduced from the music if it had no title?

JEAN **SIBELIUS**

Born : Tavastehus, Finland,
December 8, 1865

Died : Järvenpää, Finland,
September 20, 1957

*J*ean Sibelius's father, a surgeon, was keen that his son, baptised Johan Julius Christian, should study law. Nevertheless, "Janne" as he was called by his family and friends, began piano lessons at the age of 9, violin lessons at 15 and had an excellent general education.

From his early years, Sibelius loved to roam the woods near his home, with his violin tucked under his arm. Perched on a rock he performed concerts for an appreciative audience of birds. The family was therefore not surprised when, in the second year of studying law at Helsinki University, he announced his intention of switching from law to music.

Sibelius laid the foundation of his chosen profession by intensive studies in Berlin and Vienna. When he returned to Finland after two years, he found his country in revolt against Russian attempts to suppress independence, free speech and the right of assembly.

Moved by the times, Sibelius composed a symphonic poem, "Kullervo", in the folk song idiom of the people, a patriotic outcry which stirred them deeply. This was followed by a tone poem, "En Saga", for orchestra, and soon after that by "Spring Song for Orchestra" and the four "Lemminkäinen Legends" that included "The Swan of Tuonela", a touchingly beautiful work.

In 1892, Sibelius married Aino Järnefeldt, a woman of culture and distinction from an aristocratic family.

In 1897, impressed with the performance of "Kullervo", the Finnish Government voted him an annual salary, which was later readily increased. Free to compose music without financial worries, Sibelius wrote songs, pieces for solo violin and piano, and the tone poem "Finlandia", which was described as "hot with the spirit of revolt". A string quartet followed and, most important of all, seven symphonies that are considered second only to those of Beethoven, earning him the nickname "Finnish Beethoven".

In 1894, Sibelius visited Bayreuth, in Germany, where Richard Wagner had established his famous music festival. Wagner's music had a profound effect on him.

The first decade of the 20th century saw a massive growth in Sibelius's international reputation. He travelled extensively in Germany, England and the USA. Everywhere he was received with great honours.

Sibelius spent the last 30 years of his life in self-imposed musical silence. He was, it is said, deeply disillusioned with modern music, yet rated Bartók and Shostakovich very highly.

For more than 50 years Sibelius lived in a cabin in Järvenpää near Helsinki. The two World Wars interrupted his tranquil way of life. During the Russian invasion of Finland in 1940, he was forced to leave home with his family and seek safety. But he returned to live peacefully and quietly until his death on September 20, 1957.

in my spare time. The piano does not interest me. It cannot sing." He added that Chopin was the only great composer who understood the piano and wrote for it.

Sibelius was unquestionably the 20th century's greatest symphonist. His symphonies are noted for their organised growth, subtly achieved forms and refined instrumentation. His was a sovereign and independent tonal language. As a late Romantic, he created many imaginative musical pictures from the world of Finnish saga in a long series of poetic and melodious orchestral works.

Although an intense nationalist and an ardent patriot, Sibelius was not a user of folk music like Rimsky-Korsakov, Borodin and Mussorgsky. He just made his music sound like original folk music. He was Finland's unique national hero – with his own postage stamp, a special Government pension for life and other rewards befitting national stardom. He was, in short, the Grand Old Man of Finland, honoured by his countrymen from the time he was in his twenties, and by the whole world in his nineties.

chief subject of the movement proper is suggested by the strings – violins first, with derivations of the theme presented by cellos and violas. The contrasting and subordinate thematic material is divided between strings and wind. Then follows a brief period of development, ending in a climax of great intensity with the full orchestra thrusting out savagely in great masses of tone and a terrific thundering of timpani.

"The second chief theme, closely following this outburst, is sung by the flute against a transparent screen woven of the tones of violin, viola and harp. The development and conclusion of the movement is broad and free, and is built mainly upon a titanic struggle for dominance, carried on between the various thematic elements that have been introduced. There are references, both rhythmic and melodic, to the principal themes, and even a suggestion, in the incontinent cries of the woodwind, of the melody of the introduction. Rhythmically, the movement from this point onwards is for the most part developed out of the second of the two principal subjects, but the subject itself, imminent from time to time, is never permitted another explicit statement of itself and is abandoned with finality when the brass so mightily asserts itself near the end.

"The second movement is filled with a nostalgic loveliness... a gentle and pathetic desire for some remembered and intangible joy, as of a dream that, on awakening, seems both ephemeral and real. Violins and cellos sing of this sweet and pathetic desire; then the earnest voices of bassoons and other woodwinds emphasise it with a new melody. The music broods upon these subjects for a while, and presently a third theme, now in horns accompanied by a harp, intrudes. But it is a remembrance of the first theme

Sibelius's place in music history

Sibelius's admirers consider his seven symphonies to be second only to those of Beethoven. Such was the impact Beethoven made with his symphonies that even great composers like Brahms and Sibelius waited for a long time before they placed before the world their respective first symphonies.

Sibelius himself said to his pupil Bengt de Törne: "I am a man of the orchestra. You must judge me by my orchestral works... I write piano pieces

Notes on select works

Symphony No. 1 in E Minor, Op. 39

The symphony was written in 1899 when Sibelius was to some extent under the influence of Tchaikovsky and at brief intervals this is quite marked. His later symphonies depart almost entirely from any influence.

"The symphony opens with an introduction in which the clarinet sings a wandering melody – a lonely voice moving in solitary loveliness over the ominous rumblings of drums... The that brings about the most vigorous development of the movement.

"The basis of the entire third movement is the almost brutally violent figure given out by three timpani at the beginning. With all its power, this figure somehow suggests a heavy-handed humour... The second theme, though contrastingly lighter, is clearly influenced by the rhythm of the first, and only in the trio, which is much more restrained and gentle, is there an escape from the fierce assertive gesture that lies in the first thunderous utterance of the timpani. At the end, there is a swift accelerando, a growth in power, and the great drums, with the whole orchestra, thunder once again and for the last time.

"The finale of the fourth movement is like a series of three mountainous waves, rising to terrifying heights of power, subsiding to simple, if not precisely placid, fluxes of orchestral tone. The opening subject is developed clearly from the song of the clarinet in the introduction to the first movement; but its character has undergone a marked change. Where it once sang of loneliness and contemplation, it now assumes a dark and tragic significance. As if it had provoked them, suggestions of the imminent chief theme of the movement are heard deep in the strings; the theme itself appears, against ominous beatings of drums, in the woodwind. With this impetus the first great wave of the movement takes form, and rushes out from the orchestra in powerful and resistless surgings, moving toward a mighty crashing climax.

"The second theme is in marked contrast with the first. It appears, presently in the violins and, a little later, is compared with the original theme. Now the second great wave form of the movement gathers itself for another climax. It is not long in developing, and at

its peak demands almost the ultimate of the orchestral resources. A presentation of the second theme in clarinet is the interrupting idea which begets the formation of the third, and final, wave of tone which sweeps the orchestra like a storm."

Symphony No. 2 in D Major, Op. 43

The symphony belongs to the same period as "Finlandia". The same musical intuition is at work here and the same political feelings. In Finland this symphony is accepted as a symphonic drama of liberation. According to Georg Schneevoight, an intimate friend of Sibelius, the first movement was intended to depict the quiet, pastoral life of the Finns. The second movement, which is marked *lugubre*, is a lament, charged with patriotic feelings. The *scherzo*, which is like a bleak, snow-scurried landscape, portrays the awakening of national feeling. And at the end of this agitated *scherzo*, a long crescendo leads without pause into the fourth movement. This finale is a mighty chant of triumph, the dream of the fatherland which has burst its shackles. It is bold, spacious music of monumental simplicity. The simple, elemental theme of the finale climbs slowly and inexorably from the bottom of the orchestra to a climax of staggering power.

Symphony No. 4 in A Minor, Op. 63

This symphony is Sibelius's finest. "In the first movement the power, achieved by rare economy of means, is almost terrifying – almost like the elemental strivings of the brute forces of nature. The savage bowing of the low

strings on their monotonous and limited phrase is as pitiless as the grinding of great stones in some subterranean cavern. The solo cello that presently suggests a theme is not the romantic voice we know, but a grimly regretful one without passion and almost without emphasis. There is no brilliance, but only wildness and keenness even when the upper strings, bowed with ever-growing force, begin an advance toward a discordant and unresolved climax. Brasses vehemently thrust out threatening lances of tone, bright and deadly; again strings shriek like wild winter winds. From a few phrases the composer builds a brief but mighty movement, free in form, yet tremendously restrained and laconic and stern. He dwells upon this thought until it is clear, in the simplest and strongest terms; he proceeds, with merciless logic, to the next. There is no lingering upon a lonely phrase – though there are phrases of strange harsh beauty, there is no sweeping and brilliant and persuasive peroration, only a swift dissolution of the music into pale harmonies immaterial and distant as Northern mists.

"Second movement: Perhaps the uncommunicative Finn has humour like this – terse, rough and wry. A man who wrests his living from nature's grudging hands has little time for laughter. But here is laughter, harsh and unaccustomed, bold and sardonic. The peasant's cruelly acute sense of the ridiculous is almost his only stimulus to mirth, and here, perhaps, is an illustration of it. The curious cry of the oboe is almost pathetic and it is roughly elbowed aside by rude interjections of the strings. In contrast comes an almost waltz-like passage, definitely reminiscent

> " *Sibelius was unquestionably the 20th century's greatest symphonist. His symphonies are noted for their organised growth, subtly achieved forms and refined instrumentation.* "

of Tchaikovsky. Contrabassoon, and later, after a swift descent of strings, an almost painfully vehement protestation from the brass banish temporarily the mood of laboured humour and recall the fierce brazen interruptions of the first movement. Woodwinds in a graceful descending figure achieve gaiety once more, but that sullen remembrance of the preceding movement has vitiated the spirit of this one, and it dies, abruptly and unexpectedly, in a feeble flicker of tone.

"Third movement: In this truly beautiful and affecting movement Sibelius makes the closest approach to sustained melody that can be found in the symphony. Flute informs us of a lovely theme, of pastoral simplicity, clarinet continues it; both are supported by soft harmonies in the strings. A solemn chorus of brass warms and weighs the orchestra's tone, and later, a bassoon suggests a more serious thought. It is the cello, however, which holds forth upon the basic theme, against a tremulous string accompaniment. And the elements of this theme, as well as of others, are strangely dissipated through the movement, though often there are brief passages of very moving melody. The string orchestra, for a space, has almost complete possession of the composer's thought, rising to a climax that is all but passionate, and then resigning once more in favour of flute and clarinet which present their respective phrases much as at the beginning. The strange insolvent harmony of Sibelius is, paradoxically, occasionally resolved here into even such usual things as chords built upon tonic and dominant. Yet at the end, where the unsatisfying harmony gradually attenuates to a unison C-sharp in muted horns and violas, against which a succession of thematic fragments are thrown by woodwind and strings, there is no relaxation of the rigours of this

Major compositions

Symphonies (7)
No. 1, E Minor, Op. 39 (1899)
No. 2, D Major, Op. 43 (1902)
No. 3, C Major, Op. 52 (1907)
No. 4, A Minor, Op. 63 (1910)
No. 5, E-flat Major, Op. 82 (1915)
No. 6, D Minor, Op. 104 (1923)
No. 7, C Major, Op. 105 (1924)

Symphonic Poems
Kullervo
En Saga, Op. 9 (1892 rev. 1901)
Finlandia, Op. 26 (1899 rev. 1900)
Night Ride and Sunrise, Op. 55 (1909)
Tapiola, Op. 112 (1925)
Pohjola's Daughter, Op. 49 (1906)

Suites
Karelia, Op. 11 (1893) –
  Intermezzo – Alla marcia
Lemminkäinen, 4 legends, Op. 22 (1893-99)
  including The Swan of Tuonela
Scènes Historiques 1, Op. 25 (1899)
Scènes Historiques 2, Op. 66 (1912)
Andante festivo (1922)
The Lover, Op. 14 (1911)
Spring Song, Op. 16 (1894)
Romance, C Major,
  Op. 42 for string orch. (1903)
Canzonetta, Op. 62a (1911)
March of the Finnish Infantry, Op. 91a (1918)

Violin Concertos
D Minor, Op. 47 (1903 rev. 1905)
2 Humoresques for violin and orchestra,
  Op. 87 (1917)
4 Humoresques for violin and orchestra,
  Op. 56 (1917)

Chamber Music
String Quartet in D Minor "Voces Intimae"
Danses Champêtres, Op. 106
  (violin and piano) (1925)
Romance, F Major, Op. 78, No. 2 (1915)

Incidental Music
King Christian II (A. Paul), Op. 27 (1898)
  Elegy, Fool's Song (The Spider), Musette
Kuolema (Järnefelt), Op. 44 (1903)
Valse Triste
Pelléas et Mélisande (Maeterlinck), Op. 46

Songs
Autumn Night, Op. 38, No. 1
Black Roses, Op. 36, No. 1
But my Bird is Long in Homing, Op. 36, No. 2
Diamonds on the March Snow, Op. 36, No. 6
In the Fields a Maiden Sings, Op. 50, No. 3
The Maiden came from her Lover's Tryst,
  Op. 37, No. 5
On a Balcony by the Sea, Op. 38, No. 2

A Finnish stamp dedicated to Sibelius

music. It closes in a kind of hypnotised weariness, wan and without colour, given life and motion only by the ominous and inconclusive notes plucked from the basses.

"Fourth movement: It is curious that Sibelius can convey an effect of richness and colour and fantasy entirely without any feeling of warmth. He accomplishes this notably in this movement, with a hard brilliance of orchestration, and with imaginative resourcefulness not easily surpassed in symphonic music. It is with difficulty that one defines the mood of the music, or its significance, if it has any particular significance, for it encompasses every emotional state except sentimentality. There is merriment and grotesquerie, and arresting, forbidding passages of ominous portent. There are bright jinglings in the icy tone of the glockenspiel; wild bells and powerful ring out further on; an oddly syncopated figure in the strings suggests awkward dancing; eventually the trumpet beginning pianissimo and gradually forcing out a flaming tongue of tone, recalls the ominous brazen utterance of the first movement. But the harmonies are dry and hard and unrelenting, even to the end."

Symphony No. 5 in E-flat Major, Op. 82

Composed in 1915, the symphony had its first performance at Helsinki on Sibelius's 50th birthday. The reception was so enthusiastic that the concert had to be repeated three times. Sibelius, however, was not satisfied and rearranged it in 1916, aiming at a still more stringent concentration of content and form. The symphony received its final form in 1919. It is Sibelius's most popular symphony, and many regard it to be his greatest.

"First Movement: Its thematic basis is simple – first, the horn melody heard at the beginning, developed in wind instruments and timpani; second, a brief clear utterance of quite contrasting character, in the woodwind. Strings are used with extraordinary, though subdued effect, particularly where used in harmonics of ghostly quality; they are brought forward very little in the first part of the movement. There is a melancholy figure given to the bassoons and the second subject is extensively developed. The second section of the movement, because of its dance-like rhythm and much-quickened pace, is regarded by many as a true *scherzo*, and by some, including Sibelius, as a movement in itself, though there is no break between it and the preceding section. The mood becomes lighter; the texture of the music less weighty; the sentences contracted and more crisply uttered, and there is new thematic material... Towards the conclusion the orchestra once more shouts out bravely the triumphant version of the opening theme.

"The second movement, rather placid, is devoted for the most part to the exposition of a simple theme and a set of variations. The theme appears after a series of introductory chords given out by the winds, and a few tentative pizzicati from the lower strings. It comes first in the flutes – a simple, charming melody, now ascending, now descending, always shifting in outline but always borne by the same rhythmic impulse. The entire movement is devoted to the exploitation of this theme in variations that pose no problem for anyone, though the dissonant seconds that appear occasionally are a little surprising in view of the generally sweet and tranquil character of the movement.

"The third movement, *allegro molto*, features the frequent moments in the music of Sibelius when one hears almost inevitably the beat and whirr of wings invisible, and this strange and characteristic effect almost always presages something magnificently portentous. Here the strings create it and, by gradually drawing in the woodwind, intensify it; the inevitable burst comes then in the horns, with a vigorous presentation of a strong passage in sustained, forte half-notes. The theme is the very heartbeat of the movement; and in fact, it has animated foregoing portions of the symphony notably in an accompaniment figure in the slow movement. There is a subsidiary, but important, thematic role assigned to woodwind and cellos, against horns and upper strings; and there are unexpected mutations to other tonalities. That which occurs just before the coda, to G-flat Major, is rather startling in method and effective in achieving the required *misterioso* atmosphere; and it leads to the magnificent proclamation at the end which, as Lawrence Gilman has written 'is the crown of the work, and is in many ways the most nobly imagined and nobly eloquent page that Sibelius has given us'. "

Symphony No. 6 in D Minor, Op. 104

It is significant that when the terrifying news of the attack on Finland startled the world, the first thought in a million minds was for the safety of Sibelius. Few composers have in their own time commanded the attention and affection of the world as this great Finnish master.

"The first movement of this symphony has a number of curious features which set it apart from all others of Sibelius. Though loosely integrated, as most of his symphonies are, there is a unity of spirit and a similarity of thematic material running through all four movements that are really remarkable. Again, rather paradoxically, while the music represents Sibelius in his most mature period, it has passages that could quite logically have been written by a Wagner or a Debussy. This is particularly noticeable in the opening phrases... As the opening phrases grow in intensity, and especially upon the dissonant entry of basses, it is quite apparent that only Sibelius could have written that particular passage.

"The mystery and cold dark beauty of the northland make themselves felt in this music, as almost invariably they do in the music of Sibelius... Thematically the movement is loosely articulated, but its rhapsodic spirit is consistent and continuous until towards the end, when the low brasses, with some violence in tone, give sombre pronouncements and quiet the rushing evolutions of imaginary birds and half-imagined spirits...The movement, as a whole, however, is quietly rhapsodic rather than formal and we find in it no release of those mighty powers which Sibelius alone of moderns can summon from the orchestra.

"But for some change, the rhythm of the second movement, *allegro moderato*, might almost be a continuation of the first. The strange dissonant cries of the woodwinds and the quiet conflict of rhythms as well as of tones suggest a more intense emotional atmosphere. The occasional passing of unrelated tonalities produces an atmosphere of restlessness, of struggle, almost of bewilderment, and the acidulous comment of the oboe is a protesting voice rising sharply from a soul that seems to be in turmoil and confusion.

"The third movement, *poco vivace*, is probably the shortest of Sibelius' symphonic movements. The composer has often asserted that he does not use in his music the folk song of Finland. Granting that opinion, it is nevertheless true that the spirit of Finnish folk song is often present in his music, and occasionally even authentic details of folk music are noticeable... As this brief movement

develops we feel the unleashing of orchestral forces and the composer begins to call with more insistence for the orchestra's mightiest utterances.

"The fourth movement, *allegro molto*, is marked by a much brighter melodic line than the composer has so far employed in the symphony. The beautiful thematic strain introduced at the beginning is very possibly of folk-song origin, or if it is not, certainly it is modelled very precisely along the lines of many native Finnish melodies. Later we notice a marvellous effect of distance and mystery, accompanied by deft orchestration involving woodwind and horns. Still later an organ point in the brasses against a long descending figure provides a source of interesting harmonies and dissonances. The movement is almost like a succession of songs, but as so often happens in the music of Sibelius, it is distinctly episodic, and accomplishes unity of mood not only within itself but with the other movements of the work

Sibelius the proud Finn
His works express the soul of his country, the sagas of its people and the beauties of its forests and lakes

without having to labour for structural or formal unity. The music fades and dies on a long-held minor chord in the strings, bringing the symphony to a close."

"Finlandia", Op. 26

Celebrating the nobility, power and rugged beauty of her countryside and in the hearts of her stalwart children, Finland is honoured and represented in this work of her most favoured son. So remarkably has Sibelius captured here the essential spirit of his native land that it has often been assumed that the melodies used in the tone poem are folk tunes. The fact is, according to the composer's own words, that every note is original.

"There is sullen menace in its powerful chords, in brass, that introduce the music, but the antithetical phrase in prayerful woodwind and strings is contradictory. It is sad, yet soothing, and persists even against growing agitation and vehemence in the bass (strings and brass). This is followed by a subject of blazing brilliance, with powerful, strangely accented, and persistent rhythms, leading to a superb climax. Here is conflict, but here too, is a certain feeling of assurance and victory. Presently a hymn-like subject that might almost suggest mourning for the fallen in battle takes prominence in the music. In its reiteration, it reveals a growing feeling of triumph, and its final cadence is the basis for the conclusion of the music in a climax of terrific power and eloquence. It has been said that Finns would become so aroused on hearing this music that its public performance had to be prohibited."

The Swan of Tuonela, from the Lemminkäinen Suite, Op. 22

The music is based upon the mythology of Finland. It pictures the ultimate passage of the disembodied soul to the caverns of

Tuonela, the Hell of Finnish mythology, before reaching which nine seas and a river must be crossed. "Upon the darkly shining bosom of the river moves the sacred Swan in majesty, now singing her strange wild song, now floating with almost imperceptible motion among the gloomy crags, now slowly flapping her great white wings above the silent and deadly whirlpool. The Swan sings her song, a song of terrible loneliness and passionate melancholy, in the dark voice of the cor anglais; strings, con sordino, and the remote rumblings of bass drum, suggest mists and shadows through which great stony portals loom like giants. The strings reach soaring and soul-searching climaxes of passion, and sigh again, through viola, through cello, as if in brief lament for some passing soul on its journey to Tuonela.

The great climax is one of incredible intensity and beauty. The strings taking on, in place of their misty and diaphanous quality, a fierce brilliance like lightning over a sunless, subterranean sea. Then comes an exquisite pianissimo, the strings achieving a curious and effective tone by playing col legno. The snow-white pinions of the Swan are drooping as she sings once again the lovely and distant and melancholy close."

Violin Concerto in D Minor, Op. 47

For Sibelius the violin was "his instrument" as musicians say. He specialised in it as a student and excelled in playing it.

"In this concerto there is exaltation and pessimism, but the voice is the voice of the north, and the splendour that

surrounds it seems not man-made. It is like the ghostly splendour of northern lights, and its majesty is the majesty of the storm. As far as is known, there is no Finnish mythology, or painting of the Finnish landscape here, as there is in so much of Sibelius's music. But the language he speaks is the same, he uses the same vocabulary, and his melody has the same turns that hark back to the ancient Finnish runes. The concerto is in three movements.

"In the first movement over the murmurings of muted violins, a melancholy rhapsodic theme is sung by the solo violin. This is the principal melody which is soon echoed and developed by the darker woodwind instruments. There is a second, more forceful plodding theme, ending with the characteristic drops of a fifth, which also is painted in the dark colours of cellos and bassoons. As these themes begin to grow and sprout new phrases and themes, as simply and logically as a tree thrusts out new branches, there is plenty of opportunity for virtuoso display of the solo violin. But the solo part never seems ostentatious passage work or cadenzas, it remains an organic part of the growth of the music.

"The second movement begins with a poignant little phrase from the woodwinds, like the rise and fall of a sigh. It is echoed bleakly by other wind instruments, and then the violin takes up a deep-throated song of

"Sibelius created imaginative musical pictures from the world of Finnish saga in a series of poetic and melodious orchestral works. Although an ardent patriot, he was not a user of folk music like Rimsky-Korsakov, Borodin and Mussorgsky. He just made his music sound like original folk music. He was Finland's unique national hero."

almost Tchaikovskian melancholy. The movement works up to a great climax of interweaving orchestral voices built around this theme, and then suddenly breaks off and dies away with a few nostalgic phrases.

"The finale is a wild dance movement, with a savage lumbering main theme which Donald Tovey said was evidently a polonaise for polar bears! It begins with a sort of stamping figure in the drums and lower string instruments, but no polar bear could continue that dance with the dizzy leaps and whirls and somersaults in the air that Sibelius gives to his soloist. There are moments when the dance themes rumble about heavily enough in the depths of the orchestra, but always the solo violin shoots up out of that whirling mass, like a rocket into the night sky, spluttering sparks as it soars aloft, to do its own infinitely more agile version of the same dance.

"There are incredibly difficult passages of thirds, arpeggios, harmonics, double-stops and the whole battery of violinistic fireworks, without there being a simple bar of display for mere display's sake. The dance gathers momentum as it passes from one climax to another, and the end comes with a series of brilliant skyward sweeps of the violin, punctuated by sharp decisive chords of the full orchestra."

RALPH VAUGHAN WILLIAMS

Born : Down Ampney, England,
October 12, 1872
Died : London, England, August 26, 1958

Ralph Vaughan Williams was born in a rich family and therefore had none of the problems that many composers usually had in making their living. He studied at the Royal College of Music in London, took his degree of Doctor of Music from Trinity College, Cambridge, and polished his musical style with Max Bruch in Germany and Maurice Ravel in Paris.

From an early age he was interested in folk songs. This explains why he was inclined to Tudor madrigals and modal counterpoint. In 1904 he became a member of the English Folksong Society and undertook research in Norfolk before embodying the folk songs he found there in "Three Norfolk Rhapsodies for Orchestra". The ballad opera "Hugh the Drover" that he composed at about the same time bristled with folk melodies.

In 1910 he completed what has become one of his best-known works, the "Fantasia on a Theme by Thomas Tallis". Its luscious rich texture and song-like melodies complement the original 16th-century theme and has ensured the lasting popularity of the piece.

Another of his well-known works is the "London Symphony" (1914). It pictures the great Thames, the bustling Strand, the Embankment with its mingled comedy and tragedy, and the chimes of Westminster Abbey. The British Music Society pronounced the symphony a most significant work by an Englishman.

After World War I, in which he saw active service, he accepted the position of Professor at the Royal College of Music and became president of the English Folksong Society. His years thereafter were devoted to composing music in varying forms and styles.

With his death in 1958, England lost not only a fine individual musician but a statesman as well, one who spent much time trying to help young composers

" Vaughan Williams had an individual style compounded of tenderness, wit and respect for tradition, with an occasional touch of impressionism and a personal turn of expression that is his own."

and performers. He believed that a composer should "make his art an expression of the whole life of the community". The warmth and popularity of his music indicates clearly how well he succeeded.

Vaughan Williams's place in music history

*V*aughan Williams had an individual style, compounded of tenderness, wit and respect for tradition, with an occasional touch of impressionism and a personal turn of expression that is his own.

Where earlier British composers like Elgar, Parry and Stanford had remained with European musical forms and traditions, specifically of the Germans, Handel and Mendelssohn, Vaughan Williams was consciously in the vanguard of a native English idiom based on regional folk songs.

"On Wenlock Edge"
Vaughan Williams captured the flavour of Housman's poem in this popular piece revised for tenor and orchestra

Major compositions

Operas
Hugh the Drover (1910-14 with later revisions)
Riders to the Sea (1925)

Symphonies (9)
No. 2 "London"
No. 3 "Pastoral"
No. 4 in F Minor
No. 6 in E Minor
No. 7 "Sinfonia Antartica"
No. 8 in D Minor
No. 9 in E Minor

Orchestral
In the Fen Country
Norfolk Rhapsody
The Wasps (Aristophanic Suite)
Fantasia on a Theme of Thomas Tallis
Fantasia on Greensleeves
Serenade to Music (1938) for sopranos,
  contraltos, tenors and basses
Flourish for Glorious John (1957)
  (for Sir John Barbirolli)

Orchestral with solo parts
The Lark Ascending (romance for violin and
  orch. describing the flight of the lark with
  beautiful soaring melodies)
Flos campi
  (Suite for viola and chamber orchestra) (1925)
Suite for viola and small orchestra (1934)

Pieces for chorus and orchestra, songs, film music
On Wenlock Edge, for tenor, string quartet
  and piano (from Housman)
Songs of Travel, for voice and piano
  (from R.L. Stevenson)

SERGEI
RACHMANINOV

Born : Semyonovo, Novgorod, Russia,
April 1, 1873
Died : Beverly Hills, California, USA,
March 28, 1943

*" Rachmaninov was the last great representative
of the Russian Romantic tradition exemplified
especially by Tchaikovsky and Rimsky-Korsakov.
His colourful Slavic music is a valuable link
between the Romantic tradition of
the past and the harsh reality of his time. "*

*I*t was Igor Stravinsky who described Sergei Rachmaninov as "six foot two of Russian gloom". And he was not far wrong, for Rachmaninov was the very image of the melancholy Russian of literature.

As the son of a wealthy army officer, Rachmaninov spent a privileged childhood on his mother's vast estate. The family fortunes, however, declined sharply, primarily due to his father's extravagance and eventually resulted in the separation of his parents.

When he was 10 years old, his mother entered him in the College of Music in St. Petersburg, though not with any thought of her son making music his profession. She simply had to do this as the family could not afford their previous dream of enrolling him in an aristocratic school. Though talented, Rachmaninov went stolidly through his studies at the College of Music in St. Petersburg. It was only when he entered the Moscow Conservatory that his thoughts turned to music as a profession.

At the Conservatory he took his studies seriously and his musical foundations were broad and firm. On completion of his studies in 1892, Rachmaninov won a gold medal for his opera "Aleko". At the Conservatory he met many distinguished composers such as Sergei Taneyev and Anton Arensky. It was also here that Rachmaninov met the great Tchaikovsky. They became good friends and Rachmaninov benefitted from Tchaikovsky's endorsement of his work. Tchaikovsky's death in November 1893, when Rachmaninov was only 20, removed a sorely needed prop in his young life.

After the success of "Aleko", Rachmaninov composed his "Prelude in C-sharp Minor".

Though a minor composition, it made him famous around the world.

Trouble, however, was lurking round the corner. The performance of his First Symphony in March 1897 was an utter failure. That was a great setback for him. Rachmaninov began to doubt his potential as a composer and ceased composing. He was in a state of depression for three years and underwent hypnosis treatment at one point from a Dr. Nikolai Dahl. Fortunately, he responded to the treatment, his depression subsided and he soon returned to composition.

His Second Piano Concerto heralded a return to the normal and in gratitude Rachmaninov dedicated the concerto to Dr. Dahl. The concerto was a huge success from its first performance and was awarded the Glinka Prize of 500 roubles. The concerto has since taken its place among the most popular of musical pieces, second only, some claim, to Beethoven's Fifth Concerto.

Rachmaninov married his cousin Natalie Satina in April 1902 and settled down to many peaceful years of composition and conducting. His symphonic poem, "The Isle of the Dead", was well received, followed by his Second Symphony which was a great success.

In 1909, Rachmaninov paid his first visit to the United States of America. At first he was very diffident about how his concert tour would be received, but he need not have worried. Music lovers there already knew him as the composer of the famous "Prelude in C-sharp Minor". He soon consolidated his position in the USA by securing a contract as a conductor and pianist.

The deepest concern and regret of Rachmaninov's life was the Bolshevik Revolution which forced him and his family to migrate, first to Helsinki in December 1917 and then to the USA in November 1918. He was welcomed in America both as a reputed conductor and pianist, and as a major composer of his time. Although Rachmaninov took American citizenship eventually, he never forgot his homeland. To him there was no Russia after the Revolution.

Rachmaninov cultivated many friends in the United States, made much money from his piano recitals and conducting, but was always haunted by the sad fate that had overtaken his beloved homeland. He remained in the United States until his death from cancer on March 28, 1943.

Rachmaninov's place in music history

Rachmaninov was the last great representative of the Russian Romantic tradition exemplified especially by Peter Tchaikovsky and Nikolai Rimsky-Korsakov. His colourful Slavic music is a valuable link between the Romantic tradition of the past and the harsh reality of his time. He believed that a composer's music should express the country of his birth, his romantic life, his religion, the pictures he loves – in short, the sum total of his socio-cultural and intellectual experience.

Rachmaninov had no great sympathy for "modern" music and considered that many composers of his time were upsetting the laws of music before they had mastered them. Highly individualistic, his music is nevertheless marked by the conservativeness inherited from the teachers and composers he most admired.

There is in the man as well as in his music a rugged honesty, a deep and enduring sincerity which inhibited him from seeking the false gods of sensational modernism. Rachmaninov had great powers of invention and a highly developed sense of harmony. These qualities, together with his exceptional technical ability and intimate knowledge of individual instruments, gave his music an impetus and warmth of its own.

Notes on select works
Piano Concerto No. 2, C Minor, Op. 18

This is one of the most popular works in piano literature, the second greatest after Beethoven's Fifth Symphony.

"The eight solemn chords with which it begins, each individually shaded and coloured, yet progressing as a unified phrase, and with growing power, toward an inevitable climax and response – these glowing yet sombre utterances of the piano constitute one of the great exordiums of music. The response to them, low in the strings, is indeed the first theme of the movement; still lower moves the piano, in full-flowing and legato waves of tone. An accented base note at the beginning of each measure sustains the dark colour of the music that was first applied in the descending octaves at the end of the introductory eight-note phrase.

"Later the piano moves into its brighter upper register, and the liquid tones with which it overlays the shadowed voices of the strings and woodwind presently resolve themselves into a very positive and vigorous rhythm. A subsidiary idea, powerfully pushed to the front by the brass, suggests a change in mood, and the second most important theme of the movement appears in the most limpid tones of the piano. In its development, however, the piano is not the prima donna of the ensemble, but rather a partner with the orchestra in exploring, quite fully, the possibilities of the music. Almost unnoticeably there is a representation of the first theme, which appears in much the same tonal guise as originally, but with brilliant and markedly syncopated chords of the piano sounding powerfully above it. Here is a marvellously seductive foxtrot, although Rachmaninoff calls it in the score, a march (alla marcia).

"One of the loveliest moments in this whole work occurs in the succeeding section, where the horn, solo, takes up the second theme and breathes it softly, yet with passion, against a breathlessly delicate accompaniment. Later strings and piano are heard in a counter theme of the alla marcia section. Towards the end a soft suggestion of the strings sends piano and orchestra into a swift accelerando, with vigorous figures torn violently from the solo instrument, and with three powerful chords ending the movement."

The second movement starts with rich chords in muted strings and after wanderings of the piano in a wayward and pastoral melody, the central musical idea of the movement is presented by the flute and accompanied by piano. The theme is again given to the piano, with strings supplying the accompaniment.

"Still further in the serene progress of the movement the theme is assigned to the violins, the piano painting in a lovely and richly coloured background... The pace of the music then suddenly and greatly increases in a fantastic treatment of a subsidiary theme, and on a sforzando chord of the orchestra a gorgeous cadenza – exacting from the soloist exceedingly difficult requirements in the way of digital dexterity, accuracy and velocity – leads to a serenely beautiful coda."

The third movement begins with "the lower strings entering furtively, but in a sharp staccato. The phrase and its responses grow stronger with repetition, and develop into an orchestral climax of some force... A transitional passage by the piano leads to the second theme, a passionate song of piercing beauty reminiscent of the first theme of the concerto, sung by the violins... The second theme is dominant as the close of the movement approaches, but there are derivations of the first in the commentary of the piano that runs along with the chanting of the strongly bowed strings... A powerful and rhythmically eccentric figure provides a final fillip."

Piano Concerto No. 3, D Minor, Op. 30

"The very opening of the first movement is shadowed and sombre – yet within two measures a vigorous and moving rhythm is established; within a dozen, the pensive yet bright and sanguine melody which the piano sings overcomes the gloomy atmosphere pervading the orchestra...

"The chief theme of the movement occurs almost at the beginning with the first notes of the solo instrument. Strings and bassoon supply the background and contrasting colour. The piano then departs in a long and errant flight through contours derived from the theme, while the orchestra itself adopts a more explicit version of it. The piano solo, with soaring arpeggios and swift plunges into the bass, puts an emphatic period to this episode, and portentous utterances of the low strings foretell a change of mood.

"There is too a change of rhythm, as strings and piano alternate in fragments of a new motive. This quaint episode is

" Although Rachmaninov took American citizenship eventually, he never forgot his homeland. To him there was no Russia after the Revolution. "

the germ from which springs a melody of lovely lyric quality, exchanged periodically between piano and orchestra. It grows in emotional intensity and dynamic powers until a great climax is reached. Then its rhythms change, and suddenly the atmosphere of the opening of the movement returns. The thematic cycle is established and complete. But that is not its end. A development explores and exacts from both the solo instrument and orchestra the last flashing colour, the swiftest dashing flights, the ultimate variation of the theme, and the climax of this is the magnificent cadenza that occurs near the close of the movement... The cadenza involves the voices of flute, oboe, clarinet and horn, each stating in modified form a portion of the chief theme of the movement, the piano following with a suggestion of the second theme. Then follows a succession of piano gymnastics, calling for almost incredible rapidity and brilliance. The movement ends quietly with a recapitulation of its chief subjects.

"The second movement opens with a poignant cry delivered by the strings. Rachmaninov almost immediately contrasts with it a brighter thought and introduces rhythmic elements which by their vitality deliver the movement from deadliness and unmitigated sorrow.

"The woodwind is used most eloquently, its mellower voices serving as foil to the bright and sometimes crystal-white tones of the solo piano. The melodic line unfolds slowly, sending its curving curls through lovely harmonic progressions and modulations. Running passages for the piano build up from the long firm lines established by the strings and woodwind, and a sweeping climax rises out of the whole glowing mass of coloured tone. After a recession from this peak of sonority, there is an interesting transitional passage; a change in rhythm, and in a moment the entire character of the music is radically altered. The piano, glittering above the new melodic subject in clarinet and bassoon, has passage work of terrific difficulty and iridescent brilliance: the rhythmic impulses of plucked strings, curiously waltz-like, move persistently in the bass. Presently a new and brusque idea projects itself through the sonorous bass of the piano, and crashing chords lead directly to the third movement of the concerto."

In the third movement Rachmaninoff prefers to use the piano, generally, as a new orchestral colour, but this approach conceals the prodigious technical ability of the solo artist. For, this movement bristles with the most exacting difficulties but we are rarely conscious of it. "The rippling triplets with which the piano enters the final movement, the great clanging chords in the orchestra, and a second theme shared by piano and strings, evoke a succession of richly coloured musical images. Varying orchestral tones are applied; shifting rhythms pique one's interest, as does the introduction, about halfway through this section, of thematic material derived from the first movement. The agitated rhythm becomes calmer, and a retarded passage, gentle and suave, prepares us for the contrasting swift coda, with its breathless acceleration and brilliant thrusts of tone."

Symphony No. 2, E Minor, Op. 27

Rachmaninov in an interview once very gracefully dismissed the idea that he was a pupil of Tchaikovsky, though proudly admitting that he had received help and suggestions from that great Master. The Tchaikovsky influence is very definitely felt in this symphony, but though the music is for the most part grave, its seriousness passing through the purifying alembic of Rachmaninov's own personality and genius is freed of any trace of morbidity, of excess, of despair.

The symphony was composed in 1908 and was awarded the coveted Glinka Prize – the second time Rachmaninov had achieved this distinction, the first being on the occasion of the publication of his Second Piano Concerto. The symphony is rather long and is usually played with cuts authorised by the composer.

"The whole introduction is a closely woven network of melody, and of harmonies rich and dark; so that when the voice of the cor anglais appears, it stands forth in clear and solitary loveliness. With a few measures establishing a new rhythm, the curving melody of the main theme traces its way in the violins. It is vital and moving and bright now; and it gives such impetus to the orchestra that a brief climax of vigour and assertiveness is developed. There is a pause, a suggestive phrase of clarinets, and then comes the second theme – a simple figure of three notes, yet, in its particular orchestral colour and the setting against which it makes itself heard, it is one of the most poignantly eloquent expressions of loneliness one can find in music. Soft woodwinds give it voice; and strings suggest a comforting answer...

"In succeeding passages the latent power and virility of the music assert themselves; then there is a recession of the orchestral powers through a long and, ultimately, a delicate diminuendo, which continues until but one voice – a solo violin – remains. This recalls the first theme and inaugurates a period of development in which all apparent possibilities of the subject are alluringly explored. The little second theme,

Major compositions

Symphonies (4)
No. 1, D Minor, Op. 13
No. 2, E Minor, Op. 27
No. 3, A Minor, Op. 44

The Bells (Choral Symphony) Op. 35
   (based on a poem by Edgar Allan Poe)

Rhapsody on a theme of Paganini, Op. 43

Piano Concertos (4)
No. 1, F-sharp Minor, Op. 1
No. 2, C Minor, Op. 18
No. 3, D Minor, Op. 30
No. 4, G Minor, Op. 40

Works for Solo Piano
Prelude in C-sharp Minor, Op. 3 (1892) No. 2
Ten Preludes, Op. 23 (1901)
   No. 1, F-sharp Minor
   No. 3, D Minor (1892)
   No. 4, D Major
   No. 5, G Minor
   No. 6, E-flat Major
   No. 7, C Minor
Thirteen Preludes, Op. 32 (1910)
   No. 3, E Major
   No. 5, G Major
   No. 6, F Minor
   No. 12, G-sharp Minor
Serenade, Op. 3
Études Tableaux (6), Op. 33 (1911)
Études Tableaux (6), Op. 39 (1916)
Moments Musicaux (6), Op. 16 (1896)
   Oriental Sketch
   Polka de W.R.

coloured more brightly still, in its brief utterance conveying a feeling of intolerable sadness, returns momentarily. The movement is not to close in this spirit, however. A potent rhythm is introduced in the concluding measures and the music ceases after a final aggressive rush.

"The second movement constitutes what might be called the *scherzo* of the symphony. Brilliant strings establish a swift rhythm and the horns pour out a wild sweet tune, to which the violins are attracted. There is another and even lovelier cantabile from the sweeping strings and sudden secretive passages in which a return to the urgent rhythm of the beginning is suggested.

"The third movement is a tangled web of melody with an atmosphere strangely compounded of both peace and longing. In the first song of the strings one can feel it, and yet more strongly in the lovely solo of the clarinet. The whole tangle of melodies that twine themselves into this lovely fabric are nevertheless clear and individual. Near the end we are recalled to the cryptic significance of the first movement's theme again.

"In the fourth movement the music leaps out almost belligerently from the orchestra in a theme of boundless vigour and elastic rhythm, coursing freely and powerfully. For a time it is completely in control; then, its powers spent, the orchestra pauses upon a long-held note of the horn, con sordino. The basses, plucked, descend step by step into their lowest range. Then begins a grotesque little march that once more infuses vitality and mobile rhythm into the orchestra, and the bold opening subject returns.

"The strings ring a romantic melody. There is a long diminuendo, with harmonies almost visibly suspended, finally resolving in a tenuous pianissimo. There are sudden silences and sudden attacks; remembrances (flute) of the first theme in the first movement; suggestions of the quaint march of the previous section, and finally a conclusion of noble power and brilliance."

Rhapsody for Piano and Orchestra on a theme of Paganini

The Rhapsody was composed in 1934 and is in the form of a theme with 24 variations.

V. No. 1: The introduction of nine measures for full orchestra is followed by the first variation, after which the theme, stated by first and second violins is heard.

V. No. 2: Piatesso tempo is presented by piano with soft accompaniment of horns and trombones.

V. No. 3: Begins with the piano over strings to which is added a chattering of the woodwinds.

V. No. 4: Più vivo has the piano distinctly singing a melody, and after sharp chords in the piano is followed by the next variation.

V. No. 5: Tempo precedente. Here decisive chords for piano continue with soft accompaniment of strings, developing sweeping arabesques that lead to V. 6.

V. No. 6: L'istesso tempo. This variant of the theme rushes in headlong brilliance and agitation that subsides with the same phrase for piano that announced the variation.

Rachmaninov was one of the great interpreters of piano music and a successful composer in his warm style

It is followed by the mournful comment of the English horn and ends with a soft ascending scale for piano.

V. No. 7: Meno mosso e tempo moderato starts with the piano intoning a solemn melody based upon the Dies Irae, while the cellos and bassoons play the Paganini theme.

V. No. 8: Tempo 1 begins with a forte passage for the piano almost Lisztian in style.

V. No. 9: L'istesso tempo begins with a syncopated figure in a kind of galloping rhythm with the phrase ending in descending chromatics.

V. No. 10: Poco marcato. A repetition of the sombre Dies Irae theme which the piano plays forte while the strings weave fragments of the original theme. Against a whirling variant for the piano of the Paganini theme, the strings take up the Dies Irae music to which the winds add comment. Sweeping chromatics lead to Variation 11.

V. No. 11: Moderato, introduced by strings, tremolo, from which the piano emerges like the song of a bird soaring skyward. Brilliant passage work against woodwinds and harp glissando follows. Finally the piano, in a solo passage, terminates the variation with a four-note figure also suggestive of the song of a bird.

V. No. 12: Tempo di minuetto. It is one of those lilting melodies that, beautiful in itself, is made even more so by the singing accompaniment that is woven into it. Before the sweetness cloys comes the martial allegro of the next variation.

> " *There is in the man as well as in his music a rugged honesty, a deep and enduring sincerity which inhibited him from seeking the false gods of sensational modernism.* "

V. No. 13: Strings present the theme while the piano contributes strident chords. A shrill scale for piccolo, flutes and clarinets leads without break to Variation 14.

V. No. 14: L'istesso tempo which may be recognised by the vehemence with which the lower string and horns establish its rhythmic pulse. This is a stormy passage that suggests cloudy, ominous skies at the beginning, which lighten as the music progresses, and clear to show the musical rainbow in Variation 15.

V. No. 15: If this variation (*più vivo*), *scherzando,* was published anonymously there would be little difficulty recognising its composer. It is distinctly Rachmaninov. Its difficulties are prodigious and there lies the explanation of the reluctance of even the great pianists of essaying a public performance of this composition. The beginning of the variation is like a capricious wind, for the music advances now softly, now emphatic with a sudden crescendo, until, spent with the vigour of its own force, there is a pause for breath before the final chord ends this magnificent variation.

V. No. 16: It begins with a melody assigned to the oboe, while the strings furnish a wavering background. There is rich embroidery for the solo instrument, and then a return to the opening measures of the variation before the announcement of the next variation.

V. No. 17: In this variation, melody and accompaniment are both given to the piano while woodwinds supply subdued background. The calmness of this music establishes the mood for the Variation 18.

V. No. 18: Andante cantabile. This variation is a serene and expressive song for the piano, which is later taken up by strings with piano and woodwinds furnishing accompaniment.

V. No. 19: This is announced brusquely with a triplet figure for piano against a pizzicato accompaniment of strings. A quickening of tempo in the strings announces the next variation.

V. No. 20: Un poco più vivo. The piano moves along in a skipping figure, returning in Variation 21.

V. No. 21: Un poco più vivo has a triplet figure, staccato, that moves with exceeding animation to the next variation.

V. No. 22: Marziale. Un poco più vivo. Descending chords for piano mark the beginning in which a high climax is reached. The music sweeps passionately upward to a brilliant cadenza before the next variation.

V. No. 23: This variation begins simply enough but soon becomes considerably more involved. The piano comes forward at an incredible speed, engaging in a whirl of chromatics followed by four chords, pianissimo. As the solo instrument forges madly ahead in the tempestuous finale, the theme is heard at first in the woodwinds.

V. No. 24: Then, when the piano states it, the brasses and strings blare forth ominously the Dies Irae, from which the piano emerges with a fragment of the theme and ends the composition.

IGOR **STRAVINSKY**

Born : Oranienbaum (now in St. Petersburg),
      Russia, June 17, 1882
Died : New York, USA, April 6, 1971

*B*orn on St. Igor's Day and named after this patron saint, Igor Stravinsky was deeply rooted in his Russian heritage during his early years. His father Fyodor was a bass singer with the St. Petersburg Opera, and Russian opera and ballet were an integral part of his childhood.

Stravinsky was 20 years old and trying to decide between music and law, when the composer Rimsky-Korsakov made up his mind for him. Rimsky-Korsakov criticised the errors in Stravinsky's early compositions, but admitted at the same time that they were original and advised further study. He accepted Stravinsky as his young pupil who soon became his favourite disciple.

In 1908, when Rimsky-Korsakov's daughter was to be married, Stravinsky's wedding gift was a new composition, the dazzling symphonic work "Feu d'Artifice" (Fireworks). Stravinsky mailed the score in good time to Rimsky-Korsakov's country estate, but a few days later it was returned to him unopened, marked "not delivered on account of death of addressee".

Stravinsky was greatly saddened on hearing this and expressed his grief in a chant funèbre, a funeral song. For months thereafter he composed nothing.

The other great influence in Stravinsky's life was the ballet impresario Sergei Diaghilev, director of the Ballets Russes in Paris. The brilliance of "Fireworks" had dazzled Diaghilev when he heard it. He took Stravinsky on his staff in Paris and tested him with an assignment to orchestrate pieces by Chopin for the ballet *Les Sylphides*.

Those years composing music for the ballet in Paris were busy, happy and successful for Stravinsky. His scores for "Le Rossignol" (The Nightingale), "L'Oiseau de Feu" (The Firebird), "Petrouchka" and "Le Sacré du Printemps" (The Rite of Spring), all of them masterpieces, enriched the Diaghilev repertoire.

Major compositions

For Stage
The Firebird (L'Oiseau de Feu) 1910
  New orch. suite (1945)
  Scherzo
  Danse infernale
Petrouchka (1911)
  Orch. Suite
  Danse Russe
The Rite of Spring
  (Le Sacré du Printemps) (1913)
Orch. Suite (1914)
The Soldier's Tale
  (L'Histoire du Soldat) (1918)
Pulcinella (1920) after Pergolese
  Suites: For Orchestra (1924)
  For Violin and Piano (1933)
Apollo Musagètes (1927)
Le Baiser de la Fée
  (themes from Tchaikovsky)
Divertissement (Concert Suite)
Pas de deux
  (also arr. violin and pianoforte)
Ballade (also arr. violin and pianoforte)
Orpheus (1948)
The Rake's Progress (1951)

Orchestral
Fireworks (Feu d'Artifice) (1908)
Song of the Nightingale
  (Chant du Rossignol) (1913-14)
Concerto in D Major (violin and orch.) (1931)
Concerto in E-flat "Dumbarton Oaks" (1938)
Symphony of Psalms (1930)
Symphony in C (1940)
Circus Polka (1942)
Norwegian Moods (1944)
Symphony in 3 Movements (1945)
Ebony Concerto for clarinet and
  swing band (1945)
Concerto in D for strings (1946)

Chamber Music
Three pieces for string quartet (1914)
Octet for wind instruments (1923)
Tango for violin and piano (1941)
Septet for strings, wind and piano (1953)

For the first time in the history of the ballet, the music was more talked of than the gorgeous choreography.

The Petrouchka Chord, the bold harmonic innovation in employing two different keys simultaneously (C Major and F-sharp Major) introduced into the "Petrouchka" score, sparked the interest of other composers in polytonality as represented in the electrifying music of "Petrouchka".

The first performance of "Le Sacré du Printemps" (The Rite of Spring), which carried polytonality even further, was given in Paris on May 29, 1913. It made history. Half the audience stood up and cheered, while the other half stood up and booed or shouted insults. "Le Sacré du Printemps" resulted in bringing Stravinsky to the fore as a fearless new creative force.

In 1906 Stravinsky married his cousin Katerina Nossenko, and over the next few years they had a son and daughter. Switzerland, a frequent haunt of the Stravinskys, became their home during World War I.

After the War, Diaghilev suggested to Stravinsky that he adapt short pieces by the Baroque composer Pergolese, and this project produced a sparkling masterpiece in the ballet "Pulcinella".

From 1920 to 1939 Stravinsky lived in France. This period saw many works: "The Symphony of Psalms", "Concerto for Piano and Wind Instruments" and "Capriccio for Piano and Orchestra". "Oedipus Rex" and "Perséphone", both novel variations in the cantata form, premiered in Paris in 1927 and 1934.

Following the deaths of his wife and mother in 1939, and the outbreak of World War II, Stravinsky embarked for New York. The United States of America became his home for the rest of his life. He was joined in 1940 by his longtime mistress, Vera Sudeikina. They married and settled in Hollywood where Stravinsky passed his days teaching, conducting and composing.

Stravinsky's last works were short and austere. His health eventually failed. He died in New York in 1971 but was buried in San Michele, an island in the Venetian Lagoon, near the grave of Diaghilev.

Stravinsky's place in music history

Stravinsky's eminent position among 20th-century composers is permanently established. He was a highly individual, even revolutionary composer, who proved his genius by the many innovations and changes he successfully made in his musical style.

He composed amidst a galaxy of great artists and performers who constituted a new Golden Age. The names of some resound through musical and theatrical history: dancers and choreographers Mikhail Fokine and Vaclav Nijinsky, painter and scene and costume designer Léon Bakst, and artist Pablo Picasso. Stravinsky had a particular fondness for the British writers Dylan Thomas, W.H. Auden and Christopher Isherwood.

As leader of the musical avant-garde, Stravinsky startled the world of 20th-century music, then coming to terms with Richard Strauss and the Austrians, Anton Webern and Alban Berg, pupils of composer Arnold Schoenberg who invented the 12-tone system – a style called the Second Viennese School.

Stravinsky's music aroused both the fiercest antagonism and the highest praise: the "Sacré" had caused a riot at its first performance (1913), and there was great praise for his reworked Baroque and Neo-classical styles, evident in such gems as the ballet "Pulcinella" and the Violin Concerto.

Notes on select works

The Rite of Spring (Le Sacré du Printemps)

This composition made history. Its first performance, on May 29, 1913, by Diaghilev's Ballets Russes in Paris, led to one of the wildest scenes in musical history.

"The music of the 'Rite of Spring' is full of brutal, primitive strength. The most important feature is not the melody, but the barbaric rhythm, which is both stimulating and imaginative. The harmonies are daring and challenging."

The composition takes its name from a pagan ceremony filled with mystery and fear, and centres round a young girl who is chosen to dance until she dies.

As has been recounted, the music shocked its listeners when it was first performed, with half the audience cheering and the other half booing it. Present on the occasion were several well-known composers, Puccini and Saint-Saëns among them, who condemned the work, while Ravel and Debussy implored the audience to be quiet so that they could hear the wonderful music. However, when the music was performed one year later in a concert version, it was given a tremendous ovation, and many have since regarded it as one of the most important and epoch-making compositions of the 20th century. It may also be mentioned here that Walt Disney used "Rite of Spring" in his famous film *Fantasia*. He included it – after consultation with Stravinsky – to represent the creation and evolution of the world. Thus in the film violent volcanic eruptions and furious battles between giant dinosaurs accompany the wild and primitive music.

The Firebird (L'Oiseau de Feu)

The idea of creating a ballet on the Russian fairytale of the Firebird came from Diaghilev who entrusted the music to Stravinsky.

"The Firebird" was Stravinsky's first big work and brought him immediate fame. Arranged as a suite, the music soon became one of the most popular numbers of our time. To this day many consider it to be Stravinsky's most beautiful work.

The Story

"In the garden of the castle of the wicked magician Kostchei, a tree full of gold apples shines in the moonlight. Suddenly innumerable flames shoot upwards. It is the Firebird, which shows itself and then disappears. Young Prince Ivan pursues and catches it. The bird begs for its freedom and pulls out a feather which it gives to the Prince. He frees it, and it flies away rejoicing. Thirteen young Princesses come running out of the castle and one of them exchanges tender glances with Ivan. She signals to her friends to dance and the dance ends with the Prince embracing her. When day dawns the young Princesses have reluctantly to return to the castle. In spite of their warning, Ivan decides to follow them.

"The moment he opens the gate innumerable bells and gongs begin to sound. Crowds of people stream out of the dark castle in a burning red light, their cloaks streaming, helmets glittering and jewels blinking. Knights, slaves, dancers and jugglers whirl round at breakneck speed, and suddenly fall on their faces as Kostchei appears. The magician, catching sight of Ivan, advances on him

An early string quartet in performance
Stravinsky contributed three pieces for string quartet in 1914

A titan of the 20th-century musical scene, Stravinsky is credited with composing a stringent, unemotional but rhythmically vital music

performance by Diaghilev's Ballets Russes took place at the Châtelet Theatre in Paris.

The Story

"During festivities in celebration of the Russian Easter an old magician presents his puppet show in the market place before the wondering audience. By his magic he has given the three puppets, Petrouchka, the Dancer, and the Moor, human feelings and passions, and a tragedy is played out between them. Petrouchka, unattractive and ridiculous in appearance, suffers bitterly when the Dancer rejects his love and falls into the arms of the stupid and brutal Moor. Crazy with jealousy, Petrouchka comes in to interrupt their love-making, but the Moor throws him out.

"When the fair in the market place is at its height terrible screams are heard from the puppet theatre. The Moor chases after Petrouchka and kills him before the eyes of the horrified onlookers. The old magician calms the crowd by telling them

that Petrouchka is only a puppet of wood and sawdust. The crowd has begun to disperse when to his horror the magician sees Petrouchka's ghost on the roof of the puppet theatre, making triumphant gestures at him."

Pulcinella

This is a ballet suite for small orchestra by Stravinsky based on themes by Giovanni Battista Pergolese. In 1919, Diaghilev asked Stravinsky to write a ballet from fragments of unfinished dance compositions by Pergolese. Stravinsky had to decide whether to treat Pergolese's music with respect or love. He chose the latter course, with the result that many people accused him of lack of respect bordering on sacrilege. "Pulcinella" is, however, a captivatingly gay work, in which Pergolese's melodies are freely adapted to the spirit of our own age. The ballet was performed in Paris in 1920 and Stravinsky later arranged a suite from the music for an orchestra of 33 instruments.

to change him to a pillar of stone. Ivan is protected by the Firebird's feather and Kostchei is unable to cast his spell. Ivan calls the Firebird for help. An irresistible magic streams from the bird's feather and Kostchei and his followers are forced to dance until they fall exhausted. Thereupon the bird lulls them to sleep with a cradle song.

"Ivan enters the castle and returns with an egg containing the magician's soul. Hurling it to the ground, he destroys Kostchei's power for ever. The finale is the wedding procession of Ivan and his princess."

Petrouchka

This ballet was composed by Stravinsky in 1917. The story was devised by him with the painter Alexandre Benois. Its first

Line drawing of Picasso and Stravinsky
Both geniuses evoked endless controversy

Pronunciation Guide

A

Aida (Ah-ee-dah)
Ave (Ah-vay)

B

Bach (Bahkh)
Beethoven (Beh-toh-ven)
Berlioz (Behr-lee-oz)
Bizet (Bee-zay)
Boheme (Bo-hehm)
Boléro (Bo-leh-roh)
Brahms (Brahmz)

C

Caruso (Kah-roo-zoh)
Chaliapin (Shal-ya-peen)
Chopin (Show-pen)
Cortot (Kor-toh)
Csárdás (Char-dahsh)
Cui (Koo-ee)

D

Debussy (Deh-boos-see)
de Falla (Deh Falyah)
Delibes (Deh-leeb)
de Sarasate (Deh Sa-rah-sah-tay)
Donizetti (Don-ee-tset-tee)
Don Juan (Don Huahn)
Drdla (Derd-lah)
Dvorák (Dvor-zhak)

E

Elisir (Ay-lee-zeer)
Entr'acte (Ahn-tract)

F

Faust (Fawst)
Fidelio (Fee-day-lee-oh)
Figaro (Fee-ga-roh)
Fledermaus (Fleh-der-mows)

G

Giannini (Jee-ah-neen-ee)
Gigli (Zheel-lee)
Gluck (Glook)
Götterdämmerung (Ger-ter-dem-er-oongh)
Gounod (Goo-no)
Grieg (Greeg)

H

Haydn (Hai-dn)
Heifetz, Jascha (Hai-fetz, Yah-sha)
Horowitz (Hor-o-vitz)

I

Ibert (Ee-behr)
Iturbi (Ee-toor-bi)

J

Jota (Hoh-tah)

K

Kreisler (Kryz-ler)

L

Lalo (Lah-lo)
Landowska (Lan-dov-skah)
Leoncavallo (Lay-ohn-kah-vahl-loh)
Lieder (Lee-der)
Liszt (Lee-st)

M

Malagueña (Mah-lah-gay-niah)
Menuhin (Men-yoo-hin)
Monteverdi (Mon-teh-vair-dee)
Mozart (Moht-sart)

N

Nozze di Figaro (Not-zeh dee Fee-gar-oh)

O

Offenbach (Of-fen-bahkh)

P

Paderewski (Pad-er-ev-skee)
Paganini (Pah-gah-nee-nee)
Pagliacci (Pile-ya-chee)
Peer Gynt (Pair-Gint)
Ponselle (Pon-zell)
Potpourri (Poh-poo-ree)
Puccini (Poo-chee-nee)

R

Rachmaninov (Rakh-mah-nee-nov)
Ravel (Rah-vel)
Rigoletto (Ri-goh-let-toh)
Rimsky-Korsakov (Rim-ski Kohr-sah-kov)
Rossini (Ros-see-nee)
Rubinstein (Roo-bin-stine)

S

Saint-Saëns (Sen-Sahns)
Strauss (Strows)
Schubert (Shoo-behrt)
Schumann (Shoo-mahn)
Sibelius (See-bay-li-oos)
Stokowski (Sto-kov-skee)

T

Tchaikovsky (Chai-kov-skee)
Thaïs (Tah-ees)
Thibaud (Tee-bo)
Toscanini (Tos-ka-nee-nee)
Träumerei (Troy-meh-rai)
Traviata (Trah-vee-ah-tah)

V

Vaughan Williams (Vawn Wil-yimz)
Verdi (Vair-dee)
Vivaldi (Vee-vahl-dee)

W

Wagner (Vahg-ner)
Wieniawski (Veen-yav-skee)

Y

Yradier (Ee-rah-dee-ay)

Guide to Building a **Music** Collection

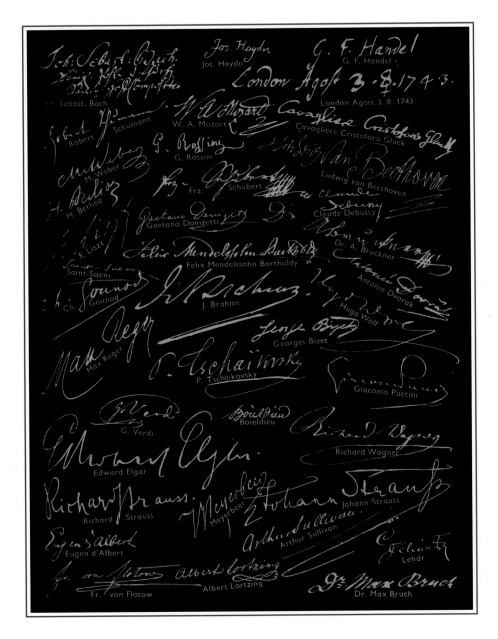

*F*or over 70 years I have listened, engrossed, to Western Classical music and it has truly enriched my life as no other leisure pursuit could have done. This has been made possible over the years by my gradually building up my own collection of recorded music of select compositions that had given me pleasure beyond words.

There are, of course, several ways in which you can welcome compositions to your collection. The most common one is through personal friendships with other music lovers who enthusiastically give guidance. Another source could be taking a liking to a particular composition heard at a recital or at a concert. Music programmes on television could be yet another venue for including certain compositions in your collection.

To enable you to smoothly start your own collection of recorded music, I have taken the liberty of preparing, over the next three columns, one each devoted separately to (i) Violin Music (ii) Piano Music and (iii) Orchestral Music. Each of these columns – 1, 2 and 3 – is also designed to mark your broadening interest from simpler compositions to progressively more complex ones.

The compositions suggested in the three separate columns are of course not to be taken as exhaustive of all the music I have listened to. I selectively mention those compositions that I have particularly enjoyed, including some that at times have been disparagingly referred to in certain quarters as "old war-horses", but which, in my opinion, have charmed generations of listeners by their inherent appeal.

I recommend that the compositions listed in the three columns be heard in stages. Start with Level 1 in all three columns, before moving on to their Level 2 and finally to their Level 3.

VIOLIN MUSIC

LEVEL 1
Schubert: Ave Maria, Serenade
Dvořák: Humoresque, Op. 101, No. 7
Saint-Saëns: Rondo Capriccioso, Op. 28
  Havanaise, Op. 83
Dinicu: Hora Staccato
Brahms: Hungarian Dance No. 7
Mendelssohn: Violin Concerto, Op. 64
Bruch: Violin Concerto No. 1
  in G Minor, Op. 26
Tchaikovsky: Violin Concerto in D, Op. 35

LEVEL 2
Massenet: Méditation from Thaïs
Ponce: Estrellita
Mendelssohn: On Wings of Song,
  Op. 34, No. 2
Sarasate: Zigeunerweisen, Op. 20, No. 1
Elgar: La Capricieuse, Op. 17
Debussy: Girl with the Flaxen Hair
Beethoven: Violin Concerto in D, Op. 61
Mozart: Violin Concerto No. 5, K 219
Lalo: Symphonie Espagnole, Op. 21
Saint-Saëns: Violin Concerto No. 3,
  B Minor, Op. 61

LEVEL 3
Beethoven: Romance No. 2 in F Major
Ravel: Tzigane
Bazzini: La Ronde des Lutins
Paganini: Caprices 13, 20, 24
Sarasate: Zapateado, Op. 23, No. 2
Achron: Hebrew Melody, Op. 33
Wieniawski: Scherzo Tarantelle, Op. 16
Bach: Partita No. 2, with Chaconne,
  BWV 1004
Brahms: Violin Concerto in D, Op. 77
Mozart: Violin Concerto No. 3, K 216,
  Violin Concerto No. 4, K 218
Sibelius: Violin Concerto in D Minor, Op. 47

PIANO MUSIC

LEVEL 1
Beethoven: "Für Elise"
Liszt: Liebesträume, No. 3,
  Hungarian Rhapsody No. 2
Schumann: "Träumerei"
Debussy: "Clair de Lune"
Chopin: Étude, Op. 10, No. 3
  Waltz, E-flat, Op. 18
Beethoven: Piano Concerto No. 5
  in E-flat Major, Op. 73 "Emperor"
Tchaikovsky: Piano Concerto No. 1
  in B-flat Minor, Op. 23
Rachmaninov: Piano Concerto No. 2
in C Minor, Op. 18
Grieg: Piano Concerto in A Minor, Op. 16

LEVEL 2
Paderewski: Minuet in G Major, Op. 14, No. 1
Rubinstein: Melody in F
Liszt: Hungarian Rhapsody No. 6
Beethoven: Piano Concerto No. 3
  in C Minor, Op. 37,
  Piano Concerto No. 4 in G Major, Op. 58
Mozart: Piano Concertos No. 19, K 459;
  No. 20, K 466; No. 21, K 467;
  No. 24, K 491; No. 25, K 503

LEVEL 3
Beethoven: Piano Sonatas
  "Appassionata" in F Minor, Op. 57, No. 23
  "Moonlight" in C-sharp Minor, Op. 27, No. 2
  "Pathétique" in C Minor, Op. 13, No. 8
  "Tempest" in D Minor, Op. 31, No. 17
  "Waldstein" in C Major, Op. 53, No. 21
Liszt: Hungarian Rhapsodies
  No. 12 in C-sharp Minor
  No. 15 in A Minor
Chopin:
  Nocturne, D-flat, Op. 27, No. 2
  Waltzes, Op. 34, Nos. 1 to 3,
  Ballade No. 1 in G Minor, Op. 23
  Scherzo No. 2 in B-flat Minor, Op. 31
  Polonaises No. 3 in A "Military", Op. 40;
    No. 6 in A-flat, "Heroic", Op. 53
  Prélude No. 15 in D-flat Major "Raindrop"

ORCHESTRAL MUSIC

LEVEL 1
Rossini: Overtures to Barber of Seville,
  Thieving Magpie, Silken Ladder
Johann Strauss: Blue Danube, Vienna
  Woods, Artist's Life, Roses from the South,
  Voices of Spring, Emperor Waltz
Johann Strauss, Sr:
  Radetzky March
  Greensleeves – Traditional
Beethoven: "Pastoral" Symphony No. 6, Op. 68
Dvořák: "New World" Symphony No. 9, Op. 95
Mozart: Symphony No. 40, K 550, G Minor

LEVEL 2
Vivaldi: "Four Seasons"
Mozart: "Eine kleine Nachtmusik", K 525
Tchaikovsky: Ballets
  "Swan Lake", Op. 20
  "Sleeping Princess", Op. 66
  "Nutcracker Suite", Op. 71
Rimsky-Korsakov: "Scheherazade", Op. 35
Beethoven: Symphony No. 5
  in C Minor, Op. 67
Tchaikovsky: Symphony No. 5
  in E Minor, Op. 64

LEVEL 3
Mozart: Sinfonia Concertante
  (violin and viola), K 364
  Concertos for bassoon, clarinet, flute,
  flute and harp, horn (all with orchestra)
Ravel: Boléro
Wagner: Overtures – Tannhäuser,
  The Flying Dutchman, Lohengrin
Beethoven: Symphonies No. 3, No. 7, No. 9
  Violin Sonatas:
  No. 5, Op. 24 "Spring"
  No. 9, Op. 47 "Kreutzer"
Sibelius: Symphonies No. 1, Op. 39,
  No. 2, Op. 43
Tchaikovsky: Symphonies No. 4, Op. 36,
  No. 6, Op. 74 "Pathétique"

Cello Concertos: Dvořák, Haydn, Lalo,
  Saint-Saëns No. 1, Op. 33

Select **Glossary**

A cappella
Designation for choral music without instrumental (Alla cappella) accompaniment (in Church style)

A tempo
Indicates return to normal tempo after deviation

Accelerando
Gradually quickening

Adagio
Slow (between andante and largo)

Ad libitum
An indication that gives a performer liberty to (i) vary from the strict tempo (ii) include or omit the part of a voice or instrument (iii) include a cadenza of performer's own invention (contrast "obbligato")

Affrettando
Hurrying

Agitato
Excited

Allegretto
Rather lively and quick

Allegro
Quick, lively, bright

Alto
A low-range female voice; (see also Contralto)

Andante
Flowing, neither fast nor slow

Andantino
At a gently moving pace

Appassionata
Passionately

Aria
Solo vocal piece (as in opera)

Assai
Very, extremely

Atonal
Music possessing no key

Bagatelle
A trifle, or short piece of instrumental music

Ballade
In piano music a romantic composition; perhaps fancifully intended to suggest the general idea of vivid narration

Barcarolle
A boat song, or instrumental imitation of such with a rowing 6-in-a-measure rhythm, or sometimes 9 or 12

Baritone
Male voice, midway between tenor and bass

Baroque
Ornate musical development between 1600 and 1750

Bass (Basso)
Lowest male voice

Berceuse
A lullaby (see also Wiegenlied)

Boléro
A lively Spanish dance. The use of castanets is a feature

Bourrée
Lively dance style (like the gavotte)

Bravura
Bravura passages for voice or instrumental display brilliant and showy expressions in performance

Brio
Vigour, spirited

Cadence
The various melodies and harmonic progressions which introduce a feeling of more or less finality and are therefore suited to closing phrases

Cadenza
An improvised flourish inserted towards the end of a vocal aria or solo instrumental movement

Cantabile
A lyrical singing style

Cantata
Madrigals and sung recitatives. Bach (among others) composed some 300 Church and secular cantatas

Capriccio
Any light composition which has unexpected and original effects

Chaconne
This is in origin a dance (3-in-a-measure, slow time), the music framed upon a basso continuo. The type was taken into pure instrumental music and developed in all manner of ways, so that it is now difficult to frame a precise definition

Chamber ensembles
(For) duo, trio, quartet, quintet, sextet, septet, octet, nonet (i.e. for two to nine instruments)

Chamber orchestra
Small-size orchestra performing in room or hall

Coda
A passage added to a piece to make an effective ending. From Beethoven onwards it often takes on a greater importance

Coloratura
The elaborate ornamentation of the female voice or melody

Concertante
An adjective corresponding to concerto, and means "in concert". When it enters into a description of a piece it generally indicates the combination of one or more instruments with orchestra

Concerto
A performance "in concert". Any group of instruments playing together, in this sense

Contralto
The lowest range of the female voice

Counterpoint
Literally, "many voiced" music, which consists of several strands, each with its own melodic interest and the whole fitting together in an effective combination

Countertenor
High male voice with instrumental quality of tone

Crescendo - Decrescendo
Indicated by the signs < and >. The usual terms and signs for increasing or decreasing loudness. For the latter, the word "diminuendo" (dim) is also used

Croisez Croisement
Indication to cross the hands in piano playing

Csárdás
A native dance of Hungary with slow and very fast sections

Da capo (D.c.)
From the beginning. Indication that the piece is to be repeated from the beginning to the end

Divertimento
A light composition for amusement. Often a fantasia or a potpourri of popular melodies

Dominant
The fifth note of the key

Elegy
Song of lamentation for the deceased

Ensemble
Small group of performers with individual parts

Entr'acte
A piece (usually instrumental) performed between the acts of a play or opera

Étude
A study (i.e. a short solo instrumental piece) developing some particular point in technique as an exercise for the player

Fantasie
Literally, "fancy". Any free-sounding, informal kind of instrumental piece. Sometimes also a string of tunes from an opera, etc. worked up into an instrumental piece

Flamenco
A southern Spanish (Andalusian) type of song performed to the accompaniment of guitars and often danced

Flourish
A trumpet call or "fanfare". A somewhat showy, decorative passage

Forte / Fortissimo
Loud / Very loudly

Fugue
Contrapuntal composition

Galop
Formal round dance with step change, or hop, at intervals

Garbo - con garbato
Graceful, elegant

Gavotte
A dance form. Sometimes found as one of the constituents of the old suites (see also Bourée)

Gigue
Rustic Scottish and Irish lively dance

Giocoso
Joyous, cheerful

Giusto
As in "con giusto" – with style, with zest

Glissando
Series of adjacent notes played up or down

Grazioso
(Played) gracefully

Gregorian Chant
Solo and unison plainsong chants of early Christian Church

Habañera
A slow Cuban dance which came to be very popular in Spain

Harmony
The simultaneous combination of notes

Heldentenor
"Heroic tenor". Powerful range of the tenor voice suited mainly to certain operatic demands

Humoresque
A fancy title sometimes attached to an instrumental composition of a humorous or capricious character, usually short

Impromptu
A quasi-extemporary short instrumental piece

Interlude
Inserted piece played between other musical passages

Intermezzo
The music intended for performance between the acts of a play or opera

Jota
A popular dance from Aragon, Spain, performed with castanets by one or more couples

Kapelle
"Chapel", with the connotation of "private or small orchestra"

Kapellmeister
The director or conductor of a Kapelle

Key signature
The sign at the beginning of a stave showing particular key of a composition

Largo / Larghetto
Slow and steady / Dignified diminutive of largo

Legato
Smoothly

Leggiero
Light (musical direction), lightly

Leitmotiv
In Wagnerian and post-Wagnerian practice and parlance, a motif of which dramatic use is made, it being associated with some personage or idea, and appearing in various shapes and colourings when that personage or idea is to the fore. A Wagnerian music drama score is, to an extent, an amazingly skilfull mosaic of a certain number of such motifs

Lento
Slow

Libretto
The text of an opera, oratorio, etc

Lied
Song. The great Lieder period begins with Schubert, from whom onwards composers made innumerable lyric and dramatic settings of Romantic poetry, with accompaniment for the newly improved pianoforte

Madrigal
A late 16th and early 17th-century choral form, a cappella and Contrapuntal in style, most popularly sung in one voice to a part

Maestoso
Majestic, dignified

Malagueña
Term for three different types of Southern Spanish folk music, usually (i) a local variety of the fandango (ii) a type of highly emotional song in free style and rhythm (iii) an older type of dance music played in parallel triads and with an improvised melody above

Mass
Main musical expression of Roman Catholic worship by various composers from the 17th century until the present. The five major parts are Kyrie, Gloria, Credo, Sanctus and Agnus Dei. Bach's "Mass in B Minor" and Beethoven's "Mass in D" are best examples of oratorio style

Mattinata
A morning song e.g. under a lady's window – a fancy title sometimes applied to short, bright instrumental compositions

Mazurka
A Polish dance performed at several speeds, moderately slow to quite rapid. Not as sensuous as the waltz

Meno
Less, slower

Mesto
Mournful, sad

Mezzo / Mezzo-forte
Half / Half-loud: neither loud nor soft

Mezzo-soprano
Female voice midway between soprano and contralto

Minuet
Dance in triple time. Originally rustic, adapted in the 17th century as courtly dance

Molto
Much, very quickly

Mosso
At quicker pace

Motet
The most important form of polyphonic music during the Middle Ages and Renaissance. It is impossible to formulate a general definition that covers all the phases of its development during the more than five centuries of its existence (1220-1750). In general, however, a motet is an unaccompanied choral composition based on a Latin sacred text

Movement
Primary sections of concertos, symphonies and other instrumental combinations, with indications of change of tempo

Nachtmusik
Literally, "night music". Any piece with which the composer wishes the romantic feelings of night to be associated can be so titled by him

Neo-classical
Style of composition in the early 20th century when composers wrote in 17th and 18th-century forms to counteract overmuch 19th-century Romanticism

Nocturne
A term introduced by the Irish composer John Field for a type of slow Romantic piano piece of the melody-plus-accompaniment order, the thing and the name then being taken over by Chopin. Other composers like Mozart used the word as the equivalent of serenade

Nonets
Chamber music for nine instruments

Obbligato

Obligatory, usually with reference to an instrument (violin obbligato) or part that must not be omitted. The opposite is "ad libitum". Through misunderstanding or carelessness, the term has come to mean a mere accompanying part that may be omitted if necessary. As a result, each individual case must decide whether obbligato means "obbligato" or "ad libitum". Usually it means the former in early music and the latter in more recent pieces

Octet

Music for eight instruments, whether all strings (Mendelssohn), all winds (Beethoven, Stravinsky) or mixed (Schubert, Spohr)

Opera

A drama that is primarily sung, accompanied by an orchestra and presented on the stage. The text of such a work, called a "libretto", is sometimes based on one or more purely literary antecedents. The music frequently begins with an "overture" and consists of a combination of "arias", "duets", "ensembles" and "recitatives". Ballet may also be an important feature. Throughout much of the history of opera, recitative served to carry forward the dramatic action, while the more lyrical or reflective moments of the drama were set musically as arias, duets or ensembles. Ensembles occurring at the end of acts, however, are often designed to bring about musical and dramatic climaxes simultaneously. In some kinds of works, spoken dialogue replaces recitative

Opera buffa

Comic opera, opposite of "opera seria"

Opera seria

Serious opera. Main operatic form in the 17th and 18th centuries, treating formal and complex mythological subjects

Operetta

Light, mostly comic opera

Oratorio

A narrative or dramatic work, usually sacred, employing arias, recitatives, ensembles, choruses, and orchestral music, but not intended to be staged. Many such works employ a narrator. The term is taken from the name of the place (oratory) where 16th-century Italian lay congregations met for prayer, readings from the Scriptures and the singing of "Laude". In its early history and style, the oratorio is closely related to opera

Ostinato

A melodic and/or rhythmic figure that is persistently repeated throughout a composition or its section

Overture

An instrumental composition intended as an introduction to an opera, oratorio or similar work

Partita

A variation. Now applied to a composite work

Passacaglia

Whatever the textbooks and dictionaries may say, this, in practice, is indistinguishable from the Chaconne

Pavane

Solemn ceremonial dance of Italian origin

Perpetuum mobile

A term used by Paganini (Moto Perpetuo, Op. 11), Weber (last movement of Piano Sonata, Op. 24) and others to denote pieces that proceed from beginning to end in the same rapid motion

Piano (musical direction)

Instruction to play softly

Più

More (as in "più mosso" – more movement)

Pizzicato

Direction for plucking, not bowing, of stringed instruments

Poco

A little (as in "poco lento" – a little slowly)

Polka

Bohemian round dance in quick time

Polonaise

Polish dance in triple time at moderate speed

Polyphony / Polyphonic

Music that simultaneously combines several lines of individual design, each of which retains its identity as a line to some degree, in contrast to monophonic music which consists of a single melody, or homophonic music, which combines several lines of similar, rhythmically identical designs

Potpourri

A medley of popular tunes, operatic arias, patriotic songs, etc, which are played in succession, connected by a few measures of introduction or modulation

Prelude

A musical piece which precedes another

Presto / Prestissimo

Quick / Very quickly

Quadrille

Popular early 19th-century square dance

Quasi

As it were, almost

Quintet

Music for five players

Ragtime

A style of American popular music that reached its peak in 1910-15. It is characterised by a march-like duple metre with a highly syncopatic melody. It was principally the creation of pianists such as Ben Harvey and Scott Joplin, though it was also performed by bands

Rallentando

Gradually slowing down

Recitative

Song in a declamatory style and rhythm, often preceding an aria

Revvivando

Quickening

Rhapsody

An instrumental piece, generally of a rather ecstatic character. The term is especially associated with Liszt who first popularised it

Ritardando

Slowing speed, held back gradually

Ritenuto

Immediately, not gradually, held back

Ritornello

A return, after a refrain, in folk song; repetition of instrumental introduction; return of full orchestra after solo passage

Rococo

Refers to decorative style in music

Rondo form

A form in which one principal subject re-appears several times with other matter interspersed. It is frequently used in Classical sonatas, symphonies and concertos for the final movement

Round

Common name for a circle "canon", i.e. a canon in which each singer returns from the conclusion of the melody to its beginning, repeating it ad libitum

Rubato

An elastic, flexible tempo allowing slight accelerandos and ritardandos according to the requirements of musical expression. Two types can be distinguishd, one that affects only the melody and another that affects the whole musical texture

Saltarello

A sprightly Italian dance incorporating little jumps

Sarabande

17th and 18th-century Latin American dance form. Later, a slow, stately version was musically incorporated

Scherzo
Literally, "joke". Applied to a brilliant type of composition, often humorous and especially to that movement which, from Beethoven onwards, often replaces the minuet movement in the symphony and sonata

Sempre
"Always", as in "sempre legato" – always smoothly played

Senza
"Without", as in "senza sordino" – (played) without mute

Serenade
Open-air evening music for instruments or accompanied voice

Sforzando
The particular note or chord so marked to be "forced" or strongly accented

Sinfonia concertante
Piece for two or more solo instruments with orchestra

Sonata
The term properly means merely an "instrumentally" sounded piece as distinct from a "sung" one (sonata vs cantata). Normally a sonata is in several movements (like a suite) but the sonata's movements are usually not in dance style as they were in the early (older) suites. From Haydn and Mozart onwards we get the Classical sonata and, in ordinary speech, today this is what the word "sonata" means

Sonatina
A short sonata, generally simpler and lighter in style

Soprano
The highest register of the female voice

Sostenuto / Sostenendo
Sustaining the tone to or beyond nominal value and thus sometimes with the implication of slackening the tempo

Spianato
Smooth, even

Spiccato
A particular kind of staccato, the bow bouncing on the strings

Staccato
Literally, "detached"; the notes played in a cat-on-hot-bricks style

Ständchen
An evening song, in the sense of a short vocal or instrumental composition, serenade

Stretto
This is (i) in a fugue the imitation of the subject in close succession, with the answer entering before the subject is completed (ii) in non-fugal compositions stretto (stretta) is a concluding section in faster tempo i.e. as at the end of the last movement of Beethoven's Fifth Symphony

Suite
Instrumental music with several movements in dance style

Symphonic poem
Programmatic single movement orchestral works

Symphony
Large-scale orchestral work, usually in four movements

Tanto
So much. "Non tanto" is not so (too) much. E.g. allegro non tanto

Tanz
Dance

Tarantella
A Neapolitan dance in rapid 6/8 metre. According to popular legend the word refers to the tarantula spider whose poisonous bite the dance was believed to cure

Tempo
The speed of a composition or a section thereof as indicated by tempo marks such as largo, adagio, andante, moderato, allegro and prestissimo

Tenor
The highest register of the male voice

Timpani
Kettledrums. Copper basins covered with parchment and tunable to particular notes

Toccata
A keyboard (organ, harpsichord) composition in free, idiomatic keyboard style, employing full chords and running passages, with or without sections in imitative style (fugues)

Tone poem
"Sound poem"
(see also Symphonic poem)

Tonic
The key note. Meaning the chief key of the piece

Tremolo
Very rapid alternation of two notes in stringed instruments

Troppo
"Too much" (as in "allegro ma non troppo" – fast, but not too much)

Tutti
In orchestral works, particularly concertos, indication for passages for the whole orchestra as distinct from those of the soloist

Upbeat
One or several notes that occur before the first complete measure and thus before the first metrically accented beat (downbeat) of a work or phrase. Sometimes also called the pick-up

Variation(s)
Varied version(s) of a tune or an original theme

Vibrato
In string music an effect of slightly wavering pitch, obtained by the motion of the fingers of the left hand as they stop the strings, equivalent to the vocalist's tremolo, but not usually objectionable. In vocal music a very rapid reiteration of the note instead of a steady holding of it, generally objectionable

Virtuoso
Refers to skilled technical interpreters – e.g. virtuoso violinist, pianist, etc; also to performances of exceptional ability

Vivace
Vivacious, fast and lively

Waltz (Valse)
A 3-in-a-measure dance derived from the Ländler. It first appeared prominently at the end of the 18th century and soon became centred in Vienna. It has a harmonic characteristic – a basis of one chord per measure with the base note of the chord on the first beat and "lumps" of the chord on the other two beats. This contributes to its swaying sentimentality. In general, the form is that of a string of seven or eight attractive tunes, in various alternations plus the introduction and the coda. Chopin, Brahms and others have taken this style and form as the basis of compositions not intended for dancing

Wiegenlied
Cradle song; German for "lullaby" (see also Berceuse)

Yodel
A special type of singing practised by the mountain peoples of Switzerland and Austria (Tirol) and characterised by frequent and rapid passing from low chest voice to a high falsetto

Zapateado
A Spanish solo dance in triple time, the rhythm being marked by stomping of the heels, frequently in syncopation

Zigeunerlied
Gypsy song

Zigeunermusik
Gypsy music

Credits

Bibliography

Classical Music, John Stanley, Reed International Books, 1994
History's 100 Greatest Composers, Helen L. Kaufmann, Grosset & Dunlap,
  New York, 1957
Oxford Dictionary of Music, Michael Kennedy, 2nd Edition,
  Oxford University Press, 1994
Portraits of Greatness, Enzo Orlandi (General Editor), Paul Hamlyn Publishing,
  London; 1967 (Beethoven, Chopin), 1969 (Mozart)
The Record Book, David Hall, International Edition, Oliver Durrell, New York, 1948
The Victor Book of the Symphony, Charles O'Connell, Revised Edition,
Simon & Schuster, New York, 1935
The World of Music, K.B. Sandved, Waverley Book Company, London, 1957

Image Credits

Unless otherwise specified (in the sources printed below) images in this book are reproduced
from *The World of Music*, K.B. Sandved, Waverley Book Company, London, 1957.

Applause – a Tribute to Zubin Mehta, Mehli Mehta Music Foundation, Mumbai, 2011
  Pages: 7, 9, 13

History's 100 Greatest Composers, Helen L. Kaufmann; illustrated by Samuel Nisenson,
  Grosset & Dunlap, New York, 1957
  Pages: 3, 20, 22, 33, 37, 86, 101, 123, 130, 132, 136, 148, 157, 164, 171, 173, 179

The Oxford Companion to Music, edited by Percy A. Scholes;
  illustrated by Oswald Barrett (Batt), Oxford University Press, 1955
  Pages: 24, 32, 62, 113, 145, 155, 181

Princes Czartoryski Foundation, Krakow
  Page: 14

Author's Note

History's 100 Greatest Composers
is a book that has been most useful
to me in gathering biographical details
of the composers.

The Victor Book of the Symphony is an
excellent publication covering symphonies,
symphonic poems, concertos and all
types of orchestral suites. It is noted for
its masterly technical appreciation of
compositions. I have not hesitated to
reproduce (within quote marks) passages
from this book describing orchestral works
because of their superb, lucid analysis,
which I strongly felt I must share with
my readers.

The World of Music, widely covering music,
opera and theatre is a two-volume set
replete with wonderful visuals. Its value
is enhanced by listings of the well-known
works of composers. The list of "Major
Compositions" in each chapter is taken
from here. I have included it to encourage
readers to listen to different works by these
composers, beyond what I have chosen to
comment on.

Acknowledgements

Thank you…

*P*heroza and Jamshyd Godrej, the Yusuf and Farida Hamied Foundation, and Dinshaw Tamboly of WZO Trust Funds – for making this book possible with such strong sponsor support.

Zubin Mehta – heartfelt appreciation, Maestro, for so graciously giving the book its warm and encouraging Foreword.

Sooni Taraporevala – your willing one-woman advisory board skills spurred on *Musical Journeys* every step of the way.

Sherna Gandhy – that experienced editing eye has kept the lines flowing free and fine throughout to give the pages crisp readability.

Farrokh Vajifdar – those additions to the text you effortlessly offered, thanks to your wide knowledge of the subject, have proved invaluable.

Ratty N. Engineer and Katy Mistry – kudos, only you could patiently decipher and convert reams of handwritten manuscripts to neat copy.

Kermin Colaço – designer extraordinaire, you are an absolute joy to work with. Your taking up our book was the happy, defining moment for its journey ahead.

Praveen S. Bhandary – for deftly making the pages assume a life of their own… to the strains of Beethoven piano sonatas!

Khushru Patel – printer par excellence with a passion for books to match and always the soundest ideas.

Sandip Thanawala – for delivering hundreds of clean and quick picture scans on demand.

Kaushal Nandu – for producing wonderful dummy editions and predicting this book should go places.

Ayesha Soonawalla – you took great interest right away in this labour of love.

Radhika Sabavala and Arnavaz Bhansali – your help eased the process of seeking permissions for images.

Sanjiv Rawell – for time and trouble spent poring over copyright laws of the publishing world.

Zane Dalal and Fareed Curmally – the care you took to study and generously recommend this effort is most appreciated.

Mehmood Curmally – you were among the earliest to cheer the project and flag it onwards.

Furtados – you endorsed the book in its formative stages and continue to walk the extra mile for it.

Khushroo Suntook – you very kindly agreed to launch *Musical Journeys* at the National Centre for the Performing Arts and present it to visiting musicians.

Mehroo Jijeebhoy – you and the Mehli Mehta Music Foundation constantly stand by us.

Natalia Ritzkowsky – it is a pleasure liaising with you.

Daraius and Pervin Dadachanji – for being there, from Sunday listening sessions and reading first drafts to sharing our excitement as the dream took shape.

Phiroze Dastoor, Shakeel Kudrolli, Shernaz Vasunia, Rumi Taraporevala, Saleem Ahmadullah, Hormusji Cama and Adi Jehangir – for a useful first look, for funding suggestions, and for thoughtful gifts of both music and music books.

Rahul da Cunha, Kunal Basu, Dilnaz Gilder, Sangita Advani and Tehmi Morris – music lover friends and sounding boards whose creative views we could not have done without.

Neepa and Ranjeet Joshipura – for your customary kindness extended yet again.

To you all and to our family – Noshir, Zarir, Ayesha and Perin – we are truly grateful.

Homi Dastoor & Meher Marfatia
Mumbai, June 2014